STEAM MOTIVE POWER DEPOTS

STEAM MOTIVE POWER DEPOTS

E.S. Beavor

LONDON

IAN ALLAN LTD

Previous page: Cheltenham shed on 9 September 1961. The right hand bay of the building is of classical GWR construction, while on the left the bay has been re-roofed with corrugated asbestos, the doors having been removed. The Class U 2-6-0 has most probably worked in from Andover via the Midland & South West Junction line.
S. C. Nash

Contents

By the same Author
Steam was My Calling, Ian Allan, 1974

First published 1983

ISBN 0 7110 1280 6

Published by Ian Allan Ltd, Shepperton, Surrey; and printed by Ian Allan Printing Ltd at their works at Coombelands in Runnymede, England

The ultimate in ash-handling equipment is seen in this photograph of 'Green Arrow' 2-6-2 No 60963 taken on 2 May 1964 on the wet ashpit at York. There were grids in the pit at normal pit-floor level — similar to those seen at the left of the picture — on which men could walk in order to rake ashes out of the ashpan. Ashes fell through the grids into a water-filled sump below, while lumps of clinker remained on the grids. A rail-mounted steam crane, fitted with a grab, was used to remove ashes from the pit into wagons as sections of grid were raised. *J. S. Hancock*

To all those who help run railway
preservation societies — may they never
run short of steam

A scene that was repeated many times in the dying days of steam traction. This is Ryde (IoW) shed, coded 70H, on 31 December 1966, the final day of BR steam operations on the island.

The locomotives are (left to right) Nos 31 *Chale*, 27 *Merstone* and 14 *Fishbourne*, all of Class 02.
J. C. Beckett

Introduction

A remarkable feature of steam locomotives is that they refuse to be forgotten, although they have disappeared from active service in most countries. It is now over 14 years since British Railways last operated a service train with one of its own standard-gauge engines. The conditions prevailing in diesel or electric locomotive maintenance depots, which almost everywhere are in keeping with modern industrial ideas, can be seen by anyone who cares to visit one of these establishments during their periodic open days. This book has been written, however, for the sake of recording the recently-departed past in steam running sheds. I readily admit to a considerable nostalgia for the sterling body of men who worked there, and for the iron horses which — for a variety of reasons — spent a large part of their lives in these 'stables', or in running 'light' to or from them.

Those societies which are operating engines in steam — even if only for a few weekends per year — may be mainly motivated by 'playing at railways' on the large scale, but they certainly have encountered, or will meet many of the problems considered in this book. Blessed as they are with volunteer labour, they will be spared the troubles of conflict with trade unions, and the immense complexity of rostering enginemen. I hope that from the following chapters they may derive encouragement in their dedicated task of demonstrating some of the locomotives whose ancestors spread the products of the Industrial Revolution around the world.

In *Steam was my Calling* (Ian Allan, 1974) I gave numerous glimpses into the activities of various depots. The present volume is offered to show features which were common to other districts, demonstrating how labour-intensive and complex was the organisation 'behind the scenes' needed to keep the hordes of steam engines ready for duty.

In this book the term 'depot' is used to cover the whole establishment which during the British Railways régime was referred to (under strong ex-LMS influence) as a motive power depot. On the LMS, prior to a certain Americanisation which invaded their top management from about 1933, these installations were called 'running sheds' — the expression by which they were known on the other railways of Great Britain until Nationalisation at the beginning of 1948.

I have generally used the word 'shed' to refer to the main building in which locomotives were serviced or repaired, except where I have employed it to avoid too frequent use of the term 'depot' — in which cases I trust that the context makes clear the meaning intended.

Acknowledgements

I am happy to acknowledge extensive advice and help freely given by friends and former colleagues. A list of these would be unduly long, so I trust that those not mentioned will forgive the omission. However reference must be made to Bryan Stone and to the photographers. In particular I would like to thank Mr MacDonald of the Central Photographic Unit of British Railways at Paddington and Mr Fletcher of the BR Eastern Region Photographic Unit at York, who have kindly supplied photographs credited to those sources.

E. S. Beavor
BSc(Eng), CEng, MIMechE, GCInstT

1

A Tour of the Depot

Many readers will have had occasion during the last few years to visit the locomotive depot of a railway preservation society; but of those in Great Britain only Steamtown at Carnforth (north of Lancaster) now possesses the equipment virtually as it was until August 1968 when British Railways operated a daily service there. So I propose to take you on a tour of that depot, and ask you to imagine how its present appearance differs from its former, busy, workaday aspect. As we go along I shall also point out how the buildings, yard layout and equipment differ from those which existed at other depots.

Each depot had its own considerable individuality, depending particularly on its surroundings and their railway functions. Examples of the installations may be seen on the lines of various preservation societies, and at the National Railway Museum at York; many are illustrated in this book.

At Carnforth — as at many other depots — one had a clear view from the station; the first impression on approaching the depot might well be a haze of smoke, which could also be smelt if the wind lay in that direction. At a few depots one could even step from an access road directly into the main shed building, while at others the principal access was over a footbridge, crossing several railway tracks. This was usually a good vantage point. The present road skirting round the north side of the depot premises is now the main entrance for visitors.

However, let us make a more imaginative approach to the depot by supposing that we have the good fortune to be riding on the footplate of *Flying Scotsman*, returning to its home depot after one of its many excursion trips.

We run under the control of signals to the South entrance to the shed where the signal letting us run into the shed yard is already at clear. Once inside the shed yard the driver brings the engine to a halt and destroys the vacuum in the brake system. He screws the valve gear into mid-position, opens the cylinder cocks, and then goes to report to the supervisor (Running Foreman in British Railways' days). The fireman meanwhile screws down the hand-brake on the tender front, and collects a galvanised bucket filled with hand tools, also the two oil-lit headlamps, one tail-lamp and a smaller oil-lamp for illuminating the boiler gauge glasses. These he will take to the lamp store before going to his locker to collect his personal belongings.

As the driver reports the arrival of the engine he will hand in a repair card noting any repairs required. Usually we shall have found an occasion for 'washing up' in a bucketful of hot water on the locomotive before reaching the depot, or we may go to the wash-room to remove coal-dust and grime from hands, neck and face. In British Railways' days the timekeeper would record the time at which the driver and fireman finished duty (often notified to him by telephone from a point at which they had handed over their engine to another set of men). Other men coming on duty would report to the timekeeper, and would read notices displayed on the notice board adjacent to the 'signing-on point'. These notices, together with the weekly printed notices — which were issued personally to drivers — were the most important communication to enginemen.

Let us suppose that *Flying Scotsman* is to be 'turned round' and prepared for another train departing a few hours later. A fresh crew will be detailed to 'dispose and prepare' the engine (on British Railways there was a fixed allowance of one hour for disposing most classes of steam locomotive). Disposal involved shovelling ash and clinker off the fire-grate and out of the ashpan, long fire-irons being carried on the tender or tank for this purpose. Char — which is like fine coke — also had to be shovelled out of the smokebox, using a firing shovel or a long-handled shovel kept on the ashpit. The name 'ashpit' refers to a long pit between the rails, with steps at each end, giving access to the ashpan.

Taking coal is also part of the disposal work, and it is a duty of the fireman to ensure that it is 'trimmed' — ie lumps of coal which might fall off the engine when running must be pushed off where the coaling is done, or so placed that the vibration of movement will not cause them to fall.

Preparation includes taking water, for which it is usual for the fireman to climb up on top of the tender or tank, so as to guide the end of the long leather sleeve of the water column (commonly called a 'bag') into the tank filler hole. A water column fitted with a movable arm is often referred to as a 'water crane', and the arm is fitted with a chain, so that the driver can move it from the ground.

Oiling the moving parts of a locomotive is part of the preparation duties, carried out by the driver, who will also visually examine all accessible items. In the meantime the fireman will collect freshly trimmed oil-lamps, unless the engine has electric lighting, in which case (on British Railways at least) oil-lamps or white discs would be carried on the lamp-brackets as train identification markers. The fireman will also obtain from the stores a bucket containing hand tools and detonators. If sand is needed he will also fetch sand in a bucket from the sand drier furnace.

If the engine needs turning this is usually done when it has to be moved for one of the purposes mentioned above. There was no set order on most railways for the functions just described, simply that in most depots the track layout and installations imposed certain sequences. Otherwise it was mainly a matter of local custom, subject to the imperative condition of avoiding conflicting movements. These sometimes did occur in fog or falling snow. Although most people were extra cautious under such conditions, it did occasionally happen in a busy depot that someone (perhaps unfamiliar with the particular yard) caused a collision, and then the blacksmith might have several hours work straightening out a footstep, buffer beam, or other exposed part.

Having taken a quick look at what is happening outside, it is time to see the activities inside that mysterious building, known by the most misleadingly insignificant of terms: 'the shed'. We shall find some engines in steam which have been parked there ('stabled' in locomotive parlance). Some may be awaiting or undergoing repairs or cleaning, or simply being held for their next turns of duty. Others will be out of steam for boiler examination or repairs, or for mechanical attention, including those stopped pending the arrival of material. Yet others may be stored, which we can see at a glance wherever a board has been placed over a chimney, so as to prevent rain from getting down the chimney and into the valve chest.

Close to the area where engines are undergoing mechanical repairs we find a workshop equipped with machine tools. At the larger sheds there was a short length of track which could be raised or lowered below rail level, this being known as a 'drop pit'. It was powered by a hydraulically operated ram, or electrically driven screws, and served to lower a pair of wheels for the purpose of changing an axlebox, or axlebox spring, or for removing a pair of wheels. Many sheds had an older type of lifting equipment, called 'shear legs'. This was a huge tripod, usually located out-of-doors, or sometimes inside the main shed building. Alternatively heavy lifting might be done with a gantry crane. If one of these installations were out of action, a breakdown crane might be used in place of it, but only if the area were free from overhead obstructions.

Every depot having mechanical staff was equipped with some re-railing apparatus, if only 'tool vans' with jacks, wooden packing blocks, chains, wire ropes and re-railing ramps. The larger depots were also provided with a steam-crane, able to lift loads of a maximum of 15ton, or other value as high as 50ton, according to its size. Such cranes (many of which have now been converted to diesel drive) were kept in steam, ready to turn out for any emergency at half-an-hour's notice, as well as for programmed lifting work for the Civil Engineer. The breakdown train was kept on an outdoor track, except at those depots which had an unusual amount of covered track-space.

All depots had offices, stores, mess-rooms and facilities for personnel which were common with industry in general. At Carnforth — as at nearly all other sheds — they were arrayed along one side of the main building and integral with it.

In many overseas countries — and particularly in North America — a railroad 'depot' meant the embryo of a town; its location was mainly chosen because it was a place where there was water for locomotives.

New features of locomotive design affected the work in depots. Robert Stephenson invented the smokebox to provide access to the front end of the boiler tubes (even *Rocket* was thus modified). In 1833 he also introduced the steam brake, followed in 1841 by dry sanding, for which each depot had to be equipped with a sand-drying furnace. In Victorian times new developments were fairly slow in forthcoming — there being few technical publications until the second half of the century. All engines had water pumps for forcing feed water into the boiler until the injector was introduced from France in the late 1860s.

Brakes were horribly inadequate in Great Britain until a number of serious accidents to expresses highlighted the deficiency in the 1870s. The various railway companies adopted different solutions, many — including the GNR — favouring Smith's non-automatic brake, in which a large ejector was used to create vacuum only when the brake was to be applied. The railways concerned were obliged to change it for the automatic brake at great expense nearly 10 years later. More enlightened companies had fitted the American-invented compressed-air brake from an early date. Sanding, power brakes, injectors and other locomotive equipment presented new problems for the maintenance men, but did not fundamentally affect servicing.

Some sheds such as Grantham (built 1852), and Leicester Central (built as late as 1898/99) were constructed mainly as staging depots for the purpose of changing engines and men — just as was done with horses and their drivers at post-houses in stage-coach days. An outward journey of 100 miles, followed by turn-round and rest, and then the same distance home was considered a long working, and indeed in this century mileage bonus payments commenced as soon as 140 miles had been completed.

1
A classic of locomotive photography. This coaling plant at the 'north' end of Doncaster Carr Shed was one of the first of many built for the LNER. Erected by the Mitchell Conveyor Co, (later Mitchell Engineering Co) in 1926, plants of this shape were dubbed 'the Cenotaph' because of the similarity of form to that of the monument in Whitehall.

The sloping south-west face was blackened by oil, grease and coal dust which had dripped out of countless wagons being raised to the height of the curved guide rails. Class A1 Pacific No 2545 *Melton* and another engine in the background carry the number on the tender, as was the early LNER practice.

It is believed that the projections extending several feet each side of the mass of concrete were part of the mechanism for changing the position of the huge steel 'flap' by means of which coal of different grades was directed into one or other of the two bunkers.

This coaling plant stood on flat, open ground, and could be seen from miles away. *British Railways*

2

Steam in Perspective

Steam traction is characterised by the limited range over which a locomotive can work before it needs to take water or fuel, and to dispose of ash and clinker. Daily attention as necessary for lubrication and to ensure that the mechanism had not developed any defect. Some of these functions could be carried out in traffic or in locomotive sidings, but wherever engines were regularly serviced proper facilities were needed. The earliest running sheds were primitive, and even many which survived well into this century were not much better. Sketches and drawings of some early depots show them to be based on horse stables. To envisage railway installations and organisation as they existed at, say, the middle of the last century, one needs to ponder the general conditions of those times. The pace of life was much, much slower than that which we consider normal with our motor transport and air travel. The only competition to the fast-developing railways for inland journeys was by horse-drawn vehicles, and the very limited waterways.

As railway was constructed, so one or more running sheds were built to serve it, their sites being chosen according to a number of criteria. For instance the starting or terminating point of regular services of trains, the presence of a town or village for the recruitment and accommodation of personnel, the availability of cheap land, and particularly an adequate water supply. In the case of a branch line, the shed might well be for one or two engines only, and situated at the 'outer' end of the branch, whence the first passenger train of the day would start and the last one end its run.

Wherever a locomotive depot was built, staff were expected to migrate to it — even if it were way out in the country. Houses of very modest dimension were generally constructed by the railway or local developers. Many of these are providing accommodation years after the influence of the railway itself has been reduced to a shadow of its former activity. For instance, Staveley Central, has been reduced to a rump of main line serving as a single-track colliery branch. Yet 99 terrace houses (address 'Railway Cottages), bounding the east side of the site where the locomotive depot stood until about 1967, are still in occupation — many by railwaymen who moved to Barrow Hill on the Midland line about $1\frac{1}{2}$ miles away, and others by retired railwaymen who never thought to see the day when 'their' railway would close.

Once a marshalling yard and a running shed were established, trains were arranged to arrive and depart there, and operating ideas fossilised around that locality. There was much duplication where 20-odd companies overlapped in various parts of Great Britain with passenger, freight and mixed sheds producing the profusion of depots built up to the turn of the century. There were hundreds of towns and even villages served by two railway companies, but many dozens were served by three or more. In each large town there was a running shed for each company or one or more sheds shared by different railways. Peterborough, for example, originally had a Great Northern shed at the end of North station on the Up side, this being retained as locomotive sidings until the end of steam traction. The GNR later built a huge depot at New England, two miles to the north. To the east of the East station the Great Eastern had a shed for its engines, closed after the Amalgamation in the 1920s. The LNWR had a shed for its Rugby line, but this was closed by the LMS which had also inherited the Midland (Spital) shed. The situation was even more complex in all the conurbations. At a railway centre like Doncaster, before 1923 seven different companies worked trains into the stations and yards there. Locomotives built by most of those companies were to be seen working there over 25 years later, after Nationalisation. In some towns two companies occupied different portions of the same depot, eg Shrewsbury where the GWR and the LNWR were side-by-side neighbours. The exercise of running powers created even more complication, as indicated in K. Hoole's account of running sheds at York; see *North Eastern Locomotive Sheds* (David & Charles, Newton Abbot, 1972).

The proliferation of steam depots had the redeeming feature that any train in trouble was seldom far from help; between Kings Cross and York there were sheds at Hornsey, Hatfield, Hitchin, Peterborough, Grantham, Newark, Retford, Doncaster and Selby. A locomotive was on other main lines rarely more than 30 miles away from a place where a fitter and one or more spare engines would be at hand. Moreover, motive power depots were wonderful training grounds for supervisors, and provided great scope for progressive promotion. The men in charge of smaller sheds were soon qualified by experience to take over one of the larger sheds, and to deal with a wide range of emergencies.

Up to World War 1 each engine was usually booked to an individual driver and fireman, who went everywhere with it — often working excessive hours. When the crew returned to their shed so did the engine, hence the depot to which it was allocated was called its 'home' shed. Footplate crews often felt an affinity for 'their' engine in a way quite unknown with the 'common user' diesels. My father-in-law (a son of a traffic inspector on 'the Midland') used to know the engines at Hasland (Chesterfield) shed by the number and the driver's name — such as 'No 223 — Jack Manton's engine' or whatever the combination of number and man's name might be. On some railways the driver's name was painted in the cab.

For maintenance and power purposes each engine was allocated to a depot, which kept its detailed repair record. Before World War 1 drivers were expected to renew woollen trimmings for lubrication and even (on some railways) to re-pack soft-packed steam glands. When a locomotive developed excessive wear, its driver would report this in writing, and often pester the management, declining responsibility until the defect was rectified.

Until World War 2 the staff were under strict discipline — even to the extent of being fined for neglect or bad work. This could not, however, prevent failures due to faulty materials, unsatisfactory design (which was frequent), or bad construction. Throughout the history of steam traction there was a steady improvement in the quality of materials, especially as wrought iron gave place to steel, and as manufacturing processes improved. The inspection and testing of materials became more sophisticated and better understood, so that in the latter days of steam locomotion the failure of a part due to inferior material was rare.

The main buildings of most running sheds were very long-lived, albeit with a number of extensions. By the 1880s most main line companies were soundly based concerns, with prospects of expansion. From that time onward their buildings — including locomotive depots — were constructed to last. However, many depots which were still quite adequate for the quantity of engines being serviced there in the latter years of the last century became congested when locomotives of greater length were constructed up to World War 1. Track alterations were necessitated by changes in buildings, particularly where new facilities were provided. At some depots new straight sheds were constructed nearby, while at others longer turntables were installed, involving expensive modification of the buildings.

Almost all the average-sized or large depots on the Midland Railway, and most of those on the North Eastern were constructed with one or more 'roundhouses' of modest diameter. This was a factor in the Midland's small engine policy, which was even perpetuated by the LMS for its Midland Division. Garratts, which did not need turning, were ordered for it in 1927, and 'Claughtons' only came into use there following delivery of 'Royal' Scots to the Western Division.

In the 1890s electric trams were introduced in several cities, and in the following decades several inner suburban lines were electrified south of the Thames, causing much reduction of footplate work. From World War 1 the Southern had surpluses of firemen during the non-summer months.

Within the five or six years prior to World War 1 superheating began to be applied to freight and passenger locomotives on many railways, and this greatly complicated the task of tube-sweepers. That war brought, among other serious difficulties, the nightly handicap of black-out from the first appearance of Zeppelins, and dreadful depletions of staff. But whatever arrears of maintenance of buildings occurred then, these were soon overcome in the first few years of peace — in stark contrast to what was to happen after World War 2.

Until World War 1 brick walls and slate-covered timber roofs were commonly used for the construction of locomotive sheds, although the superstructure of many of the smaller ones was in timber only. Some railways had built quite large sheds in wood. From World War 1 re-inforced concrete (then called ferro-concrete) began to be used as a building material. A few new sheds were so constructed in the inter-war years. One of the last locomotive developments on the LSWR was the ordering of a new depot at Feltham, opened in the spring of 1923, as described in the 9 June 1923 issue of *Modern Transport*. In 1926 even the parsimonious Southern Railway, which was concentrating its slender capital resources on electrifying suburban lines, was obliged to build a new shed and coaling plant at Exmouth Junction, Exeter. This shed replaced a mainly timber structure on the same site, which was in such bad condition that it was literally falling to pieces.

By the huge Amalgamation at the beginning of 1923 the 120 plus competing companies came under new ownership, and a great deal of rationalisation became possible. This depended on developing traffic patterns and on existing connecting lines. A good example of this was at Lincoln, where the Great Central had a running shed east of Pelham St Crossing, and the Great Eastern had a small one at Pyewipe Junction, some two miles north of the city, at the connection of the GN&GE Joint Line with the original GNR line to Doncaster. Locomotives were transferred to the Great Northern depot, a short distance west of Central station. This being only a four-track dead-end shed, soon became badly congested; some relief was effected by building a mechanical coaling plant there in the mid-1930s. The Great Eastern shed was demolished, and its site abandoned; the Great Central shed was demolished and converted to carriage sidings, the turntable being retained. In the 1950s the former GCR shed site was used to build the present DMU depot.

The LMS conglomerate inherited a motley collection of under-powered locomotives, and a very indifferent assortment of running sheds from its constituent companies. During the next 10 years, while the various divisions and sections of the company tried to behave as if the grouping had never occurred, little was done about improving either the power or the depots.

It was left to Stanier to introduce from 1933 the fleet of adequately powered, Swindon-inspired locomotives for which he became renowned. The total stock of engines was reduced from 8,226 at the end of 1933 to 7,691 three years later — a decrease of 6.1% while still working a similar number of trains. This was largely due to less double-heading, following the progressive deliveries of more powerful engines, but was also in part due to the more efficient working of depots as a result of shed analysis, and to the effects of modernisation works which were carried out in depots. A considerable improvement in morale resulted from these developments, and the company reaped valuable benefits better timekeeping of trains, as well as by reduced staff costs.

The *Railway Magazine* of July 1937 contained an article entitled 'Reorganisation of LMSR Locomotive Depots'. This referred to a scheme inaugurated in 1933, embracing 47 depots. Besides major renewals and the modernisation of facilities the principal objective was the re-arrangement of tracks where this would avoid conflicting movements in depot yards. New machine tools were also provided — something almost unheard of on the other railways, where running sheds had to be content with cast-off machinery which had outlived a normal life-time of intensive use in the main works.

At some depots coaling stages, with manual filling of tubs, were replaced by mechanical coaling plants. Ash-loading equipment far superior to that provided by other railways in Great Britain was installed. The new equipment greatly reduced the time spent by engines in depots, while a much decreased stock was able to work trains conveying a greater tonnage. Having a 'concentration depot' in each motive power district, with the other depots mainly responsible for running work and minor examinations, dated from this reorganisation.

The Southern was obliged to construct about 1930 new dead-end sheds at Hither Green and Norwood to replace old ones at New Cross Gate and Croydon respectively. These were near to marshalling yards, so reducing light engine running over heavily occupied lines. Bricklayer's Arms ('The Brick') was modernised in the latter 1930s, mainly to avoid sending engines from the London area to main works for intermediate or light repairs. This was the reverse of a tendency on other railways to concentrate such repairs on the works. (See H. Holcroft, *Locomotive Adventure*, Ian Allan.)

In 1932 the LNER built the shed at Frodingham (Scunthorpe) to replace the old, South Yorkshire depot at Keadby, on the east bank of the River Trent. When I knew the shed at Frodingham, where I relieved the Shed Master in 1949, it was in such poor condition — due to the concrete having deteriorated in the damp, sulphurous atmosphere that the roof was shored up with heavy timbers.

Many depots of the LNER and the Southern remained notoriously bad in their lack of modern facilities for repairs. A few had drop-pits, or had electric winding-gear fitted to old shear-leg hoists. However, apart from mechanical coaling plants, power-operated turntables and water softening, most of them survived until the end of steam traction more or less as they had been taken over in 1923.

Several parts of the country were, however, little influenced by such moves. The Great Western was only affected by the Amalgamation to the extent of acquiring a number of small railways in South Wales, and its already well-advanced standardisation continued unchanged. The railways in Scotland were not able to achieve much rationalisation, since the Caledonian and the Highland, which did not compete with one another, passed to the LMS, while the North British and the Great North of Scotland — which did not overlap — became parts of the LNER.

At many places separate lines, served by different sheds, suited the operating patterns better than would a single depot in the same town. At Leeds Neville Hill a shed would have been very inconvenient for trains working into Central station. Apart from such cases as these, it was sometimes impracticable, due to lack of space, for one depot to absorb the engines of a neighbouring one. The LNER would have liked to combine in a single shed the locomotive facilities which it had inherited at Retford: these consisted of the GNR depot immediately west of the station and the GCR depot just over a $\frac{1}{4}$-mile away at Thrumpton crossing. Several schemes designed to achieve this purpose had foundered owing to the company's chronic lack of capital. By the time I relieved the Shed Master there in 1949 a single shed administration, and the concentration of all passenger engines at the GN shed were about all that had been achieved.

World War 2 brought much worse civilian conditions than the first one, including frequent heavy aerial bombing. One direct hit on York shed during the night of 29 October 1942 exploded between Class B16 4-6-0, No 925 and Class A4 Pacific, No 4469 *Sir Ralph Wedgewood*, which was standing minus its driving wheels after having been on the drop pit. Both were damaged beyond repair.

Numerous other sheds sustained severe bomb damage, but had to carry on under stringent 'black-out' precautions and in spite of frequent air-raid alerts, the staff often taking cover in dank underground shelters. Damaged buildings were given only minimal amounts of patching up. Many running sheds — particularly on the LNER and the Southern — were in no shape to cope with the arduous exigencies of war. Moreover, many locomotives (most of all Gresley's) deteriorated rapidly when maintenance fell below the standards of 1939.

Spare parts were often in short supply, so that the sheds had often to 'make do and mend' with worn-out components and machinery long overdue for replacement. The main Works were in similar difficulties, and so could not ensure peace-time standards of workmanship, besides having to overhaul many obsolete, Victorian engines, which under normal conditions would have been scrapped.

Electrification usually spells the closing of steam sheds, but the Manchester-Sheffield-Wath scheme, prepared in 1938-9, and deferred because of World War 2, included the building in 1944 of a new steam depot at Darnall, east of Sheffield Victoria — near to where the postwar electric traction was exchanged for steam haulage of freight trains. This depot, constructed during the war, replaced the cramped, Neepsend shed, built by the Manchester, Sheffield & Lincolnshire Railway on the west side of the city. For some 80 years or more an average-length shunting operation at that shed had necessitated the occupation of the adjacent main line.

Nationalisation of the railways at the beginning of 1948 was the ultimate in amalgamation. However, numerous running sheds could not be closed until overlapping commercial areas and operating lines had been rationalised. The new regime naturally had many uncertainties to contend with, and one of its early pre-occupations was to formulate a motive power policy. After much investigation of diesel traction in North America and elsewhere, it was decided to continue with the existing steam locomotives, to supplement these with some new building to the latest designs of the four main line companies, and to construct a range of locomotives according to British Railways designs as a hybrid of the best existing practice.

The dilapidated state of many sheds, which persisted through most of the 1950s, was a monumental disgrace. Several accompanying photographs show buildings with the roof over the tracks missing, or in various states of chronic disrepair. On staff welfare grounds alone there was a crying need to effect drastic improvements in most steam depots, and in the worst affected places a certain amount of reconstruction was done, in the form of new mess-rooms, etc. Such renovation of shed buildings as was done — and many of them were very old, as well as sadly neglected — was in most cases limited to pulling down roofs or walls which were scarcely safe, and patching up the rest.

When I took charge of Staveley Central on 1 January 1951 it had a 12-track 'dead-end' shed with the roof over the tracks mostly missing. During the subsequent 18 months a new roof was installed over the two tracks nearest the offices etc and the next three tracks adjacent to them were roofed over for about an engine length nearest to the shed front. New, adjacent outer walls were constructed, and the east wall of the old building was demolished (This is the more correct version of the account given on page 102 of *Steam was my Calling*.

Most sheds had to be content with more modest treatment, often consisting of the installation of electric lighting, replacing early, inadequate electric lighting — or even surviving gas lamps.

A surprising number of large depots remained on sites close to main stations until the end of steam traction. These included Cambridge, Peterborough Spital, Rugby, Crewe North, York and Leicester Midland.

The prophets of dieselisation had been preaching mainly in vain for almost a generation when British Railways plumped heavily for diesel traction and electrification under the Modernisation Plan of 1955, under which the Government belatedly placed huge sums of capital at their disposal. From then on it took remarkably little time for the throb of the diesel or the whirr of electrics to be heard all over the country. Some modernisation of steam sheds was allowed for, and a few running shed buildings, including Immingham (Grimsby) were reconstructed using steel frames and asbestos sheeting.

From the mid-1950s there was a heavy decline in traffic — especially freight. This had many causes, including changing Government policies, which favoured road haulage at the expense of rail. But worst of all was the most damaging strike in British railway history, when the Associated Society of Locomotive Engineers & Firemen virtually shut down the whole system for 17 days in 1955. Not only was a great amount of traffic turned away at that time — while most of the management's expenses continued undiminished — but a crippling blow was struck at British Railways' reputation as a reliable public carrier. Hundreds of thousands of customers who found alternative means of transporting themselves and their goods never again returned regularly to rail.

It was altogether against the general run of developments that a big, new straight 'through' shed, and a round house (nick-named 'the bull ring') plus a large new coaling plant were constructed at Thornaby-on-Tees in 1958, although authorised some time earlier. This was widely taken to mean that in the north-east at least serviceable steam locomotives would have an extended lease of life. In the event, however, heavily declining freight traffics and the dwindling patronage of stopping passenger trains forced a reduction in the number of lines and services, and led to a rapid diminution in the work of many locomotive depots. Massive deliveries of diesel locomotives under the Modernisation Plan hastened the closing of many a steam depot. Then in 1963 was issued the Report on the Re-shaping of British Railways — a long overdue exercise — quickly followed by the Beeching closures. For the running sheds it became a matter of maintaining the existing facilities at minimum expenditure.

Traffic continued to decline, and further rationalisation took place as more and more diesels were delivered, until on 5 August 1968 — after more than 140 years of valuable public service — unsued the complete demise of commercial steam traction in Great Britain.

The earliest duty of horses on railways had much preceded locomotives; this form of traction was to last virtually as long as steam, Shire horses being retained for moving single wagons at Newmarket until 1967. They were able to step easily from one track to another directly, while a shunting engine would have to make awkward to-and-fro' time-consuming switching movements.

As a 'tailpiece' to this historical perspective, steam traction had much more affinity with the work of horses than most people recognised. In the last century many thousands of men were recruited to railway work from agriculture, and it was not surprising that they should bring farming terms with them. In the earliest days of steam engines 'she' or 'he' were often applied to them — often as expressions of affection or abuse. The feminine form was more common (as with ships) in spite of many locomotives having such robustly masculine names as *Dick Turpin*.

Water is common to both engines and horses; filling up a tank at a water column was sometimes referred to as 'giving her a drink'. Officially the water forced into a boiler was 'feed water', but coal was more logically a locomotive's food, and indeed one sometimes spoke of 'feeding' coal into a firebox. When fed with an excess of coal, a fire would not burn properly (indigestion). Shovelling ash away was removing the waste product (manure), while putting an engine in the shed until it was required for the next turn of duty was frequently called 'stabling'. Indeed, a short length of dead-end track provided for stabling a single locomotive — particularly one of the stub-end tracks leading off the turntable of a round-house — was popularly known as a 'stall'.

A locomotive which would not steam freely was sometimes 'thrashed' with full regulator and long cut-off of the valve gear to 'liven up' a sluggish fire, or to charge at an incline with a heavy load, (the fireman had to do a lot of sweating). When an engine was working hard hauling a train up a steep gradient, it was said to be 'pulling against the collar'. Another which was creating an unusual noise, or giving other signs of defect (symptoms of sickness) would be driven less hard than one in good order, and was thus being 'nursed'.

An engine which was run-down (eg with valves or valve-gear worn) might be 'coaxed' but driving it with less than full regulator uphill, while one which had broken down was commonly called a 'cripple' — and so on. Some locomotives seemed to have almost as much individuality as the men who drove them — which was saying much. Steam engines were surely the nearest machines ever made to an animal in performance — even at times appearing to have a will of their own. If not properly treated (for example tubes clogged), they would refuse to steam well. Certain engines would acquire a reputation for running as fast as the wind, while other engines of the same class were downright lazy — when they had a full head of steam they would not pull as well as their stable-mates. (This was mainly a matter of valve-setting.)

And what better way was there to describe the action of a willing horse than 'running'? — as was applied to engines in traffic everywhere in Great Britain. By the way that some 'loco running' men were talking after 120-odd years of steam traction, one might have been forgiven for thinking that the most modern of iron horses needed at least eight hours rest in every 24.

Many readers will be able to supply other examples of 'ferroequinology'. But to crown all these animal analogies, one writer even lamented, following British Railways' decision in 1956 to build no more steam locomotives after its 1958 programme, that 'the breed would no longer reproduce itself'!

2
Class A3 Pacific No 84 *Trigo* as re-numbered by Thompson from 1946 in postwar livery, seen under the coaling plant at York on 30 May 1947. The fireman is observing the coal which has piled up above the loading gauge. The black marks across the lining above the letter N are probably due to oil which has dropped down from the plant, and to which coal dust had adhered. *BR Eastern Region*

3

Fuel for the Iron Horses

It was the burning of coal (or oil) which caused steam locomotives to be enormous dirt-producers, contaminating themselves, their crews and others who had to work on them, and much of their close environment. They thus contributed heavily to the general grime of industrial areas. From the earliest days of steam railways Parliament stipulated in the Acts by which various railway companies were incorporated the obligation that 'engines must consume their own smoke'. Coke continued in general use until brick arches, constructed of refractory bricks, were successfully developed for use in fireboxes from the latter 1860s. These made it possible to burn coal almost smokelessly *when a bright fire of good quality coal was maintained, with an adequate draught being drawn over the fire.*

There were millions of cases when these conditions were not satisfied, due to poor coal, or bad firing, or both, and this provoked innumerable public protests. But the railways carried on practically with impunity, often regardless of this very inefficient consumption of fuel. When specifications were drawn up for a new running shed, built at Doncaster Carr in 1875, they included two coke stages — one at each end of the shed yard.

Coal was graded for locomotive purposes according to its suitability for various classes of train working. Coal from particular collieries was considered to fall within one or other of these categories, although different seams from the same pit might yield coal of quite different quality. Yorkshire Hards are considered to be some of the best steaming coals, particularly from a number of pits in the neighbourhood of Doncaster. The lumps are not friable (do not crumble), they burn with long yellow flames, and combustion is virtually smokeless when provided with ample 'top air'. Over a hundred years' innumerable sparkling runs were made with this fuel on the East Coast main line.

Mixed traffic depots were supplied with different grades of coal in proportion to the amount of trains of each kind which they worked. Dozens of the larger depots had coaling plants containing two or more bunkers for the various grades. Some enginemen were prone to fill up their tenders with better grades than that warranted for the type of train they were to haul, supervision being difficult, particularly during the hours of darkness.

Firemen naturally did not like shovelling coal from any further back in the coal space than could be avoided, so whenever possible enginemen would find occasion to go under a coaling plant to take extra coal. Sometimes they would drive an engine round to an ashpit to rake out ashes, although it had already been disposed when it came into the depot. Often these were genuine moves to make a locomotive fit for extra hours in traffic, but sometimes it was more a matter of creating additional work, such as oiling around an engine which did not really need it.

Tender engines consumed up to nine tons of coal per day, but the average was nearer to three tons. At the peak of steam traction in Great Britain it was reckoned that the railways were absorbing some 7-8% of the total output of all the collieries in the country. Thousands of wagons were allocated exclusively to the carrying of 'Loco coal', and often whole trains were run conveying this commodity alone. In order to maintain a constant check on the quality of the fuel being delivered, each railway employed a number of coal inspectors who visited the pits and the depots periodically, taking samples which were analysed by the Chief Chemist's staff.

Only certain grades of coal were designated as suitable for locomotive use. However, during the 1940s and well into the 1950s inferior kinds had to be used from time to time in certain localities because fuel of the requisite quality just was not available. From the early 1940s persistent shortages of underground workers necessitated the increasing use of coal-cutting machinery, which often broke up the coal smaller than was done by hand-hewing. Picking out dirt and shale was not done with prewar thoroughness, so that a certain amount of mineral rubbish came through. I have often seen lumps of fairly hard ash, up to the size of a man's hand shovelled out from a fire-grate. These were known in South Yorkshire as 'bats', and were the remains of pieces of semi-combustible shale.

During the war and the 1950s maximum-quantity production of coal was pursued at almost any price. In wartime long hours were worked, and discipline 'went for a Burton'; coal of inferior quality could all too easily be dumped on the persistent 'seller's market'. However, during the 1950s distribution gradually improved and better qualities became available, though not to 1939 standards. But the prices continued to soar, and this was one of the principal factors leading to the suppression of steam traction.

The coaling of locomotives was for decades done by hand, shovelling direct from a wagon into tenders and tank-engine bunkers. This method persisted throughout the history of steam locomotion at hundreds of depots where there were only one or two engines. In some cases, the coal-wagon track was built at several feet above the engine track, so as to reduce the upward throwing required, and thus to speed up the operation. In many cases not even the most rudimentary shelter was provided, although the coalman often managed to rig up some protection with old tarpaulin and ropes.

A very early invention was a narrow wooden stage, constructed to about the height of a wagon floor, on to which coal was stacked. Locomotives came alongside this stage, whence coal was shovelled into the tenders; this was much easier than digging coal out of a wagon. Furthermore a reserve of coal could be transferred to the stage when the coalman was not occupied with engines, and so a wagon could be released earlier. Such a stage was in use at the engine turn-round point at Rickmansworth, whence Metropolitan (later London Transport) trains were worked forward by steam locomotives until the line was electrified in the early 1960s. Up to World War 2 manual labour was incredibly cheap, so that many an agricultural worker with little security of employment, and even lower pay than the lowest grade of railwayman was glad to take a steady job shovelling coal at a running shed. (In parts of Africa and Asia men and women still load baskets with coal from a wagon, using their hands; they then raise the basket on to their heads and stagger with it up a plank to tip it into a tender.

From medium height stages (such as existed at many of the smallest depots to the end of steam traction) it was a natural development to construct the elevated stages of the larger sheds.

At many depots whose yard was too small for an elevated stage, four-wheeled steel tubs were loaded on a platform near ground level by hand-shovel from wagons — usually under an ample roof. The tubs, which had one end hinged at the top were raised by jib crane; this was originally hand-operated, but in many cases was later equipped with an electric motor. By this means the tubs were tipped over tenders. Up to a dozen tubs were kept loaded on a narrow-gauge track, where they were filled from wagons by hand, and whence they were raised by an electric hoist. Elevators of this type were used at locomotive turn-round points; Kings Cross and Marylebone station yards, Barnstaple junction, Barnsley and Retford (ex-Great Northern) were just a few of which I had personal knowledge. At the latter place an antiquated tub-hoisting jib-crane was kept as a reserve facility, while the ex-Great Central shed there was still using in the 1950s an old radial crane, with hand-filled tubs. By then it was becoming difficult to get men to do this heavy, dirty, unskilled work.

When unloading coal wagons by hand the usual procedure was to release the top fastenings of a side-door, allowing it to fall under an avalanche of coal — this being a possible cause of accidents. Where coaling was done by hand, or by hand-filled tubs it was common for an ashpit to be installed alongside the coaling facilities, so that ash disposal could be done at the same time.

Almost all elevated coal-stages were constructed with the coal-wagon rails and the steel-plate covered floor, on which the tubs were loaded and pushed around, at a height of about 13ft above the level of the track on which locomotives were coaled. The tubs were trundled to a tippling point, where they were tilted so that the coal shot out of the hinged end on to tenders of engines standing below. When there were no locomotives being coaled the coalmen filled empty tubs, so that a reserve of full ones was ready to tip on to the next engine to arrive.

Wagons were raised at an elevated stage by being propelled up a ramp which was in many cases as steep as 1 in 20, and occasionally even steeper. It was quite a sight to watch a shunting tank, or sometimes a tender engine push a rake of wagons at full regulator over a hundred yards or more, using the impetus to storm up the stiff incline until the wagons were on the upper level of the coal-stage. It sometimes happened that a driver unused to this tricky task (especially by bad weather in the dark) pushed one or more wagons through the buffer stops at the end of the elevated track.

All coaling stages were draughty places, but elevated ones were particularly exposed. They had to be open along most of one side for access to the engines, and open at each end for the access and outlet of wagons.

As each wagon was emptied it was moved by means of a pinch-bar and direct pushing to the top of the gradient; its descent was then controlled with the lever-type hand brake, using a shunting pole to prise against any convenient part of the wagon's anatomy, and then pinning the lever in the brake-applied position.

Nearly all the larger depots in Great Britain had an elevated coaling stage until the 1920s, although a few mechanical plants were installed before World War 1. (See K. Hoole's account of the one brought into use in 1916 at Hull (Dairycoates), his book *North Eastern Locomotive Sheds,* David & Charles, 1972.)

The Great Western, which had very much its own ideas about coal (as about many other matters), used South Wales coal almost exclusively, and its engines all had narrow fire-grates on which this was usually burned in a 'haycock' pile. Since this coal was very friable (tending to crumble when dropped) no GWR shed had a mechanical coaling plant.

Apart from the elevated type of coal stage, there was an arrangement known as 'coal-drops'; these were derived from the coal-staithes by which coal was discharged from wagons into river craft or coastal ships. They were considerably higher than coal-stages, for below the wagons were bunkers into which coal was unloaded by hoppers in the wagon floors, or sometimes by shovelling out the wagons. From the bunkers coal was released by gravity into locomotive tenders or bunkers. This system was favoured for the larger sheds on the Queensland Railways; it was also used at Liverpool, Edge Hill.

The most direct possible way of obtaining coal was to be found at a colliery near the foot of the Worsborough Incline between Wath and Penistone. There the LNER Garratt and other engines on banking duties used to go under the coal-screens and took coal from the same chutes as were used to load wagons.

On the West Coast main line most of Stanier's Pacifics were provided with a steam-operated coal-pusher, which could be heard by passengers riding in the front of the train. Almost all of the LMS Garratts, working mainly on the Midland Division, were fitted with slightly inclined rotary bunkers, which fed the coal forward, but these had a tendency to break the coal into small lumps and dust. A photograph of one of these locomotives and a description of maintenance problems with the bunker is given by W. G. F Thorley in *A Breath of Steam* (Ian Allan, 1975).

The LNER and LMS installed mechanical coaling plants from 1926, and by 1939 almost all their sheds with an allocation exceeding 40 engines was equipped with such a plant. Those at Kings Cross, Peterborough (New England), York, Gorton and some other sheds on the LNER, as well as various depots on the LMS were of a type which raised a wagon, together with a section of track which formed a platform, and raised it to around 60ft above rail-level, where it was tippled through about 130°.

Coaling Plants of this type built by the Mitchell Conveyor Co were nick-named the 'Cenotaph', because their shape was reminiscent of the War Memorial in Whitehall. Their great height caused them to be prominent landmarks, so that across open country, as at Doncaster Carr, they could be seen from miles away. Early during World War 2 lubricating oil was found streaming from the bottom of the bunker of the coaling plant referred to above. Urgent enquiries revealed that a wagon loaded with barrels full of oil intended for the shed stores had, by mistake, been shunted among the wagons of locomotive coal. The coaling plant attendant had quite unsuspectingly discharged this into the coaling plant bunker, and then tipped other wagon-loads of coal on top of them — so bursting the barrels. One may imagine what a filthy, Herculean task it was to clear the obstructions out of the 40ft deep coal hopper.

It was found that the first generation of mechanical coaling plants consumed an exhorbitant amount of electric power in raising a wagon containing some 20 tons of coal, plus the heavy platform-section of track on which it stood, to a height of over 60ft. Later plants, constructed by various contractors (including Henry Lees & Co) were therefore built with a wagon-tippler at ground level, or used hopper wagons. A skip which descended below the ground received the coal, and automatically hoisted it. These had capital cost much less than for a 'Cenotaph' type.

The largest coaling plant of all was at Stratford, which had by far the largest allocation of locomotives. In this the coal was raised by two parallel conveyor belts; this had the advantage that by a simple system of diversions from the belt coal could be fed in different grades to several bunkers. This plant was never completely out of action during the whole of its long life.

An important advantage of a coaling plant in a cramped shed yard, such as at Boston, was that it needed considerably less space than an elevated stage, with its long ramp. For reasons of minimising the disturbance to existing depot track and building layouts, it was usual to instal a coaling plant in close proximity to the stage which it displaced.

Drawings of all the various types of coaling plant mentioned, and descriptions of their operation may be found in H. C. Webster's book *Locomoitve Running Shed Practice.* Notes about coaling and a photograph of the twin-bunker coaling plant at Rugby are given in *Locomotive Management:*

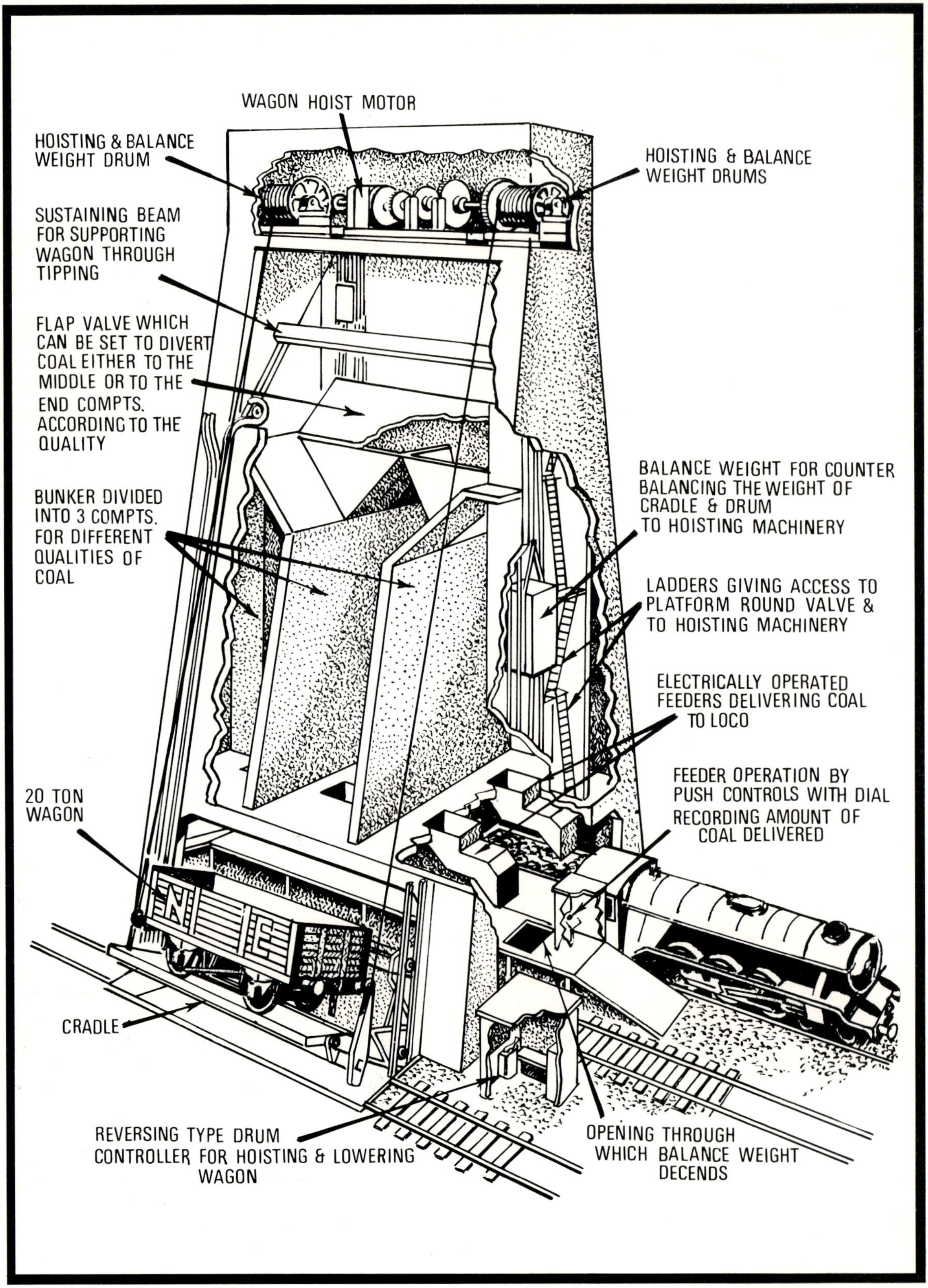
WAGON HOIST MOTOR
HOISTING & BALANCE WEIGHT DRUM
HOISTING & BALANCE WEIGHT DRUMS
SUSTAINING BEAM FOR SUPPORTING WAGON THROUGH TIPPING
FLAP VALVE WHICH CAN BE SET TO DIVERT COAL EITHER TO THE MIDDLE OR TO THE END COMPTS. ACCORDING TO THE QUALITY
BUNKER DIVIDED INTO 3 COMPTS. FOR DIFFERENT QUALITIES OF COAL
BALANCE WEIGHT FOR COUNTER BALANCING THE WEIGHT OF CRADLE & DRUM TO HOISTING MACHINERY
LADDERS GIVING ACCESS TO PLATFORM ROUND VALVE & TO HOISTING MACHINERY
ELECTRICALLY OPERATED FEEDERS DELIVERING COAL TO LOCO
FEEDER OPERATION BY PUSH CONTROLS WITH DIAL RECORDING AMOUNT OF COAL DELIVERED
20 TON WAGON
NE
CRADLE
REVERSING TYPE DRUM CONTROLLER FOR HOISTING & LOWERING WAGON
OPENING THROUGH WHICH BALANCE WEIGHT DECENDS

Cleaning, Driving, Maintenance (7th edition) pages 36-7.

The immense weight of a coaling plant, built to contain — as a rough average — some 300 tons of coal, and itself weighing around that much, posed serious problems of foundations). During a shed analysis on Neasden in 1950 we were surprised to find the unique feature of *two* coaling plants very close to one another. This had come about because the original plant (the first installed on the GC main line) had begun to tilt in the manner of the Leaning Tower of Pisa, so that it was impossible to keep the machinery in working order. A new one was therefore constructed a few yards further along the track. By the time I was appointed to that depot in 1954, the old plant had been demolished, and the new one was functioning as coaling plants should.

However, I found that the maintenance fitter was riding to the top of the plant in the skip, and was only prevented from being thrown into the bunker when the skip tippled over by his mate switching off the hoisting movement at the appropriate moment from ground level. I remonstrated with him for thus risking his life, but he pointed out that it was less dangerous than climbing an unprotected steel ladder in wind and rain. Having ascended coaling plants by such death-daring ladders at six or seven other depots I had to concede that riding in the skip was indeed safer. (See *Steam was my Calling*, page 125.)

The usual means of mounting to the top of a 'Cenotaph' type coaling plant was to ride on one end of the platform-section of track, with nothing to hold on to but a wagon buffer. There was only steadiness of nerve and sureness of foot in all states of the weather to prevent one's falling some 60ft to the ground when the moment came to step off the moving platform on to a fixed narrow one, just as the wagon began to turn upside down to discharge its load into the bunker below.

The coaling plant of a heavy freight depot, such as Frodingham, having about 85 engines allocated, would have to supply them with some 250 to 300 tons per day. The controls for the release of coal from the bunker were installed in a cabin on a platform at about the level of the cab floor of a locomotive, so that after the engine had been set under the chute, the driver or fireman could step straight out of the cab to set in motion the 'jigger' or 'shuffler' which regulated the outflow of coal. The lever which started the mechanism also turned on water-sprays, thus drenching the coal falling on to the tender, and so laid most of the dust.

At Nottingham Midland and some other depots the old elevated coaling stage was kept in reserve in case of failure of the mechanical plant, particularly as at Woodford and other sheds where the main water tank formed the upper part of the structure.

The economy-keen Locomotive Department of the Great Northern and of some other railways operated a very meticulously applied coal bonus scheme for their footplate men as a means of making savings with this expensive commodity. On some of the early LMS and LNER coaling plants a recording apparatus was mounted in the operating cabin, and on this the driver composed the number of his engine, which was then printed on a paper roll. A mechanical counter registered the number of horizontal strokes made by the 'jigger' mechanism, and a nominal amount of coal — supposedly corresponding to the quantity of strokes (or 'shuffles') was also recorded on the roll. A realistic measure might have been so obtained had the coal been regularly of a consistent size, but this could not be guaranteed — so the amount of coal dispensed could only be indicated approximately.

Whatever the method of coaling no engine should leave with coal which might fall off when the engine moved; however, this was easier ordered than enforced, and shed masters, running foremen and inspectors frequently had cause to speak to men who had not trimmed their coal properly. This was particularly so with engines making long runs — as on the East and West Coast main lines. At Kings Cross and at Edinburgh, (Haymarket) special attention had to be paid to packing coal by hand on the top of the tender of the Pacifics used to haul the 393-mile summer-time non-stop London-Edinburgh (from 1928 to 1939 the 'Flying Scotsman', and from 1953 'The Elizabethan'). This remained the world's longest non-stop run. The coal was stacked to somewhat above the loading gauge, but the tender carrying its maximum complement of coal and water was down on its springs, and the coal would vibrate down in passing over the first few dozen rail joints.

However, on other workings the coal was seldom so carefully trimmed; in spite of the best efforts of supervisors, there was often much spillage of coal around mechanical coaling plants, and a certain amount scattered alongside the tracks leading from there toward the preparation pits and to the shed outlet. From Polmadie (Glasgow) there was even a sprinkling of coal for a mile from there toward Glasgow Central station.

Most depots had one or more coal stacks. The best form of base for a stack was a concrete surface with drainage gulleys, but this was rarely provided. It was considered that a thick base of large lumps of chalk, levelled off and rolled flat with a dressing of ash, on top was nearly as good. Sometimes the ground surface consisted simply of consolidated locomotive ash, as found in running shed or marshalling yards. I have also known instances of coal being dumped on rough grassland.

The site for a walled coal stack was staked out to about 6ft from the near rail of the siding. Along this line a wall was built, using large, long lumps — in the manner of dry-stone walling. As this proceeded, the space behind it was filled in. From World War 2 an excavator was often hired for the purpose, as also for lifting a stack. Coal storage was thus yet another of those duties ancillary to steam traction which called for rough, out-of-doors labouring work.

When the storage was done correctly — as it generally was until 1940 — only large lumps were put into the stack, good weathering grades being supplied specially for the purpose. However, from that time inadequate supplies of good-quality coal sometimes led to coal being put to stack which was not really suitable for storage.

It was normal to replenish the stacks in summertime, when coal was plentiful, and sometimes seasonally cheaper, although it might be done at any time when supplies were in excess of current use.

Shortages of labour often prevented reserve coal from being lifted, so that it was subjected to much weathering. Crushed coal therefore accumulated at the bottom of stacks and tenders, so that when the coal on an engine was running low after extended hours in traffic there would be only 'nutty slack' to draw on. This would depress the firebox temperature unless the engine could be thrashed at full regulator, thus creating an unusually strong draught on the fire.

When a stack was cleared the material at its base was lifted with the coal unless it was readily distinguishable, especially when mechanical handling equipment was used, since a drag-line, or other machine was not sensitive to the difference between slack coal and other kinds of soft material.

With coal being generally used for domestic heating it was an attractive commodity, especially when it was rationed in wartime. So when labour was available the tops of the stacks were made level, and their vertical and horizontal corners were whitewashed, so that any considerable amount of pilfering would soon be apparent. The whitewashing served further purposes in improving the appearance of the yard, and also made it easier to find one's way about in the dark. The latter consideration was particularly important during the black-out which had to be imposed during the two World Wars.

Centralised dumps were provided by some railways, so as to ensure a greater reserve than that which could be accommodated at depots with restricted suitable ground space. This was, however, only economical if machines such as mechanical shovels, skimmers, excavators or mobile cranes fitted with grabs were used. Some of these could be used for lifting ashes. None of these machines is, however, suitable for unloading a wagon. When there was a surplus of wagons coal would be held in reserve in them, so avoiding putting it to ground and lifting it again. While it was uneconomic to hold revenue-earning wagons in this way for more than a week or two, it was quite justifiable to use condemned wagons for this purose.

Putting coal to stack is not a likely subject for anecdote, but Neasden depot — where I suffered as Shed Master for 15 hectic months in 1954 and 1955 — was capable of producing complications in the most hum-drum of activities. There had been a number of serious shortages in the country during the early 1950s, so several train-loads of American coal were sent from a wharf in East London for storage at various depots. However, the London Midland Operating Department unwittingly came to our aid. First they said that they could provide any additional footplate crews, so we made considerable efforts to supply drivers and firemen. They then agreed, but as soon as the next train was due to run they scratched it, saying this time that they had no guard available.

So after all this, a contract was placed for the coal to be ferried several miles across the highly-congested built-up area by a fleet of tipper-lorries. This solved our stacking problem, since the lorries unloaded themselves — albeit in low piles on to rough ground, instead of stacking it to a height of about 6ft. Next came heavy rain to complicate the proceedings, and so the lorries — loaded to over 20 tons gross — soon got bogged down in mud. Not to be beaten by this little difficulty, we hauled out the stranded tippers by hitching them with a steel hawser to a steam locomotive. There was ample power, but we had to be mighty careful not to damage the lorries. In a few days the job was completed — but what a way to deliver coal, which had already been standing in wagons, to a railway depot!

An incident was related to me by one of the lorry-drivers, which had nothing to do with railways, but is well worthy of being retold here. He, with several others, had been employed on moving a large quantity of building materials from one site to another. The area from which the stuff was being removed was urgently required for clearance, with a penalty to be paid for every day of delay. The contractor at that site therefore offered the drivers a bonus of £1 a day to clear the site as quickly as possible. So the tempo of turn-round was stepped up, but the material then started arriving at the delivery end in such a flood that the place became inundated with it. The Clerk-of-the-Works asked the lorry-drivers to ease off the rate of delivery, but they said that they were under pressure from the despatching end to complete the job rapidly, However, if he would agree to pay them £1 per day per man then they would revert to the former pace of working. So by making pretences of hurrying and offering excuses for traffic delays at the clearance site, and by dawdling about at the delivery end, the rascals had collected £2 a day tax-free bonus for driving normally between two points!

At various times of severe national coal shortage several railways of Great Britain experimented with oil firing, notably in 1921 and again 1947-49. In the 1920s coal was imported from the Continent (especially Poland), and this made good the shortfall.

Richard Hardy, in *Steam in the Blood*, (Ian Allan, 1972) gives an account of his exploits with an oil-fired WD 2-8-0 in 1949. At about that time fuel tanks and pumping houses were installed in many of the larger running sheds. However, it was considered more economical to import large amounts of coal from the USA, than to equip a considerable number of locomotives with oil-firing apparatus. Full-scale oil-firing was never adopted in any section of railway in this country.

3
Coaling plants were of many shapes and sizes. This one was photographed on 2 March 1968 at the end of steam traction at Buxton. The water tank is supported by a massive limestone wall, which was part of the original coaling stage, as was typical of a considerable number of north-country depots. *J. S. Hancock*

4
Normanton depot yard on 7 October 1967, after steam locomotives allocated to that shed had all been withdrawn. The line of engines in the picture were being serviced after working in from the London Midland Region. Two diesels are at the right and two near the coaling plant. That plant was of the type which lifts a wagon bodily to the top of the bunker. The main line is at the extreme left. *J. S. Hancock*

5
A steam crane at Fratton discharging a coal tub into the tender of a BR Standard Class 4 2-6-0 on 22 May 1957. Another tub is being loaded from the wagon on the right. The two tracks in the foreground have pits.

After the electrification of the Portsmouth-Waterloo and Brighton-Portsmouth lines, Fratton had very few locomotives left. *H. C. Casserley*

6
Class 47xx 2-8-0 No 4707 on the ashpit alongside the coaling stage at Southall about 1960. Note the hydrant for quenching hot ashes, installed in a very exposed position. Great Western depots did not have fixed ash-handling plant. *J. S. Hancock*

7
The LMS had a considerable variety of ash-handling plants. The one at Buxton was pictured here on 2 March 1968 in the last days of steam power in the Peak District. A skip was raised on the inclined rails, and discharged ashes into a wagon. *J. S. Hancock*

8
45xx 2-6-2 Great Western tank No 4555 is here shown taking water at an unknown date and location. This engine is preserved on the Dart Valley Light Railway; note the central gap in the back of the cab by which the fireman could obtain access to the bunker — also the shield at the top of the bunker to protect a lamp placed on the top lamp-iron. *J. S. Hancock*

9
Class 5XP 4-6-0 No 45646 *Napier* being re-victualled at the north end of Nottingham Victoria Station, while working a Poole-Leeds/Bradford train in the last years of operation of the Great Central main line. The engine is blowing off while the fireman holds the leather hose in the tender filling hole. At the light patch about 2ft from the back of the tender two pencil-sized leaks are squirting out on to the platform. The driver of the train just off the picture to the right is sitting on a pile of sleepers, waiting for his turn to depart. The coach is of post-Gresley LNER construction.

Note the water-storage tank at the upper ground-level beyond the tree. The site of most of this huge white elephant of a station is now occupied by the Victoria Centre.
J. S. Hancock

10
Kennicott 10,000 gallon water softening plant at Carlton, near Gowdall Junction, Hull & Barnsley Railway, as described in *The Locomotive* magazine of 15 November 1912 pages 241-3, showing 2-4-0 No 41A. The water tank was typical, with its water gauge having the indicator at the bottom when the tank was full. *The Locomotive*

11
A locomotive with four tenders!? Yes and no; the last three are tenders converted to sludge carriers, conveying sludge in 1962 from the water softening plants at Scrooby Troughs (near Bawtry) and Doncaster to a dumping ground near Ranskill. Part of this can be seen beyond the bushes ahead of the smokebox of Class K1 2-6-0 No 62014 heading south on the East Coast main line. *J. S. Hancock*

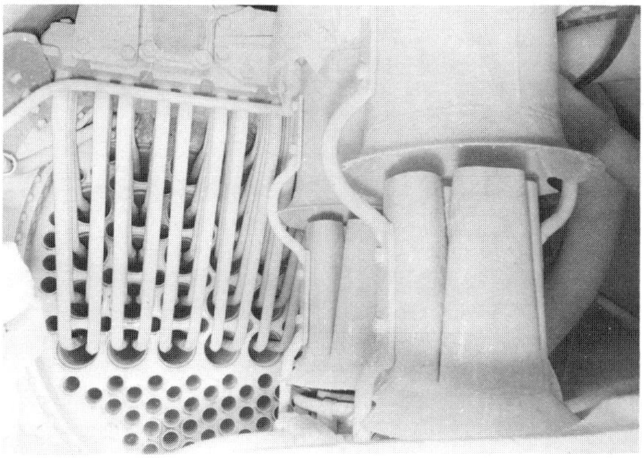

12
Tube-sweeper's view of a boiler, but this boiler has not yet been fired. It shows a smokebox with a 'Kylchap' double blast pipe and twin chimney cowls. The position of this equipment ahead of the superheater header explains why the chimney had to be well forward on the smokebox. At the left may be seen the flanges of a main steam pipe. The small sloping pipes are the superheater elements, expanded into the superheater header. The pipe running across the smokebox just below and ahead of the header conveys steam to the blower rings on top of the blast pipe.
British Rail Engineering Ltd

13
The boilersmiths' department. A view of a Pacific firebox taken in 1964 through the firehole, giving a splendid impression of the brick arch. Fireboxes were never as clean as this, even when new; the effect has been obtained by photographer Ben Burrell by spraying the surfaces with whitewash for the sake of the picture. It shows how the heating surface was maximised by placing small tubes alongside and between the superheated tubes. Note also the huge fire 'bricks' which were used in wide LNER fireboxes — thus greatly simplifying the work of building the arch. Smaller bricks were used in the middle of the front row where the fire was probably hottest due to flame passing between the front of the arch and the throat plate. The riveted joints between this plate and the wrapper plate, and between these and the tube-plate can be clearly seen. A lead plug is just visible between the roof stays near the front of the middle of the firebox crown. *British Rail Engineering Ltd*

14
Close-up of the drop pit at York on 30 May 1947. The two men in the pit (one of whom cannot restrain his interest in the photographer) are there for the purpose of guiding the axleboxes into the horn-plates as the drop-table is raised hydraulically. The frame, etc, of the Class V2 2-6-2 are in typically filthy condition for that period, and the men's overalls are correspondingly dirty. Note an axlebox spring, coupling rods, and a portable paraffin bath (for cleaning pins and other small items). *BR Eastern Region*

15
The drop-pit at New England, Peterborough, with the table partly lowered, taken in 1928. The crank-axle is from an ex-GNR 0-6-0, the axle being machined from a single solid forging. *John Crawley collection*

16
Ex-North Eastern 0-8-0 (LNER Class Q6) No 63450 on the drop-pit in the repair shop of Darlington depot on 24 April 1965. The front pair of wheels had been removed, hence the heavy timber baulks supporting the front end of the engine. The repair pit was narrower at the point, so as to allow concrete strengthening where the pit ran into the drop-pit. A spring, a leading coupling rod, a bottle-jack and a pinch-bar are clearly visible.

Left of the baulks can be seen the extension of the drop-pit from which wheels were hoisted for re-turning in the machine bay beyond.

This shop was much more light and airy than most running shed repair shops. It formed part of a building containing seven straight-through tracks, constructed in 1939 to supplement the hopelessly inadequate, small roundhouse which dated from 1865. *J. S. Hancock*

17
Class D13 4-4-0 No 7772, photographed at Norwich on 30 June 1936. Its proportions scarcely conceal that it was re-built from a 2-4-0. The generously roomy cab and low tender were typical of Great Eastern practice. It was common at the larger sheds to see one or more locomotives stabled minus a pair of wheels, while axle journals or tyres were being turned.

In the background is a Class J21 0-6-0, far from its native North Eastern Area. *H. C. Casserley*

18
Who says there was never a 2-8-0 in the BR Standard range? — well, if you don't mind running about with a rear axle missing! Class 9F No 92201, photographed at Doncaster on 13 December 1964, towards the end of steam traction it illustrates the fact that hot axleboxes were never overcome so long as plain bearings were used.

Beyond the front end of this engine can be seen the London & North Western shed, closed in 1932, then used as a wagon repair shop, and which survived in derelict condition until about 1971. *J. S. Hancock*

19
Running sheds sometimes carried out very extensive repairs. Here 0-6-2T No E737 *Earl of Mount Edgcumbe* is seen standing at Plymouth Friary on 12 July 1924 with all its coupled wheels removed for tyre-turning, or (less probably) axlebox overhaul. It is still in London & South Western livery. Many engines of that company carried an E (for Eastleigh) in front of the number for several years after the Amalgamation of 1 January 1923. *H. C. Casserley*

20
LMS 2-4-0 No 20267 waits outside Wellingborough shed on 3 July 1937, while its trailing coupled axle is being turned. *H. C. Casserley*

21
Kirtley double-framed 2-4-0 ('Outside swinger') No 60 pictured at Kentish Town on 31 May 1924, with its leading axle removed. It is still fitted with Midland oval shed-code '15'. The cylinder and ram of the hydraulic sheer-legs are mounted on the left-hand pair of legs.

The young man is H. C. Casserley, on of the best-known locomotive photographers, who has over half-a-century of this activity to his credit. *H. C. Casserley*

22
'Schools' class 4-4-0 No 928 *Stowe* being lifted at Bournemouth on 19 July 1937. This type of travelling crane (by the Chatteris Engineering Co) was probably unique at a locomotive running shed. The front buffer beam is seen resting on timber blocks, the trailing bogie wheels being clear of the rails. *H. C. Casserley*

23
Class Q6 0-8-0s Nos 63379, 63455 and 63360 at Tyne Dock on 26 February 1966. It was a remarkable testimony to the 1913 design of these solid, hard-slogging engines that the 120 of them built up to 1921 survived long after many more modern classes had gone to the scrap-yard. The commonplace rusty patch on the smokebox door of No 63459 was due to air being drawn in, so causing the smokebox char to burn red-hot. Locomotives of this class were used to haul heavy iron-ore trains up to Consett Ironworks, returning with coal from the surrounding area.

The type of direct-acting hydraulic crane shown, giving a lift of about 4ft, was probably used only by the North Eastern. In the twilight of steam the Civil Engineer had decided not to renew the roof, but simply to take it off.
J. S. Hancock

24
Great Central 'Coronation' suburban tank No 170 photographed at Neasden on 1 July 1922; the class was so nick-named for the coronation of King George V, and later became LNER Class A5.

The hoist was for transferring materials to and from wagons; a similar one (if not the same one) was there when the author was the Locomotive Shed Master there in 1954-5. Part of the sheer-legs for lifting locomotives is seen to the right; inside the shed building was another set of sheer-legs constructed of heavy timber baulks, and two shallow drop-pits. *H. C. Casserley*

4

Disposing of Ashes

The servicing operations in steam depots did not follow a universal sequence, since their order depended on the shed and yard layout. However, disposal was usually the first function carried out after the arrival of an engine in a shed yard. This most unpopular of engine duties consisted of clearing ash and clinker from the fire-grate and ashpan, and shovelling 'char' (fine, partly burned bits of coal) out of the smokebox. This procedure had to be carried out once — and sometimes twice a day on every locomotive.

Char is combustible, and the LMS made commendable economies in recovering it. Alongside each of their ashpits a bin had been installed at ground level, into which enginemen were instructed to throw it. Being similar to fine coke, it could be used in furnaces. H. Holcroft, in his book *Locomotive Adventure* (Ian Allan) mentions having obtained 11,205BThU per lb from a sample of it. He relates how it was used to heat one of the workshops at Ashford. At Colwick (Nottingham) the Great Northern had installed a gas-producer plant which used char as fuel, but at the majority of other depots for most of the history of steam traction it was simply thrown away with the ashes.

During the last three decades of steam traction in Great Britain different types of so-called self-cleaning smokeboxes were installed in many of the modern locomotives. These consisted of wire-mesh screens and steel plates forming a 'box' around the blast-pipe and the chimney cowl (or petticoat). On British Railways engines the fitting of such equipment was indicated by a small, oval cast iron plate on the smokebox door, bearing the letters 'SC'. This equipment was intended to blow the fine char away with the exhaust, and to prevent the ejection of burning cinders. In total lineside fires and fires on trains had cost a fortune in compensation. Even small ones were a time-consuming administrative nuisance. Notices to enginemen were posted approaching forested areas, standardised pictograms still being seen in the form of a black silhouette symbolic of a fir tree on a yellow circular background.

Much experimentation involving running sheds was needed before plates and screens were developed which did not impair an engine's steaming capacity. Some were even abandoned because of this difficulty. This topic is considered here mainly because it complicated life for anyone who had to clear ash away from the tube-ends. The person most affected was the tube-sweeper, whose task was horrible at the best of times; it will be considered in Chapter 6.

With a two-cylindered inside-cylinder locomotive it is desirable to stop over the ashpit with the cranks on the front and rear upper quarters, so as to give the maximum clearance for access to the ashpan, and also to keep them as far away as possible from the fine ash which is liable to blow about.

Removing hot ashes and partly burned coal from a firebox is arduous at the best of times, but is even more disagreeable if the grate is clogged with clinker from low-quality coal. This usually appears in a dark brown or dark grey form — often with a dull gloss. It can burn at high temperature (which is one of the virtues of maintaining a hot fire), but at lower temperatures — eg with too thick a fire, or one cooled by an excess of fresh coal — it can adhere to anything which is not burning. By blocking some areas between the firebars it may concentrate the draught into adjacent spaces. This can then raise the temperature so that the clinker and and bits of coal lodged between the bars burn fiercely like the fire on a blacksmith's hearth. This would be fine above the bars, but between them it causes the bars themselves to be burned.

Most Gresley engines, and many of other designers, had a 'drop grate' — a section of the fire-grate about 2ft square — hinged so as to open downwards when a screw was turned in the cab. Thus a gap was created through which ash, clinker and partly burned coal could be pushed into the ashpan below. Other locomotives, notably some of the later LMS types and the BR Standard range had rocker grates and hopper ashpans. Such ashpans were operated from ground-level by inserting a bar (carried on the locomotive) into a short hollow lever located on each side of the ashpan.

Rocker grates are usually divided into halves, containing a number of rocker sections, each half being rockable while the engine is running so as to break up clinker. The fireman has to be careful in using this equipment, because ash or clinker could become jammed between the halves, thus preventing one half being closed. Rocker-sections could be turned through 90° for dropping the fire over an ashpit. If a rocker-section should be blocked partly open it could be impossible to maintain steam pressure.

A drop-grate or rocker grate much facilitated the removal of clinker, but it still needed much prodding and levering with a long, heavy fire-iron, known as a 'dart' or pricker, carried on the tender. Where there is only a plain fire-grate, clinker and lumps of ash have to be strenuously and awkwardly shovelled out through the firehole door, using a shovel whose handle may be as much as 9ft long. This has to be swung around so that it is pushed out through the gap between engine and tender, and the clinker, etc thus dumped on the ground alongside.

In some depots a fire-dropper or a fireman would occasionally avoid this tedious chore by taking a piece of steel rod, bent into a crude hook at one end, and use it pull a few firebars out of position, so as to drop clinker and ash (and probably those firebars) into the ashpan. Such an action was only admissible if the engine were to be stopped for cold-water washout, or repairs were needed which would involve the engine being out of steam for a day or more. This was because an engine with a few firebars dislodged was effectively immobilised until they were replaced — a job which could not be done without considerable difficulty and discomfort while the firebox was hot.

If such an engine were required for traffic within the next hour or two, then the running foreman had to persuade a boilersmith's mate to replace the bars in the hot firebox. This persuasion was often achieved by the granting of some favour — such as being allowed to go home early without loss of pay — but the job was seldom done without strongly expressed feeling against the culprit who had dropped the firebars. The avoidance of such troubles (though seldom acknowledged) was one reason for fitting special grate sections.

When it was known that coal with a propensity to cause clinker was being supplied to a depot, it was common to throw fire-brick — broken into small pieces — across the grate before making up the fire. When clinker formed while an engine was in traffic, with a possibility of standing awhile, it was sometimes possible to rake the burning coal to one side of the grate, remove the clinker from the exposed bars and then scatter shovelsful of ballast stones across them. Then the fire would be pushed across to that side of the firebox, and the same process repeated on the other side. It was insufferably hot and laborious, but could make all the difference between getting home without further difficulty and struggling to get back with much loss of time.

It was not uncommon to find a burned firebar, lumps of clinker, or firebricks in ashpans or ashpits. Whole firebricks sometimes came from collapsed rows of a brick-arch.

Clearing out ashpans necessitates a deep pit between the rails, while this and the ground surface on either side of the track has to be so made that hot ashes can be thrown on to it. On occasions when ashes have to be raked out 'on the level', the men concerned have to resort to some awkward and even dangerous antics, besides which there is little likelihood of the job being done satisfactorily. Ashpits were therefore provided not only in depots, but also at most turntables and places were fires were cleaned 'in traffic'.

Since ashes were often red-hot or dusty, it was usual to provide hydrants and short lengths of slacker hose, either inside the pit — just below the rail level — or, less commonly, alongside the ashpit. The latter position was most undesirable, since the hydrant caused a dangerous obstruction — especially during the hours of darkness. Due to their exposed position and their proximity to hot ashes and smouldering coal, the cocks were often damaged and the hosees burned, crushed or severed. They thus needed frequent maintenance, and where this was difficult to provide the equipment was frequently out of order for days on end.

On locomotives not fitted with hopper ashpans the clearing of ashpans was a manual operation, using a scraper blade on a long steel handle. If the ashpit water slackers were out of use, powder ash was liable to blow about over the unfortunate individual who had to rake out the ashpan.

Hopper ashpans were operated from ground level by inserting a bar into a short hollow lever located on each side of the ashpan. When the mechanism was not being actuated the lever was held in the closed position by a pin chained to the engine frame.

Generally it was the job of a fireman to carry out the disposal tasks described above, but in Great Western and North Western depots, at Kings Cross and some other sheds it was the thankless task of fire-droppers to do this appalling work throughout a shift. (In *Steam was my Calling* — page 95 — I explained how staggering the hours of these unfortunates at Kings Cross 'Top Shed' was instrumental in curing severe congestion at the 'inlet' side of that depot in 1950.) While firemen were relieved of this detested duty at the depots concerned, the practice had a negative effect in terms of fuel economy. Since they could regularly leave the fire-droppers to do this heavy, dirty work, Great Western enginemen in particular tended not to care at all about bringing an engine into the shed yard with a firebox heaped up with live coal to be thrown out. It was most disturbing to get coal dust in one's eyes, but specks of hot ash or burning coal could be very painful, and even cause long-term injury. Since fire-dropping was so horribly disagreeable, its inclusion in the duties of footplate staff also depressed the recruiting of cleaners at many depots, and often caused drivers to discourage their sons from following them into locomotive work.

Disposal was so strenuous for fire-droppers and firemen that by the early 1950s it was in many places difficult to get men to do it. This was a strong reason why over 60 trains per day (passenger and freight) had their engines changed at Grantham or Peterborough, instead of being worked through to Kings Cross. Had steam locomotives not been superseded when they were by more modern forms of power, then drop-grates would have had to be much more widely adopted and wet ashpits would have been installed at many more depots.

During the two world wars, there was the most difficult problem of concealing the glare from locomotive fire-holes and the glow of red-hot ashes at ashpits from observation by enemy bombers. On the engines themselves tarpaulin sheets were fitted across the gap between the cab-roof and the tender, also over the aperture at the sides of tank engine cabs. These sheets made the cabs most uncomfortably hot — especially in summer-time. They had, of course, to be maintained by the running sheds.

The only satisfactory means of concealing glare at the ashpits was to erect a shed over the area where ashes were liable to be dropped. This was not practicable at many places due to inadequate clearances, and would have complicated enormously the lifting of ashes by mechanical means. Such sheds were, however, built at some Great Western depots, of which Didcot was one. The other railways coped with this problem by suspending fire-dropping during air-raid alerts, and by slaking any piles of glowing ash in the pits or alongside them.

After ash, clinker and char had been dropped into an ashpit, or thrown on to the ground at either side of it, there was still the problem of loading it into wagons. This was the duty of ashpit labourers, who had shovelling to do under all conditions of weather. Where the ash loading was entirely manual, the ashes in the pit had first to be thrown up to ground level, whence all the ashes were heaved up into low-sided wagons.

At many sheds various forms of mechanical aid were provided in order to speed up this tiresome toil. The most usual type of equipment for raising ashes was an inclined conveyor belt, powered by a petrol motor, and mounted on flanged wheels so that it could be pushed along the ashpit rails. The ashes were shovelled into the lower end of this contraption, which then conveyed them up into the wagon.

Unfortunately those elevators (of LNER design) which I saw at a number of sheds were mounted on a framework made up of old boiler tubes; thus even when the maintenance fitter managed to keep the petrol engine operative, there was always a risk that someone (probably in the dark, or in a mist) would bump an engine into the elevator and damage it. The one which was at Lincoln when I was there in 1948 was particularly unfortunate in this respect. After one such collision, several days were spent in putting it back into working order, only for a further careless engine movement to smash it up worse than before.

In *Steam was my Calling* I described how a wheeled agricultural trench-digger had cleaned up the ashpits at Woodford in double-quick time. It was a great pity that the authorities had not experimented with such an appliance. That one's performance was so impressive that they would surely have bought a quantity of them for use at many depots.

The LMS went to the considerable expense of providing ash-elevating plants at most of its depots, and these saved a great deal of the roughest manual labour. The most advanced type comprised a concrete ash-tower, which looked much like a miniature version of a coaling plant — save that it had to have full loading-gauge clearance around vehicles standing on the single track which it straddled. One of these towers has survived at Carnforth, awaiting restoration.

With such plants, however, it was still necessary to shovel the ashes from locomotives into a hopper-trolley, mounted on a narrow-gauge track, and to push that along the pit to the inlet of the elevating machinery, where the trolley was emptied by bottom-discharge. At most depots the trolley ran on a narrow-gauge track at one or both sides of the pit, and there was usually another running on a track in the bottom of the pit. With the latter it was possible to rake ashes directly out of the ashpans into the trolley, and so avoid shovelling them altogether.

I had some experience of one of these installations when I was Acting Locomotive Shed Master at Peterborough Spital in 1952. Discharging ashes from the base of the tower into a wagon was a very dusty operation, notwithstanding slacking of the ashes with the sprinkler apparatus. When there was a wind, it was thus desirable to defer this work whenever possible until it had dropped.

At a few of its largest depots the LNER had provided a much more sophisticated installation in the form of 'wet ashpits', which eliminated virtually all shovelling of ash in the ashpit area. Colwick (east of Nottingham) and York were two of the depots so equipped. These pits were very deep, being decked over at the normal depth between the rails, and at ground level outside them, with heavy steel grids. Men could walk about on the grids to rake out ashpans, examine engines, and so on, but the ash fell through into water below. Large lumps of clinker and partly burned coal were shovelled into the water by raising hinged sections of the grid. These were also lifted by ashpit men, whose duty was to empty the pits, regularly using a steam-crane fitted with a grab.

This type of ashpit greatly reduced hot powder-ash being carried in the air, and settling on any exposed surface — whether of men, or of locomotives. Drawings of ashpit sections and ash-elevating plants are given on pages 54-61 of *Locomotive Running Shed Practice* by H. C. Webster, Oxford University Press, 1947.

The Queensland Railway gave a lot of thought to the problems of ash-lifting, for several of their depots had skips which descended into the pits, and were hoisted hydraulically on inclined rails, so that they could tip ashes into wagons standing on an adjacent track. Another method used by that railway was an overhead runway which transport bins containing ash across several parallel shed-front tracks.

While ashes were an unmitigated nuisance to running shed supervisors and staff, they were most useful to the Civil Engineers for many an in-fill job, or for surfacing yards. Ashes not so used were often locally sold to farmers, or others who used them for making tracks across muddy fields, etc.

The drainage of ashpits was liable to be troublesome; short of having wet ashpits, the best arrangement was to have a gutter running the whole length of the pit, this being covered by removable sections of perforated plate — so that the gutter could easily be cleared with a narrow shovel. Others had a sump, which tended soon to become clogged up, unless it was regularly cleaned out. This was a particularly disagreeable job, since oil and grease collected there, making the sump stinky as well as extremely filthy. Even with oil-traps, the effluent was so highly polluted, and very acidic, that there were often complaints about it from river boards and local authorities.

When the ashes in a medium-sized depot were not cleared up within the ashpit-men's day-shift (as could easily happen in bad weather if the foreman did not keep a close watch on the work), then enginemen and others would be stumbling around over piles of hot ashes in the dark. Piles of smouldering ash would also soon accumulate in the pits themselves.

H. Holcroft, on page 180 of the book cited earlier in this chapter, refers to the Southern Railway having spent so much capital on electrification that (in 1934) 'there was no money to spare for improving and modernising locomotive depots, many of which were inadequate for the number of engines allocated to them . . . Salisbury shed, at a most important point on main and intersecting cross-country lines, was a dreadful example. Built about 1900 without provision for future extension, it became in the course of time much congested by the increasing number of engines allocated to it. There were inadequate facilities for fire-cleaning and coaling arrangements were slow and out of date. The consequence was that while waiting for coal, cleaning of fires, ash-pans and smokeboxes was done on the approach to the coal-stage and the two roads leading to it would get piled high on each side with clinker and ash, through which the footsteps ploughed. Periodically the Divisional Engineer sent in a train of empty wagons and a gang of men during a quiet time of the day to clear up, after which the accumulation would make a fresh start . . . Conditions at Tonbridge, on the Eastern Section, another such important point, were very much the same'.

The coaling and ashpit facilities at Salisbury depot had not been improved by the mid-1950s, but the work of the depot had considerably diminished, especially by the general reduction of freight.

From shed analysis experience I had learned that a Running Foreman's office ought to command a view of the ashpits, since these needed the most supervising. After all, engines being prepared each had a set of men on them, whose duty was to take the engine off the shed at a booked departure time, or to get it ready for a set who would be signing on duty, generally within the hour. On the other hand, an incoming set of men placing an engine on the ashpits had one prime purpose, namely to occupy themselves with any other activity which would enable them to abandon the engine and be near the end of their turn of duty before the foreman discovered their arrival. In this way they would hope to avoid the unenviable task of disposing of the ashes, etc from the engine and having to put it away before they could go off duty to rest or recreation.

The Running Foreman's Office in the various running sheds in Great Britain was to be found in locations which ranged from the convenient to the downright awkward. In very few depots was its size, position or amenity suitable for the supervisor who — in the absence of the Locomotive Shed Master — was responsible during two shifts out of three (and at weekends) for the hour-by-hour operation of the depot. Unfortunately most running foremen's offices, including those at many very important depots, did not provide views of anything significant.

C. H. Read, who came over from the London Midland Region on one of the first inter-Regional promotions to become the District Motive Power Superintendent of Colwick (Nottingham) District had an uncommonly good appreciation of the need to keep the ashpits in a depot as well supervised as possible. At Annesley he had moved the Shed Master from his prestigious bay-windowed office on the front of the shed building, in order to install the Running Foreman with his Assistant and the List Clerk there. The Shed Master had to content himself with the former office of the Running Foreman, which had a window looking out on to wagons or an engine parked at the side of the shed. At Woodford the Shed Master had escaped this indignity, since his office was at the side of the shed away from the ashpits. Instead, a little box of a building (described in *Steam was my Calling*) had been built alongside the ashpits for the use of the Running Foreman and the enginemen.

At most depots artificial lighting in the vicinity of the ashpits was generally minimal, but in the last four decades of steam traction it had tended to improve as gas lighting gave way to electricity, and as early electrical installations became obsolete or deteriorated beyond economic repair.

One could often form a fair impression of the adequacy of the manual labour at a depot and of the quality of its supervision by the state of its ashpits. If they were constantly piled up with ashes, then there were not enough shedmen or the management was indifferent — or both. But if the ashpits were in good order, this usually signified that the rest of the shed was ship-shape.

25
Throwing ashes out of the smokebox of 'Green Arrow' class 2-6-2 No 978, here pictured on the wet ashpit at York on 30 May 1947. The firedropper's apparel is typical, his overall trouser-bottoms being secured with bicycle clips, so that they would not catch on lamp-irons, etc, and ensuring that ash would not get into the top of his boots. The cap was worn to keep ash and rain out of his hair. A normal firing shovel was used for this work. In the middle of the smokebox door can be seen the 'dart', by which the smokebox door was fastened, while left of the man's elbow is the horizontal bar across the front of the smokebox, with which the dart engaged. The inscription 'L7' above the figure 8 was a power classification used in the latter days of the LNER. *BR Eastern Region*

5

Steam Engines are Thirsty Brutes

In revenue-earning service in Great Britain the more hard-working engines had a daily water consumption of over 10,000 gallons. Their tanks had to be replenished several times a day; some of the more cautious drivers would no more willingly pass a water-column than a dog would pass a lamp post. Water-columns were familiar objects in stations and engine sidings, and at many unlikely places where trains might stop. They could deliver up to 1,000 gallons per minute.

There was a great variety in their design, the simplest being a plain stand-pipe, with a huge leather sleeve — called a 'bag' — clamped on the top of it. Because water-columns were the most durable of articles, many of them were very old, and the design of most of them went back to pre-Grouping days. Thus, just as the buildings of many running sheds were stamped with the architecture of their pre-1923 owning company, so the water-columns still existing in the latter days of steam traction bore silent witness to the company which installed them.

The more sophisticated ones had long radial jibs which could be swung around in any direction, and were therefore generally known as 'water-cranes'. Since the jib was heavy — especially when full of water — some of them had a wheel to support the weight of the jib. There was a danger of the jib being left foul of a train, so in a later development the jib-wheel was mounted so as to run on an inclined circular track. When the enginemen let go of the jib it returned by gravity to a safe position parallel with the track.

It was common logic in depot layout that water columns should be placed where some other function should be carried out while water was being taken. Thus there was a water column alongside almost every preparation pit, and next to many ashpits. A water-column was frequently found near to a turntable, since besides engines often needing water at the same time as they had to be turned, there were many locomotives which could only be turned on a balanced table with reasonable effort if the tender tank was full.

In 1949, late in my motive power training, I had the odd assignment of going around Doncaster District to visit all the hundreds of water-columns. The intention of this exercise was to make an inventory of the various types and dimensions of valves in use. A motley variety they were too, most of them going back to the pre-Grouping railways. Many of these watering points were in outlandish locations, and could only be reached by infrequent mineral trains, or by travelling by bus and then walking a mile or two along a rough line-side track. Some of them were cylindrical tanks standing on a fat column, looking just like a giant's toilet cistern, with a giant-size chain to operate the water valve. They were popularly, but inaptly known in some areas as 'parachute' columns.

Quite a number of the valves were leaking, and the water-column or crane was thus constantly dribbling; there were many causes of this, including corrosive water, or water with solid impurities in it, while most water-columns also had very frequent use. Moreover, it was a heavy, unpleasant job to take out a valve and renew the valve faces, besides which many valves were not well designed for the unfortunates who had to repair them in outdoor locations at all seasons. The main supply had to be cut off before work, and restored afterwards, and this sometimes meant two long walks to the valve.

As an alternative to having a multiplicity of water-columns between several parallel preparation pits, some of the larger depots — such as Peterborough, New England — had an overhead water gantry. This was a large diameter pipe, spanning all the pits, having a valve and leather hose just above the centre of each track; this avoided the space between the pits being encumbered with columns, and was a much less expensive installation.

Train heating by steam is a hang-over which has survived from steam traction in many countries, though diminishing in Great Britain and on other railways which are converting to electric heating. It has provided boilermakers with a type of work which is far more complex and sophisticated than their traditional craft. Indeed an oil-fired train heating boiler can sometimes give more trouble than the boiler of a steam locomotive which was producing enough steam to haul a heavy train, and yielding steam to heat it as an incidental. Although the amounts of water required for train heating were minimal compared with those needed by the iron horses, some water troughs were retained, and certain classes of diesel locomotives were fitted with pick-up gear.

Almost every depot and most of the larger stations had a big water tank (sometimes two) on the premises or close by; this enabled a nearly constant head of water to be maintained, and so smoothed out most of the irregularities of supply. In case of a single source being cut off it enabled the shed to keep going for a few hours. Where there was a softening plant it was usual to have one tank for raw water and another (or a separate portion of the same tank) for the treated water. At many sheds — notably on the Great Western — the tanks were roofed over to exclude atmospheric dirt (mostly smoke, which is sulphurous), and to avoid the growth of weeds by keeping the water in darkness.

A float in each water tank actuated a water-level indicator — usually in the form of a pointer moving against a scale visible on the outside of the tank. Others had a remote electrical indication in the running foreman's office. The upper level of water was controlled by a ball-valve — as in a lavatory cistern.

During the last century, where railways drew water from their own local sources, there was nearly always a steam-driven pumping plant, whose boiler was in many cases a down-graded locomotive one. These plants were progressively replaced when reliable electric pumps became available, but a number of them survived until the 1920s.

At most locations in Great Britain where it was desired to install a locomotive depot there was little difficulty in obtaining ample quantities of water, even with engines taking up to 3,000 gallons at each re-fill. Isolated columns, fed directly from a town supply, were usually restricted as to the size of main which could be permitted to them. Municipal supplies were generally preferred, but in a considerable number of places either the supplies were insufficient, or cost more than the railways were prepared to pay. In those cases, as also in many country areas, local sources had to be tapped — usually by bore-holes.

In the early years of railways in Great Britain town drinking water was often derived from rivers; at Doncaster, for instance, there were complaints from the Corporation about the railway works polluting this source. In numerous places the railways also took their supplies from rivers, but by the latter decades of the last century many of these were too impure for locomotive use — some being too acid or alkaline. While it is possible to neutralise fairly constant pollution, this was often inconsistent downstream in industrial areas.

During my motive power training it had been well drilled into me that adequate supplies of water and coal must be available at all times in every depot. It therefore became a matter of daily habit to check these vital commodities, and to ensure that other supervisors did so frequently.

The fittings of water supplies rarely gave trouble so long as they received periodic maintenance, and were kept free of weeds and dirt, but disaster could strike if corrosion caused failure of the iron stays supporting the sides of a rectangular tank. Many of the older tanks were built up of cast-iron plate sections bolted together, and provided with stays. At Lincoln the main supply for the shed was brought in via a large tank, dating from Great Northern days, and situated on the roof of the stores, which formed part of the main building. One day in the early 1950s, one of the stays inside the tank rusted so thin that it failed, throwing sudden extra tension on to others which had also corroded. The whole side of the tank, which contained water to a depth of about six feet over an area of some hundreds of square yards, collapsed outwards without warning. Tens of thousands of gallons of water came deluging down into the premises below, flooding out the stores, and causing damage, havoc and panic over quite an area — fortunately without loss of life or serious injury.

Several of the stays had simply wasted away through corrosion, without anyone being aware that this was taking place. Immediate examination of all other water tanks and water softening plants throughout the country was ordered forthwith. Many of the tanks of water softeners were found to have accumulated several tons of solidified sludge.

A large, old water tank, still in use for non-motive power purposes, such as carriage cleaning, filling carrige roof-tanks, and supplying stations needs, is often a sign of the former presence of a steam running shed.

One of the most troublesome conditions affecting the operation of a locomotive running shed was frost, especially in freezing winds. Both the engines themselves and the water supply equipment had to be protected against this nuisance. Injectors are not lagged, mainly for reasons of accessibility, nor are the pipes leading to them; being exposed to cold air they are liable to freeze solid unless frequently used.

For these reasons, whenever frost was forecast, motive power depot yards would be dotted about with small fires wherever engines were left standing, so as to keep these vital components free from ice.

These tended to be smoky, and in still air added noticeably to the pollution which was all too common in depots. In winter a shed yard was thus sometimes illuminated by such fires; by night there were thus patches of eerie contrast where slushy puddles reflected the flickering of these fires. Such fires were lit in preparation and inspection pits, and locomotives stabled over them to prevent the tanks of tenders and of tank engines not in steam from freezing. Braziers ('fire baskets') were used in those few depots where someone had thought to provide them. It was, of course, necessary for one or more steam-raisers, cleaners or labourers to go the rounds with a wheelbarrow full of coal, or to throw coal off locomotives in order to replenish the fires by day and night until the frost abated.

It was equally important to give similar protection to all water-columns, and various means were used to prevent their freezing. The most usual was to keep a brazier alongside, but most of the heat only reached the surface it was supposed to warm only when the wind happened to blow toward it. Okehampton shed had the column encased in timber, so as to afford some protection against the icy winds which often prevailed in winter in the exposed situation on the northern edge of Dartmoor.

The most economical method of warming water supplies during frosty weather was to install a gas ring close to the part to be warmed, eg inside a water-column. Once lit this needed no further attention, except to check occasionally that it was still alight, and to extinguish it when no longer required.

Water-columns abounded at places other than running sheds. Their frost protection depended on local operating staff, or on the crews of freight trains which stopped there for water. The most effective anti-frost precaution for them was a latter-day development, consisting of a valve which drained the column automatically when the hand-valve was shut.

Water tanks were also susceptible to freezing up, with the added danger that water expanding into ice might fracture a tank plate (often of cast iron), or even burst the tank with disastrous results. Thus during severe frost it was also necessary to maintain fires under the tanks, although the space below — often called the 'tank house' — commonly served as a mess room, store or workshop, and so had a fireplace where the staff using the place kept a roaring fire going anyway. Frost precaution fires, although not provided for staff welfare, nevertheless often afforded some means of thawing out for the unfortunates who had to work in the vicinity.

Whatever the water source concerned, vigilance had always to be exercised to ensure that not only was the water-crane, etc maintained at a sufficient temperature, but also that the valves did not become iced-up.

In spite of conscientious attention being almost always given to this important hazard, a locomotive injector or a water supply valve would occasionally freeze, or an engine would come in with an injector frozen. If it were convenient to do so, the usual practice was to pour copious quantities of hot water over the part concerned; an alternative method was to wrap rags or wads of cotton waste around it, soak them with paraffin, and then ignite it. Yet another means was to play a gas flame around the part affected until it was thawed out.

Whatever the type of shed, there were often occasions when men had to work on locomotives out-of-doors. It was not at all agreeable to have to brush snow off the footplating before one could commence work, and it was hardly practicable to erect a screen against a blustery wind. Both inside a shed and outside it one could light a coal-brazier close to the place where work had to be done, and this at least afforded opportunities to thaw out frozen fingers, and to leave tools close to the fire where they could be warmed when not actually in use.

6

Keeping Boilers clean

Ensuring an acceptable standard of steam production from a boiler requires regular and careful cleaning of its heating surfaces. The chief trouble is caused by deposits of scale, which occur with all waters except those which have been collected on land surfaces, or have been softened to near zero hardness. Since scale has low conductivity, it causes serious reduction in the heat transmitted, and has often been a significant factor in cases of engines not steaming properly.

Scale has therefore to be removed regularly — along with loose sediment — by boiler-washing. This involves emptying the boiler, and then flushing it out with fresh water while surfaces to which scale is adhering are poked and scraped with long steel rods — a process known simply as 'rodding'. To wash-out most locomotive boilers, excluding the time taken for removing and replacing the wash-out plugs, takes half-an-hour to an hour, depending on the size of the firebox, on the number of wash-out holes and the quantity and nature of the scale to be removed.

Any scale left in a boiler is liable to cause local overheating, and hence unequal expansion — if this occurred around stays or tube-ends it could lead to leakage. Boilersmiths were therefore always on the look-out to see that the boiler-washers did their work satisfactorily.

In view of the vital necessity of keeping boilers free of scale, boilerwashers were among the most highly paid of the under-remunerated shed staff. Their work was most uncongenial since it involved working almost continuously in heavy, cumbersome oilskins, — often getting wet where this protection was not entirely adequate. This was all the more disagreeable in the draughty conditions prevalent in most depots. No skilled training was needed for boiler washing, but the work required a considerable degree of conscientious effort to remove scale which often lodged in awkward positions. The design of some firebox water-spaces was open to criticism in this respect. Between the tubes where it was virtually impossible to provide access, the scale used to build up progressively, until tubes had to be removed for the purpose of dislodging it, and of facilitating boiler inspection: this was known as 'sifting'.

If there were not enough cleaners available, the engines could go out dirty — although no conscientious supervisor could be content to see that happen. But if boilerwasher Joe Bloggins should report sick, or should send in some excuse for absence because there was an attractive local football match, then a temporary promotion at short notice would have to be arranged among the other shed grades. And at a depot suffering serious staff shortages this kind of situation often posed considerable difficulties. Such re-arrangement devolved on the Running Foreman, (whose duties at the smallest depots were covered on the day-shift by the Locomotive Shed Master); the worry involved was seldom understood, and even less appreciated by higher levels of management.

At many depots the water pressure in the mains was only that available from the water tank at a little above the height of the shed roof. Since this was insufficient for effective washing out (the firebox crown being some 10-11ft above rail-level on most locomotives) a booster pump was often installed to give a more satisfactory jet of water.

The period between one wash-out and the next depended on the amount of scale which formed at each particular depot. This was a function of the hardness of the local supply and of water which locomotives of that class took elsewhere; it was one of many sound reasons for keeping engines on regular workings. The other determining factor was, of course, the quantity of water evaporated in the interval. There was in practice no more satisfactory method of determining the wash-out period than reckoning the number of days which a boiler had been in steam and stipulating a limit according to previous experience for each depot. Generally if a locomotive was washed-out within the time laid down there would be no trouble with priming. However, it might be necessary to have either intermittent blow-down or a small, continuous blow-down.

Depots other than an engine's 'home' shed were supposed to advise the home depot of trips which an engine had performed on the foreign depot's workings, and the home shed had to advise others when one of their locomotives was due for washing out.

On the LMS from the 1930s, and on those areas of British Railways which inherited LM Control offices this was looked after very well; elsewhere it was a matter of supervisory contact whenever the home depot knew from which 'foreign' shed one of its engines might be working.

Until the present century all boiler-washing was done with cold water. Steam was blown away to atmosphere, and then boilers were allowed to cool for some hours before the water was run out, it being considered essential that all parts of a boiler should cool simultaneously. This was usually from five to eight hours, depending on the size of boiler; the LMS achieved the shortest times by means of a system using a special valve to obtain a controlled rate of flow from a hydrant.

Scale and sludge from boilers was swilled out in considerable quantities, with risk of it blocking the drains of pits, so causing trouble for anyone who had to go under locomotives in these locations. This, together with the oil, grease, ash and coal dust used to drop down from engines to produce a high pollution in the drainage effluent.

Cold-water washing-out was commonly done on the day-shift, after the boilers concerned had cooled down since the afternoon or evening of the previous day. After filling up with cold water it was a slow process to heat up the boilers to working temperature again; the loss of availability used to amount from 15 hours to a whole day.

Since boilerwashing had traditionally incurred much loss of engine availability, a lot of attention was given to water softening and to hot-water washing out. The LNER and some overseas railways therefore installed hot-water wash-out plants at most of their large running sheds. These also achieved the enormous advantage that the boilers did not contract and re-expand to the extent involved in cold-water washing-out. Hence the very costly replacement of broken stays and leaking tubes was greatly diminished. Much saving of heat was also effected by steam from the boilers being blown back into the system.

Steam from a locomotive could be blown back into the hot-water wash-out plant down to about 25lb/sq in, and this would take up to 20min depending on the amount of residual pressure and the size of the boiler. The remaining pressure would have to be dissipated by blowing to atmosphere unless there was waiting time before the boilerwashers were ready to proceed. Then the wash-out plugs had to be removed. This would take from 15 to 30min according to the class of engine. For hot-water washing-out, and for filling up, water was delivered at pressures to about 80lb/sq in, with temperatures between 70° and 85°C.

Occasionally a wash-out plug would leak after washing-out after the boiler had started to create steam; I have seen an intrepid running foreman tighten one up while the boiler was under pressure. This was at considerable risk to his own safety, since fine threads on a tapering diameter were used. If the plug had been inserted 'cross-threaded' it might have blown out against him along with a stream of scalding water!

Carelessness in boilerwashing sometimes caused much trouble by water splashing into the oil-trays of axleboxes, thus floating away the oil. Detailed design should have guarded against this possibility, and I would aver that this was a contributory cause in many a case where a heated axlebox was not properly explained.

After washing-out all plugs had to be carefully replaced (with fresh asbestos joints around the mudhole 'doors' of most LNER engines designed after 1923), and the boiler then refilled via the hot water connection to the plant. The regulator and cylinder cocks had to be open, so as to let air out of the boiler, until water was just showing in the gauge-glasses. Then by closing the regulator some initial pressure could be obtained in the boiler by adding more water until the level reached about half the height of the gauge-glasses.

Soot in the tubes, on the superheater elements and on the firebox plates considerably reduced the transmission of heat. Some grades of coal produced more soot and char than others, but this effect was largely dependent on firing methods. Although soot was cleared out at wash-outs, boilers were never entirely free of it.

The tube-sweeper's job was undoubtedly the most disagreeable of all the many dirty tasks in a running shed. Traditionally it was done with rods and brushes, much like chimney-sweeping — except that the tubes were horizontal, and of the order of 2in internal diameter, with the brushes shaped accordingly. These small tubes were commonly called 'smoke tubes', although smoke went just as much through the considerably larger superheater tubes, in which the elements were inserted.

At most depots in Great Britain, at least from the inter-war years there was a compressed-air supply, which besides driving portable pneumatic tools was also used by the tube-sweeper. He had to spend all his working hours in sooty smokeboxes to ensure that tubes were clear of soot, ash and char. Sometimes tubes were blocked with a mixture of these dirty products, and then he had to force a way through with rods, having variously shaped ends.

But he had to be careful about using compressed air on such tubes, for a blast of soot-laden air might back-fire on him. Some soot-blowing lances were of a sophisticated design, giving impulses of air at much higher pressure than the 100lb/sq in, which was the normal order of air-line pressure.

The LMS and some overseas railways used soot-blowers on many of their more modern locomotives. When turned on by the fireman this blew a blast of steam against the tube-plate. This was intended to stir up ash, etc lying on top of the brick arch and to blow it together with other deposits in the tubes through to the smokebox, whence the exhaust through the blast-pipe would discharge these waste products to atmosphere. These blowers were items of capital expenditure, which also required regular servicing — hence the reluctance of most Chief Mechanical Engineers to adopt them.

A vital part of the anatomy of a boiler of which amateurs were little aware was the brick arch. This humble component — introduced by Kirtley on the Midland Railway in 1859 — could, according to its condition, make all the difference to an engine's steaming. Building this arch with refractory bricks of special shapes, cemented together with fireclay, was a semi-skilled job. At some of the largest depots the brick arch man and his mate would do little else except demolish old arches and remove the debris, build new ones and repair damaged ones. The arches had a life which varied widely from depot to depot, and from one type of duty to another. Their maximum duration in Great Britain was six months, at which they had to be knocked down for the examination of the firebox by the Chief Mechanical Engineer's boiler examiner. Some arches lasted scarcely longer than a month, and often it was necessary to replace one or more rows of bricks — usually the rear ones. These were susceptible to damage if they should be knocked by fire-droppers or firemen using fire-irons.

Distance pieces were fitted in most fireboxes so as to maintain a narrow space in front of the brick arch, allowing hot gases and flames to pass through the gap. Since the brick arch sloped downward towards the front, ash dropped down through this space instead of accumulating on top of the arch.

Most troubles in boiler maintenance could be traced to unsatisfactory feed water because of hardness or corrosiveness. Water treatment was not available on a large scale until about the turn of the century. Generally in mountain areas and in most parts of Scotland the water supplied by local authorities is very suitable for locomotive use. In England, however, most water is pumped from boreholes, having been in contact with limestone strata.

Hardness in water is 'temporary', giving rise to easily removed, soft, chalky scale or sludge, or 'permanent', including silica salts, which produce hard, troublesome scale. A boiler inspector once brought me a sample of this at Staveley, where we had untreated water; this was baked on to a smoke-tube like a coating of rock about 3mm thick. It would have been difficult to remove — even by chipping — making it necessary to renew the tubes concerned. Since scale has low conductivity it was a major cause of engines not steaming properly.

Before the 1923 Amalgamation the Great Western, the North Eastern, the Great Central, the Midland and some other companies had a few isolated softening plants treating particularly troublesome sources. Unfortunately, even until the end of steam locomotion, many depots which could have benefited greatly from water-softening did not have it because of the high capital and running costs of treatment plants. Besides requiring chemicals by the wagon-load, such plants also needed an attendant on duty — in many cases throughout 24 hours — this being one of the several semi-skilled grades of motive power staff. His duties included feeding the installation with the prescribed doses of various chemicals, and doing simple, repetitive chemical analyses, so as to ensure the continuing effectiveness of the treatment.

During the latter 1920s the four main line companies had tried to find an alloy to resist corrosion in fireboxes better than the arsenical copper then in use. In 1930 H. N. Gresley created a position of Chief Chemist & Metallurgy to the LNER and appointed to it T. Henry Turner from Birmingham University. Turner recommended tackling the corrosion at source by neutralising as far as possible the impurities in the feed-water (ie by rectifying the liquid environment instead of changing the metal). His survey of the water supplies along the East Coast main line revealed that those between Kings Cross and Doncaster were much the worst. It was therefore decided to instal a chain of lime-soda softening plants at 13 places on this route. At most of these locations tens of thousands of gallons of water per day had to be treated continuously 'round the clock'.

The treatment plants on the LNER prevented thousands of scale-forming salts and sludge from entering boilers, thus obviating numerous failures, as well as avoiding loss of time caused by priming. The plants were typical of many dozens of others used, particularly on the LMS from the mid-1930s; from 1930 the LNER used sodium aluminate to precipitate magnesium salts, (so preventing the formation of hard scale) in addition to the traditional lime/soda process.

Every effort was made to avoid corrosive waters being taken into locomotive supplies, but the quality of a source might vary. In times of drought dubious water might be taken — even at some risk of corrosion — rather than cancel trains. Corrosion in boilers generally takes the form of localised 'pitting', somewhat like pock-marks. On the tubes it can also appear as 'necking'; this means an annular groove near the firebox, and is aggravated, if not indeed caused by electrolytic action between steel tubes and copper firebox plates.

An extensive problem in water treatment was incurred with the necessity to dispose of the vast quantities of chalky sludge which were produced from the plants. This odourless, but otherwise rather disagreeable waste was piped away to nearby settling pits. Where these could not be provided locally, the sludge had to be transported away in old tenders converted to sludge carriers, and then dumped. Some of the solid waste which settled out could be used for rough whitewashing jobs, such as lining platform edges, and at least one firm used it as a constituent in the manufacture of cleaning paste. These uses were, however, minimal in proportion to the quantities of sludge to be disposed of.

There was an occasion at one sludge pond where a quantity of the stuff flowed out across a considerable area of a cornfield. The farmer claimed compensation, but while the legal process dragged on the part of the crop affected produced a better yield than the rest of the field! The claim was dropped, the farmer having learned by this experience that his land had a deficiency of lime.

The overall saving in repairs due to the use of softened water relieved the work of depots in numerous ways over the next 30-odd years. Softened water also constituted a major and quite unrecognised contribution to that high standard of locomotive performance for which the East Coast main line became famous in the 1930s. Ten further plants were therefore installed on the Great Eastern Section. The provision of further plants was unfortunately suspended during World War 2, but in 1941 there were 41 lime/soda plants in operation on the LNER. In addition there were stationary boilers at over 60 locations where specially adapted systems of treatment were installed, and these very largely counteracted corrosion and scale-formation.

While most softening plants were at running sheds many water pick-up troughs had a plant close by. A depot monitored the level of water in the troughs, shown by electrical indicator, or as reported by drivers picking up water. In case of difficulty a fitter had to be sent post haste. For example the troughs at Werrington were the responsibility of Peterborough New England (later Spital) depot, and the author had to deal with such problems while acting as Locomotive Shed Master at the latter depot in 1952. If the supply could not be restored quickly, then emergency notices had to be telegraphed to the depots whose drivers would normally use the troughs.

O. V. S. Bulleid wanted to use the French TIA system for the all-steel boilers which he constructed for the Southern Railway from 1941. However until summer 1945 he was prevented from doing so by wartime conditions; by the time this was introduced the deterioration of these boilers had reached serious proportions. The system involved putting briquettes of various chemical compositions into canisters in the tanks of locomotives. At the larger depots, simple regular tests were made of samples of the raw water and of the treated water. Briquettes were dispensed according to the results of these tests, and to the amounts of water to be taken at different sources.

The treatment included the neutralisation of corrosive constituents in the feed-water to near zero. The water was also softened to such an extent that the period between washouts at some depots (notably Exmouth Junction, Exeter) was prolonged to as much as 56 working days on several classes of engine, thus greatly improving availability. Corrosion was also reduced in steel fireboxes to much less than that which was occurring in copper ones.

The foregoing remarks are based on notes made in 1941 by F. S. Lilly, Chief Clerk to the Chief Chemist & Metallurgist, and on material kindly supplied by T. Henry Turner.

It is indeed surprising that the TIA system, which was remarkably successful on the Southern, and which did not need fixed installations, was not widely adopted elsewhere in England.

Besides the huge volumes of water consumed by locomotives during their normal work, there were also large amounts used in the sheds by engines standing around in steam, and by the daily activities of the boilerwashers.

A serious operating trouble caused by bad feed water is 'foaming'; this occurs when certain impurities in solution or suspension reach a given degree of concentration for the prevailing boiler conditions. A large amount of particles of water will then pass through the regulator along with the steam. This phenomenon may be demonstrated by pouring a small quantity of milk into a pan of boiling water, whereupon there will be a considerable frothing or foaming. Anti-foaming briquettes can be put into a locomotive water tank to reduce the tendency to foam, and may be particularly useful if an engine is almost due for washing-out, but it will not cure the trouble once it has started.

Webster, in his book *Locomotive Running Shed Practice,* goes to some length to explain the difference between foaming and another phenomenon called 'priming', which also caused waterspray to come over with the steam. As the effects were the same in each case, the term 'priming' was commonly used to describe both types of occurrence.

Priming will take place if a boiler is filled too full of water (especially one having a relatively small steam space at normal water level), and if at the same time there is a sudden opening of the regulator at long cut-off the valves. When priming or foaming occurs it is quite disconcerting — the engine sounds as if it is being choked, and there is a considerable loss of power. Opening the cylinder cocks reduces the hydraulic 'hammering' in the front end, but also still further decreases the power output, and therefore the speed. Thus a bad case of priming would usually involve serious loss of time. In addition to the effects already described, priming and foaming both wash away cylinder lubrication. (A superheater can evaporate quite a considerble amount of spray carried over; drying wet steam is one of the principal virtues of superheating.)

Somehow the concentration of dissolved matter must be substantially decreased, either by completely changing the water, as at wash-out, or by 'blowing-down' — ie discharging an appreciable amount of water from the boiler, and replacing it by fresh. Either way a great deal of heat is lost, and this is one of the serious losses of efficiency with steam traction. Many locomotives built from the 1930s (especially on the LMS) were fitted with an automatic blow-down valve, which came into action when the driver opened the regulator, or had a valve operable from the cab.

The automatic system embodied a fundamental fallacy, since for most of the time that it was operating the water being blown down had either very low concentration of dissolved solids, or at least much less than were likely to have caused foaming, and into the bargain it was accompanied by an appreciable loss of heat. To make the matter worse, as J. Dearden found when he was detailed to investigate why the right-hand running rails were getting more wear and fractures than the opposite rails, these were being corroded by the blow-down effluent, which for some years had been discharged above the right-hand rail.

7

Shortage of steam — Boiler Repairs

One of the most frequent causes of lost time with steam locomotives was the general malady known as 'shortage of steam' — often abbreviated most approriately to 'SOS'. There were multifarious causes of this trouble, which may be summarised as follows: inferior fuel; bad firing; indifferent driving; dirty heating surfaces, scale on the water side and soot on the hot gases side. Restriction of draught, due to air drawn into the smokebox; steam blows in the smokebox; fire-grate partly blocked with ash and clinker; foaming and/or priming; valves and/or pistons leaking steam.

There were very good drivers, while others were of inferior skill, generally through ignorance of the combustion of coal and of the expansive working and superheating of steam. A good driver not only worked with the shortest cut-off possible for a given set of conditions, but also made exceptions to this when a minute or so of sharp blast was needed to liven up a sluggish fire. There were many not-so-good drivers who just did not bother to correct their mates when excessive smoke was created, often leading to blowing-off shortly afterwards. Making smoke indicated clearly inefficient combustion and a fire whose temperature was lowered — thereby reducing the degree of superheat.

Poor driving and bad firing were known collectively as 'mismanagement' they were more often due to ignorance and inexperience than neglect, and were present at many depots to a disturbing extent from 1940 onwards. A great deal of improvement could have been achieved by more adequate and imaginative training.

Shed fitters and boilersmiths looking for causes of engines booked 'SOS' had to have some acquaintance with footplate practice, and if nothing could be found amiss with the locomotive then it was often arranged for an inspector to ride with the enginemen on the engine concerned. Two items to be checked were the dates of last wash-out and of the last boiler inspection. Insufficient draught was commonly due to loss of smokebox vacuum. Instances of bad design affecting steaming were legion — especially concerning the smokebox and/or blast-pipe proportions, or those of the ashpan. None of the engines of some classes would steam satisfactorily, short of 'illegal' modifications being carried out at depots.

The access of air to the underside of the fire-grate soon became restricted if ashpans were not regularly and thoroughly cleaned out. Many 4-6-0s had their ashpans so designed that accumulations of ash quickly occurred; this not only impeded the steaming, but also led to the ashpan plates being burned. This point is clearly illustrated by Dr W. A. Tuplin in his book *British Steam since 1900* (Pan Books). Once the ash built up under the fire-bars to touch them in one or more areas there was little that the fireman could do about it with an engine running, except feed coal to the brightest areas of the fire, and allow generous top-air through the fire-hole whenever smoke was produced at the chimney top. But not all firemen were so observant or resourceful.

If air was being drawn into the smokebox, this was usually due to char having been trapped in the door joint. The air rushing in at that point would cause a local fire by creating a draught on hot char against the door, and this would then damage the joint or distort the door. Numerous engines with short, inadequate smokeboxes were liable to build up a considerable depth of hot char there. Many of the older 4-4-0s and 0-6-0s, designed long before self-cleaning smokebox equipment was dreamed of, were particularly bad in this respect. Since they had only a fastening device in the middle of the door, they tended to draw in air, and so these old-timers often ran about with a fire in both ends of the boiler! Any heat gain to the cylinders, or to the smokebox tube-plate was almost certainly offset by the loss of smokebox vacuum.

It was characteristic of some of these engines to see them with a tell-tale segment of corroded plate at the bottom of the smokebox door, where the paint had burned off, and the plate had become distorted. Then it would look a rusty mess, and impede proper steaming until it was rectified. In the absence of this evidence, such a leak could generally be found by inserting a thin feeler gauge. Other air leaks sometimes occurred around the joint where the steam pipes passed through the sides of the smokebox to outside cylinders, or around the vacuum ejector exhaust pipe, or anywhere else where pipes or fittings had necessitated the cutting of a hole in the smokebox plate. Old smokebox plates would occasionally corrode so much that holes (often in concealed places) were caused by rust. It was not unknown for a boilersmith to agree to be shut inside a smokebox so that he could look for daylight coming in — but this was no occupation for anyone with tendencies to claustrophobia!

To find a steam blow in a smokebox it is necessary to apply the brakes, put the valve-gear in mid-position and open in turn the various valves admitting steam to pipes which pass through or into the smokebox. In the absence of other loud sounds a steam leak can be heard, and can generally be located by fastening a piece of hemp or lamp-wick to the end of a rod, saturating this with paraffin and igniting it, then holding the flame in the vicinity whence the sound is coming. The likeliest source of a blow is at the superheater header, and it is often not easy to find which one of a battery of several dozen element joints is the culprit.

A blow of steam in a smokebox can be an unholy nuisance, since even more importantly than constituting a direct loss of live steam, it reduces the smokebox vacuum — and so doubly impairs the engine's steaming capacity. Furthermore, if it is only a slight blow, it may persist unnoticed for days, until the locomotive being repeatedly reported 'shy of steam' causes a thorough investigation to be made.

A superheater element with a leaky joint, or an element which has started to fracture or develop a hole can, of course produce the same kind of trouble. These blows may be tricky to find, but on the other hand a burst element can give violent evidence of itself, especially if its seam splits at the 'torpedo' end, ie where the tube doubles back sharply through 180°. In this case there will be a heavy blow into the firebox, with a serious danger of flames and steam blowing back on to the footplate.

If a steam blow in a smokebox is reported or suspected, and the boiler is not in steam when the defect is to be located, it is usually sufficient to connect a compressed-air line to the boiler, and fill it with air at whatever pressure is available. If compressed air is not at hand, or if an air or steam test fails to indicate the exact location of a blow, then a hydraulic test will certainly do so. Such a test has the great advantage that the escape of water can be seen.

Boilersmiths used occasionally to go into hot fireboxes, as is vividly described by E. S. Cox in his book *Locomotive Panorama* Vol II. In Great Brtain this was not a systematic practice, but sometimes when a running foreman needed an engine urgently for traffic leaky stays or tubes would be reported, and an intrepid boilersmith could go into a hot firebox in order to satisy himself whether he could 'let it go' or not. This was entirely a matter of goodwill — at least in the latter days of steam traction — for a supervisor could not order a man into a situation where he might have been overcome by heat, fallen unconscious and died of heat exhaustion.

(This never happened to my knowledge, since the staff were well aware of the danger, and had a slim, agile mate standing at the firehole door in case of difficulty. I well remember Tom Thurley, my portly Leading Boilersmith at Woodford, coming into his office after such an exploit, streaming with perspiration, and still sweating profusely a quarter of an hour later.)

While it was not good for the firebox, it was not unknown under the circumstances for the staff concerned to let a compressed air pipe blow into the ashpan, so as to provide a current of cool air, or to place a compressed air jet-ring in the smokebox, blowing up the chimney, thus drawing air through the firebox.

In a smokebox fitted with 'self-cleaning' apparatus one might locate a steam leak without having to remove anything more than loose screens. But to replace one or more boiler tubes, renew a superheater element, remake a steam-pipe joint or remove the blast-pipe nearly always necessitates dismantling part of the framework of the screens, or taking down a 'fixed' screen. Their fastenings are usually so corroded that nuts have to be chopped off with a hand chisel (often in a position which requires the fitter to be a contortionist), and the remainder of the bolt then punched — or even drilled out of its hole. Finally the whole ensemble of dirty plates has to be restored to its original position, making sure that none of them is displaced.

Detecting and rectifying a case of 'SOS' might thus require team-work between a fitter, a boilersmith, their supervisors and a footplate inspector.

The inherent dangers with boilers, highlighted by a succession of dramatic failures during the last century gave rise to maintenance standards being prescribed, backed by legal powers of enforcement with Board of Trade Regulations.

In order to ensure constant compliance with these requirements, district boiler inspectors were appointed to the staff of the Chief Mechanical Engineer of each railway, not being under control of the Locomotive Running Superintendent. Their principal duty was to carry out rigorous examinations of every locomotive boiler and every stationary boiler in service, with a maximum period of six months between examinations. They also had to inspect any boiler on which a plug was 'dropped', a plate burned, or other serious defect found.

Whatever the dicey mechanical state in which many steam locomotives were allowed to run about during World War 2 and for some years afterwards, bad maintenance could never be tolerated in their boilers. If the roof-plate of a firebox became 'uncovered' — ie without water over it when there was a fire in the box — there was a grave danger of the plate becoming scorched and distorted, and of roof stays becoming stretched or breaking.

In order to avoid an explosion occurring under such circumstances, fusible plugs were invented at an early date; these were fitted in the crown-plate of fireboxes, and became a universal safety fitting. They were so constructed that if the plate became dry the plug would overheat, and the lead insert would melt. The centre of the plug would then drop into the fire, leaving a hole of about ½inch diameter through which steam would rush, quickly damping the fire. If the engine were standing, there would be a blow of steam noticeable on the footplate, but if the engine were working hard, the steam would be partly drawn off through the tubes by the blast; it may occasionally have happened with the footplate crew being unaware of what had happened until the fireman opened the firehole door.

There were one or more lead plugs in the crown of each firebox, so that if one did not fuse as soon as the crown-plate became over-heated there was every probability of the others doing so.

If an inspector discovered scorching of plates or distortion of stays, he would usually order a hydraulic test at about 50% above the working pressure. One or two cases were discovered at depots under my control, but fortunately water had been fed to the top of the firebox before anything more than incipient scorching could occur. Occasionally a driver on whose engine a plug had failed would stoutly maintain that water was showing in both gauge glasses when the calamity had happened, but few boiler examiners would ever believe such an assertion, especially if inspection of the gauge glasses and their waterways revealed no defect. After all, shortage of water in the boiler was the most serious allegation against driver and fireman, and they had every motive to escape culpability if they could.

Boiler work in motive power depots, being on pressure vessels, was always considered as requiring apprentice-trained boilersmiths. Much the greater part of their work was inside fireboxes, access to which was through the fire-hole door. On Great Northern engines, and on engines of LNER design, as well as on engines in many other parts of the world the fire-hole was of oval shape, conforming somewhat to the cross-section of a human torso, thus making the access easier than through a round hole. An oval hole also made the fireman's work easier, since that shape lent itself better to spreading coal across the width of the firebox.

Although being of only medium build, I often had difficulty in wriggling through a fire-hole, stretching one arm above my head, and keeping the other alongside my body. But I could not understand how, at depot after depot, well-preserved boilersmiths, with a girth of around 46in, used to squeeze their abdomens through a fire-hole having a periphery of about 45in — especially the round variety. The latter was the standard Great Central shape, and for a boilersmith to manoeuvre himself through such a fire-hole seemed to be part of the mystique of GC training!

Sometimes tubes, or even stays would leak due to unequal expansion. Seepage of water into the fire-area was so prevalent at some depots cursed with corrosive water that the boiler staff virtually had to live with it, and could only hope to keep it within manageable limits. Occasionally in a cold boiler, water could be seen steaming over considerable areas of the firebox plates.

The remedy for these defects was caulking — hammering with a tool like a blunt-nosed chisel — the edges of stay-heads and plate seams, and beading (curving over the ends of tubes). These became so worn by repeated caulking and by the corrosive and abrasive action of the fire that an engine would have to be stopped for extensive renewals of the parts affected.

At depots having heavy corrosion and erosion of the stay-heads, and even pitting of the firebox plates around them, it was not at all uncommon for a locomotive to be accepted into the main works for a general overhaul on account of the run-down state of its firebox, whereas its mechanical parts could have been kept traffic-worthy for several months longer.

Pneumatic tools were introduced in various main works from the 1880s, but these did not appear in running sheds until about the time of World War 1, and even then many years passed until compressed air or electric power tools were available in most motive power depots. These not only greatly reduced the physical effort required from boilersmiths (and some other grades) but also speeded up the work enormously.

As in the main works, pneumatic tools used on boiler-work were infernally noisy, but the noise was seldom being created on more than one boiler at a time. Furthermore, although the men working in a firebox were subjected to the full intensity of the din, those outside were largely shielded from it by the insulating lagging, and by whatever water happened to be still inside the water space.

Unfortunately there were many small depots at which it was not considered economic to install compresed air supplies; even those which had electric power points provided could only use electric hand tools of a rotating type, such as drills and (possibly) tube expanders. Thus rivetting stays and rivets, chipping and caulking plate edges, and some other jobs were done by blacksmiths at these sheds using hammers and hand-tools until the end of steam locomotion. And unless or until electric power points were available even drilling and expanding had to be done by tediously slow, laborious hand-ratcheting. So whenever any fairly extensive boiler-work was found to be necessary at a small depot, the engine was almost always sent to a larger depot in the same district where power tools could be used.

Changing tubes at running sheds was relatively easy, but cutting out portions of boiler plates and patching them was an expensive main works job. Superheater tubes, being considerably larger than ordinary ones, were difficult to expand, and to keep water-tight if they started to leak. They were therefore screwed with fine threads into the firebox tube-plate, and were very seldom changed at a motive power depot.

Stays were changed at all depots where there were one or more boilersmiths, and at some sheds it was a fairly frequent task. Many railways imposed a limit on the quantity which a shed was permitted to change in one area of a firebox, above which number the locomotive had to be sent to the main Works. Even some of the latest types, such as the British Railways Standard 2-10-0s were plagued by defective stays.

Renewing stays in the fire-area of narrow fireboxes was difficult for running shed staff, since that part of the firebox was located between the frames, and thus there was no access to the outer ends of the stays, unless the designers had thought to provide large holes in the frame-plates in that vicinity. Steel stays, which were used mainly in steel fireboxes, were always fitted with nuts at the fire end, due both to the difficulty of riveting over the steel, and because of the danger of distorting the plate which might result from such hammering. These nuts tended to waste away — particularly in the 'fire area' (the area in contact with the burning coal) so that it was common to have to replace them.

Small cracks used to occur in steel firebox plates; these were at first welded in the main works, and later also in the main running sheds.

There were many causes for the demise of steam power, but foremost among these were the limitations imposed on a locomotive's working range by the nature of coal and its dirty products.

26
New Cross Gate depot was closed shortly after World War 2, but such were the staff shortages and other difficulties at neighbouring sheds that its repair shop — although bomb-damaged and roofless — was still carrying out heavy depot repairs when this picture was taken on 29 July 1947. The engines shown here are Class D4 0-4-2T No 2253 and Class B4X 4-4-0 No 2067. *S. C. Nash*

27
Bird's eye-view of Bulleid Pacific No 34069 *Hawkinge* on the turntable at Exmouth Junction, Exeter, about 1962. The man nearer the camera is standing near the catch lever, and the other is operating the vacuum tractor. Fastened to the side of the table is a vacuum reservoir. Behind the coal bunker are the four vacuum reservoir cylinders of the locomotive, and behind these the water-filler hole cover has been left open (coal could thus fall into the tank under the coaling plant!)

Beyond the turntable, left, is a typical pile of oil drums, beyond which is the track used by wagons coming away from the coaling plant. Beyond that the depot territory was limited by the dead-end reception road of Exmouth Junction marshalling yard, beyond which are the Up and Down main lines to and from Waterloo. Beyond those — due to lack of space in the depot yard — was the coal dump. Cameraman J. Parsons, who was a fireman at Exmouth Junction at the time, took this shot from a very high water tower which stood at the back of the shed. *J. Parsons*

28
Cosmopolitan collection at the 'north' end of Doncaster Shed, as seen from the coaling plant on 5 April 1936. The offices in the background still exist, as does the running shed, but it has been shortened at this end, and re-roofed.

There was a frequent pushing of engines, by day and night, through the shed to the far end, where preparation was done. The locomotives seen here from top to bottom, and left to right are: a Class A7 4-6-2 North Eastern freight tank, an 'A3' Pacific, and a 'K3' 2-6-0, 'A1' 4-6-2 No 4477 *Gay Crusader* and another 'K3'; 'A1' Pacific No 4473 *Solario*, a GNR 4-4-0 and a GNR 0-6-0; two GER 0-6-0Ts of Class J67 or 'J69' and two GNR 0-6-0STs; a Class 04 2-8-0, L&Y 0-6-0 No 12583 and a GNR 0-6-0; 'A1' Pacific No 4471 *Sir Frederick Banbury*; a 'Q4' 0-8-0, a 'C2' small Atlantic and another '04' 2-8-0; a 'J39' 0-6-0, and another 'C2' 4-4-2. *J. S. Hancock*

29
Saffron Waldren, typical of the smallest sheds — often found at the end of a branch line — having only one or two engines, plus three sets of men, one of the drivers being in charge of the depot. The shed roof is of timber, and to the right of it is the water tank. Class G4 0-4-0T No 8139 is stabled in the shed, while Class F4 2-4-2T No 7174 runs round its train. *H. C. Casserley*

30
Severn Tunnel Junction depot, photographed when it was new on 2 June 1908. Note the typical coaling stage, with a roofed water tank above, and gas lighting in the yard. The locomotives are a 28xx being coaled, and 0-6-0 saddle tanks. *BR Central Photographic Unit*

31
With true Scots economy the Highland Railway built their round-house at Inverness without any roof over the middle of the shed, and without doors to the 'stalls'. They also painted the name *Clan Fraser* on the splasher, as was also North British practice, instead of providing brass name-plates. It seems that the long continuous splasher was intended to cover up the Walschaert's valve gear, which many designers considered unsightly — never minding if it made life difficult for erectors, fitters and drivers.

The management had to put the LMS number 14763 on engine and tender, but by 16 May 1928, when this photograph was taken had still not succumbed to putting the initials LMS on it. Note the automatic tablet-catcher on the cab-side. *H. C. Casserley*

32
A Lancashire & Yorkshire 'Crab' 2-6-0 north of the Border; No 42918, photographed at Dumfries after it had come from the elevated coaling stage seen in the background. At least the turntable had a modern drive, the vacuum-motor equipment being visible in the foreground. *T. G. Hepburn*

33
Locomotive depots often provided striking contrasts. Here Ivatt Atlantic tank, LNER Class C12, No 67382, built for suburban services in 1901 poses at Grantham depot in the early 1950s alongside 'A1' Pacific No 60118 *Archibald Sturrock*, built in 1948. The latter locomotive was named after the Locomotive Engineer of the GNR who established Grantham depot in 1852.

The coaling plant can be seen above the bunker of the tank engine. *T. G. Hepburn*

34
West Coast main line freight depot: Crewe South in 1966. The very tall pylon is a lighting mast for floodlighting the locomotive shed and the marshalling yard beyond it. All of the engines in view are later LMS or BR Standard types.

The details between the shed building and the water-tank at the left are: left of the extreme left locomotive, the outer wall of a shed building from which the roof has been removed, the tracks of which were retained for preparation and stabling. Beyond the wall is the coaling plant and behind that a high water tower for boosting mains pressure. *J. S. Hancock*

35
Stored locomotives always looked dejected, especially when they were kept in the open air, where they usually became rusty. Here BR Standard Class 2 2-6-0 No 78021 is seen at Leicester Midland shed on 21 May 1966, with little prospect of further work.

On the extreme right is the skip-type coaling plant; the other towers are for elevating ashes. *J. S. Hancock*

36

Reading locomotive running shed seen from the direction of the station at the same time as the previous photograph. To the left is the line to Southampton, and to Taunton (via Westbury): to the right is the main line to Bristol and South Wales. The tower in front of the water-tank was apparently a water-softener. The water-tank still exists, and the site is now occupied by a diesel maintenance depot.

Note the gas lamps with glass partly obscured so as not to give light in directions which might impair drivers' views of signal lamps at night. *BR Central Photographic Unit*

37

The close surroundings of some depots reflected the activity of the locality, and in some cases the work of the shed itself. Here a huge coal-fired power station forms the back-drop for a picture of engines on the shed-front at Wakefield in August 1965. The trio of 'Austerity' War Department 2-8-0s includes No 90698; its neighbour is sending up a column of smoke which might probably have been avoided by turning on the 'blower' jet.

The dark silhouette at the top of the photograph is the outline of the end of the smoke-chutes which run the length of the parallel tracks in the shed. *Ian Krause*

38
Unfortunately for the neighbouring residents, steam locomotive depots were often very close to housing. A particularly bad example shown here was Neepsend, built by the Manchester, Sheffield & Lincolnshire railway on a cramped site in the west of Sheffield. No smoke was being produced when this picture was taken (almost certainly on a Sunday) about 1935. Shed masters of depots in such locations used to receive irate complaints from housewives whose washing had been spoiled by smoke and soot.

The 4-4-2T shown here is of LNER Class C13.
J. S. Hancock

39
One of the duties of the larger depots was to keep an engine ready to replace at a moment's notice any locomotive which might fail. On main lines an express passenger engine was kept so prepared, either in the shed yard, or even at the station of principal towns. Thus on the east coast main line, one was held in the locomotive sidings adjacent to the turntable at Peterborough North. Another was kept at each end of Doncaster station, since a train might stop there for a fresh engine at extremely short notice. A further one was kept at York shed, and yet another at Darlington.

'A3' Pacific No 60036 *Colombo* is seen here covering the latter duty on 6 March 1964 — ready to turn if necessary — after dieselisation of the principal expresses. The reservoir cylinders of the vacuum-operated turntable are clearly visible. *J. S. Hancock*

40
Some locomotive depots were close by the sea, where any unpainted steel was quickly rusted by the salty marine air. Here is St Leonards, Hastings, photographed on 27 April 1947 against a background of seaside hotels. This was a typically cramped Southern depot.

The locomotives shown are all SECR 4-4-0s or 0-6-0s, except the engine with two head-code discs which is a 'Schools' 4-4-0. This was the depot's largest type, used for working the London expresses. *S. C. Nash*

41

Bird's-eye view of Redhill shed on 26 July 1964. The building is of the type of construction used by British Railways Southern Region to renew roofs (and in this case the walls) of locomotive depots which could no longer be economically repaired.

Redhill is at the junction of the London-Brighton main line with the Reading-South Kent cross-country line. It is surprising that the depot should have acquired three high snow-ploughs. The locomotive on the right is a visitor from the Eastern Region, Class B1 4-6-0 No 61318. Next to it is BR Standard Class 3 2-6-2T No 80138, while an engine of the same class No 80149 is seen near the centre of the photograph. All the other identifiable engines are of the Southern's ubiquitous 'Woolworth' 2-6-0s, of which No 31850, next to its isolated tender, is in an advanced state of demolition by the shed staff. *S. C. Nash*

42

Occasionally motive power depots were called upon to participate in the particularly interesting work of testing a locomotive. This photograph, issued by the Southern Region Public Relations & Publicity Department on 26 June 1956 shows modified 'Merchant Navy' Pacific No 35020, *Bibby Line*, ready to work the 10.30am Exeter Central-Waterloo.

The members of the group include (from the left): Chief Loco Inspector Sam Smith of Exmouth Junction District, a technical assistant equipped for communicating with the dynamometer car behind the locomotive, an operating department inspector, Mr S. O. Ell — Chief of the Testing Station at Swindon, and (from the right) top link Exmouth Junction crew — driver A. Bennett and passed fireman R. Bartlett.

The tube and cable attached to the handrail are for analysing smoke-box gases and recording their temperature. *British Railways*

43
Still steaming after years of decrepitude. The sad remains of SECR No 98, photographed at Ramsgate on 2 July 1949; it served a most useful purpose in heating carriages for many years, after almost all removable parts had been stripped from it. Locomotive depots had to maintain a variety of stationary boilers in all sorts of locations. *H. C. Casserley*

44
LMS Class 4MT 2-6-0 backing into the round-house at Manningham, Bradford. The shed is a typical piece of Midland Railway 'cathedral' architecture in local Yorkshire limestone. The groups of three round-topped windows were characteristic of that railway's buildings. The notice reads:

'Midland Railway. Notice to Drivers, Firemen and all Enginemen. Stop. All engines requiring to enter this shed must be brought to a stand at this board. By Order.'
J. S. Hancock

8

A Host of Troubles

Repair work on steam locomotives is a very different proposition from that of more modern forms of traction. In particular one can usually detect in a matter of minutes, or even seconds, exactly what is wrong with a steam engine, (although this is seldom so in a case of shortage of steam).

In a steam depot one would encounter the examining fitter — usually identified by his carrying a 'tapping' hammer. This had a small head and a long shaft, so enabling him to tap parts which would otherwise have been out of reach. He would generally be one of the most experienced men in the depot, since his duties needed knowledge of all the various defects which might occur — however infrequently. He was responsible for checking that every locomotive leaving the shed was fit for its day's work. Often the keen observation of these men avoided engines going into traffic with defects which might have produced failures.

During a visit to a depot we would probably have seen fitters with their mates, working on various engines around the yerd. Most of these would have been 'running men', which meant that they had to carry out repairs on engines in steam, already booked for particular duties. Sometimes they would find a defect which necessitated that an engine should be 'stopped', in which case the 'running foreman' (responsible for engines in steam) would have to find a substitute engine at short notice.

The heaviest repair work in a steam running shed was the removal of wheels — usually for re-metalling hot axle-boxes, or for re-profiling tyres. For this purpose the principal depots had a drop-pit deep enough to permit the biggest diameter wheels (6ft 9in on most British railways) to be lowered by a hydraulic ram, or electrically driven screw-hoist to well below rail-level. The pit was usually some 9ft deep. Some drop-pit tables — like the still-existing one at Carnforth were fitted with extension pieces, so that they could lower a bogie complete. Many drop-pits were constructed by manufacturers of turntables, such as Cowans, Sheldon of Carlisle. With a bogie, or a pair of wheels lowered, bridging rails were moved in laterally to close the gap. The locomotive was then towed away and stabled while the wheels were re-turned, or an axlebox remetalled or renewed.

Most depots not equipped with such a drop-pit had a massive tripod (called sheer legs), or a gantry under which one end of an engine could be raised, so as to remove one or more pairs of wheels. Working with such a means of lifting was frightfully laborious, and can best be described by way of example. Suppose, for instance, that a 4-6-0, with drive to the middle coupled wheel-set had a hot axlebox on that axle, necessitating the removal of that pair of wheels. The successive operations would include the following:

Parting the engine and tender draw-gear.
Parting the intermediate water and brake hoses.
Removing the tender, and probably stabling it elsewhere.
Disconnecting the brake-gear adjacent to the middle and trailing coupled wheels; removing brake pull-rods.
Disconnecting the connecting rods at the big end, and
tying them up out of the way.
Taking down the coupling rods.
Taking down the horn-stays below the axleboxes.
Removing sand-pipes adjacent to middle and rear coupled wheels.
Removing oil-pipes from the axleboxes of those wheels.
Packing up the frame of the engine under its front buffer-beam.

Only then could the middle and rear pairs of coupled wheels be run out, and the offending axlebox lifted off its journal. In some circumstances an axlebox could be lifted off once it was clear of the horn-guides without an adjacent pair of wheels being removed: it very often happened that the journal also needed re-turning, in which case running out the other wheel-set could not be avoided.

Nearly all of this was dirty, heavy work, and at many depots had to be done out of doors, whatever the weather. At a number of round-houses, notably on the Midland, and on the North Eastern the sheer-legs were, however, indoors and some of them were hydraulically operated.

The stripping down detailed above represented over two days work for a fitter and mate. All this had to be done again in reverse order — plus re-setting four axlebox wedges — when the re-metalled or new axlebox, and the wheels, etc were ready to be put back into position. Sometimes it was possible to take advantage of the occasion to carry out one of the major examinations, or a boiler inspection at the same time, but even this was not done if the engine was from a 'foreign' depot.

Besides the work involved when a heated axlebox had to be removed for re-metalling, there was often remedial work to be done to the bearing surface (the 'journal') of the axle. This might be scratched ('scored'), so that a couple of long, slow, running-in trips would suffice to make it fit for normal service. Or the normally bright steel surface might be roughed up like corduroy, in which case it would have to be re-turned in a wheel lathe. Most large sheds were equipped with such a machine, although in some areas this type of turning was done only at principal depots. Most wheel lathes at running sheds were quite ancient, many being in dubious condition; in spite of this the turners usually managed to make a fair job of turning a journal. To overcome chatter in worn gears it was often necessary to burnish with emery cloth soaked in oil, so as to obtain a mirror finish.

If a journal were severely damaged, or if there were any suspicion of cracks being caused by overheating, or if the work were beyond the capacity of the depot, then the pair of wheels concerned would be loaded into a wagon and sent away to main works. Such 'outdoor' work was a nuisance to the Works, since it interfered with their main flow of repairs, and it was often two or three weeks before a depot would get its wheels back again. In the meantime an expensive locomotive would be standing idle — but this would be of no financial consequence to the Mechanical Engineer's Department.

It was very desirable that the machine shop should be located close to the track where engines were lifted for re-metalling axleboxes, and where the fitters did their heaviest work.

A less frequent, but even more troublesome type of defect, was excessive wear on tyres. These sometimes wore 'hollow' — ie concave across the width of the treads — or the flanges might wear sharp, due to heavy side-thrusting when running on curved tracks. Occasionally 'flats' were produced when a locomotive skidded down an incline with its coupled wheels or tender wheels locked. When these kinds of wear exceeded the strictly prescribed limits, it was necessary to remove the wheel concerned for re-turning.

Where more than one pair of wheels required this attention, then the engine might even go to the Works for a 'Light Repair' — especially if extensive boiler repairs were needed at the same time. There was a certain art in getting the Shopping Bureau to accept such engines, but keeping other engines in traffic beyond the average mileage often helped.

A frequent type of repair, though mercifully necessitating much less work that that described above, was heated connecting-rod and coupling-rod bearings. These suffered similar lubrication troubles to axle-boxes, but one annoying feature was loss of oil due to missing corks. Surprising as it may seem, the oil-cavity in the rod-end above the bearing was fitted through a hole having a screw thread, which was then sealed off by a medicine-bottle cork, screwed into the hole! During 1957 we had a spate of coupling-rod bearings over-heating at Exmouth Junction, with 'Merchant Navy' and 'West Country' Pacifics coming in off the Waterloo expresses. The rod-ends would be blue with heat due to fast running without oil, after the cork had been thrown. I traced the trouble to the change-over of crews at Salisbury, where a 6min stop was always made for taking water. The Exmouth Junction men were in the habit of going round removing the corks and replacing them 'just to make sure that there is enough oil' — this after only 83 miles running from Waterloo. I pointed out to some of the drivers concerned that on the region where I came from a Pacific was expected to work the 393 miles non-stop between London and Edinburgh, without anybody checking oil-levels on the way. So if bearings were cool at Salisbury, it would be as well to let them alone and trust that the Nine Elms driver had done his preparation work properly. The message must have gone home, because over-heating due to lost corks became very rare.

Heated big ends of connecting rods driven by inside cylinders were a particular nuisance because the big-end brasses had to be taken down in an awkward position, necessitating the engine being placed over a pit. The big-end itself was of heavier construction that that of an outside rod, and in between the frames it was often not easy to see what one was doing. Also it was vastly more difficult to hand-trim and polish the scored journal of an inside crank than that of an outside crank-pin.

One of the commoner repair jobs was making sanding gear work. If stones were found in the sand, it meant that the sand had not been properly riddled, or that the equipment was out of order at the depot where the engine's sandboxes were last filled. It was often troublesome to remove wet sand from places where it had become blocked.

A frequent complaint with many classes of locomotives was 'riding rough'. There were many causes of this — mainly concerned with the adjustment of axlebox wedges, about which running sheds could take effective action, but many more — mainly due to poor design — about which they could not. The number of classes in which it was common for engines to ride rough before they had completed 20,000 miles was evidence enough that drawing offices, and particularly Chief Mechanical Engineers who took all the credit for their designs, occupied themselves very little with this problem.

There were also cases of bad balancing, and the incredible example of the North British Locomotive Co, which although it constructed many thousands of engines for numerous countries, had no wheel-balancing machine at all!

Two particular sources of heavy knocking were worn axleboxes and the coupling between engine and tender. Many designs of locomotives had wedges fitted immediately behind the coupled wheel axleboxes — the rear face of the horn block being inclined correspondingly. The wedges were very beneficial so long as they were correctly adjusted, and could be maintained in the adjusted position. Unfortunately under the deteriorated standards of workmanship and supervision which became all-too-common during World War 2, the heavy task of setting and re-fastening wedges (which had to be done in a greasy, dirty pit — and often in a cold draught) was one of those jobs which tended to be improperly done, deferred or dodged altogether. Furthermore the fastenings — while they looked adequate on a drawing — in many cases did not stand up to the knocking and vibration of engines working hard on heavily loaded trains. It was only by repeated attention on the part of the fitters that these fastenings were kept tight. When that attention was lacking, the wedges sometimes fell down to their lowest position, thus producing a much worse condition than badly worn axleboxes not fitted with wedges.

A fairly common defect consisted of one or more plates of a leaf-spring being fractured, although coil springs could also be broken. Running sheds did not repair springs because of the heat treatment and tempering required, and furthermore a spring with a broken leaf was also liable to have incipient 'hair-line' fractures in other leaves. So defective springs were always sent to main works to be stripped down and overhauled. At the sheds a broken spring was therefore a matter for re-placement with a spring of identical dimensions.

A factor usually overlooked in changing springs, or in replacing wheels was that the weight distribution was liable to be changed. This should have been checked — a task for which very few sheds were equipped. It was difficult to find a piece of dead-level track in most depots. Moreover, since locomotives seemed to run satisfactorily enough without such verification, it is not likely that running sheds bothered with this procedure — which was, or course, normal practice in the main works. Unequal weight distribution aggravated the tendency of some engines to slip, and was sometimes a partial cause of derailments.

Steam locomotives are characterised by yards of pipes of various sizes carrying water, steam, lubricating oil, vacuum and/or compressed air and sand. These are liable to failure — often with very serious consequences — either by slacking back of the nuts securing the joints, or by brittle fractures of the copper pipes. These defects were provoked by the vibration, to which all components of steam locomotives were congenitally subject. Dismantling of the joints usually presented no special difficulty, except sometimes in respect of access, the pipes often being adjacent to hot plates, particularly in such locations as the steam manifold. On some engines this was tight up in between the top of the boiler and the cab roof. Occasionally one could hear a stream of florrid language from some unfortunate fitter whose fingers had come into painful contact with a sharp, hot part of a boiler in steam.

If a pipe or its flanges needed repairs, this was the work of a coppersmith, whose duties covered all metallic, non-ferrous parts. One of the tricky jobs in pipe repairs was to ensure that the flanges had exactly the same relative position after repairs as before. The coppersmith was also the specialist on whom one relied for re-metalling axleboxes and side-rod bearings — often in a hurry. There was quite a variety of other jobs requiring his attention (especially where running shed staff also did outdoor machinery maintenance). Such work would include brazing on brass-bodied valves of all sorts. He was often quite a factotum, who would also do the tinsmithing required on oil-burning head-lamps and gauge-lamps. And if one wanted anything from a cigarette lighter to a motor-bike fuel-pump mended, then the coppersmith was usually the chap to fix it!

At smaller depots a blacksmith would undertake the work of a coppersmith, or vice versa. Blacksmithing was a dying trade, mainly due to the replacement of smithing by welding, but several blacksmiths became expert welders and oxy-acetylene cutters.

It was surprising how much work the blacksmith had to do at some freight depots in straightening footsteps, guard-irons, hand-rails, footplating etc, which suffered from the knocks and bumps of marshalling yards. Every day in a fair-sized depot a number of fire-irons needed knocking back into shape, and repeated attention was needed to see that other tools and equipment were kept in good condition. For instance, if the head of a cold chisel became de-formed (cauliflowered'), and if this were not trimmed in time, a piece of steel could fly off it when struck, possibly causing an injury to eye or hand. All in all, a good blacksmith was a very useful fellow to have around a depot and was worth his weight in gold as a handyman.

Most of the bigger depots had a character who was appointed as a handyman (often a semi-skilled carpenter) who could make a fair job of repairing or renewing the wooden floorboards in a cab, and was often a 'dab hand' with a paint brush.

A regularly recurring repair job at all steam depots was changing brake blocks and adjusting brake rigging. Some of the larger depots had one or two Grade II fitters and mates, who were engaged whole-time on these duties, plus the freeing of blocked sanding-gear. It was rough repetitive work, not requiring the use of special tools, to which semi - skilled men, including fitters' mates, were promoted.

The most important nut or bolt in any machine is the loose one, and nowhere is this more so than with a steam locomotive. For some months early in 1950, during my motive power training I kept the records at British Railways Eastern Region Headquarters of engines which had become total failures, or lost more than five minutes in running.

A disturbingly frequent type of casualty, covering a great variety of fittings was collated under the heading of 'parts loose or detached'. This common phenomenon was due to heavy vibration which almost all steam locomotives inflicted on themselves. Gresley locomotives were particularly prone to this malady, sometimes due to inferior workmanship at the sheds, but more often due to unsatisfactory design.

'Grover' spring-washers — consisting of a single coil of helical spring, fitting around a bolt under its nut — are remarkably tenacious, and in locomotive applications make the use of any other locking device unnecessary.

This book is too short to consider brake defects in detail, so that a few general remarks must suffice. Much the most common group of causes of trouble is the leakage of vacuum or compressed air at flexible hoses, at brake cylinders, and at joints in the pipework. The locomotive brake gauge will indicate if there is a leak, and the hoses with their connections are the first items to examine.

Difficulties with vacuum brakes were sometimes due to foreign matter being drawn in, such as bits of cotton waste issued to the footplate staff. Occasionally an unthinking driver would place a wad of the stuff on top of the ejector (usually located in front of his chest), and then strands of cotton were liable to be drawn in without his being aware of it happening.

Rolling rings in vacuum brake cylinders were one of the recurring causes of failure with that system — these being somewhat tricky articles to install correctly, and also subject to deterioration after long periods of use. Faults in the adjustment of brake rigging might also occur, this being mainly due to inexperience on the part of staff.

Much trouble and anxiety was caused to footplate staff when an injector would not work correctly (hence this vital component was always duplicated except where a water-pump was fitted).

Up to 1940, steam locomotives had been maintained to a high standard by employing on them large quantities of skilled and semi-skilled staff to whom discipline was the accepted norm. From that year onwards the standards of maintenance fell regrettably low, due to the call-up of skilled men to the Armed Forces, and to their partial replacement by 'dilutees' and others who were not railway-trained. Wartime also produced severe shortages of materials, tools and equipment, so that badly worn parts were kept in use, and damaged parts often bodged — with consequent liability to failure. Labour shortages led to a deterioration in disciplinary standards; the ultimate sanction of dismissal became virtually impossible for bad work, and was only adopted in cases of wilful disregard of duty. In a labour market which had become highly competitive there were many depots which had great difficulty in recruiting apprentices for maintenance.

Many shed buildings suffered progressive deterioration, especially where the maintenance of old structures (many of them built nearly a hundred years earlier) was sorely neglected due to shortages of materials and skilled staff. To make matters worse, in World War 2 many sheds suffered damage by aerial bombing. In areas liable to repeated attack only makeshift repairs were made to keep the depot functioning. But even the most serious damage never caused a depot to be abandoned. On 29 October 1942 York shed sustained a direct hit which destroyed two engines, one being an 'A4' Pacific No 4469, *Sir Ralph Wedgewood*, standing with a pair of wheels removed.

There was also the black-out, which made matters difficult in numerous ways. Anyone who has to maintain machines realises the importance of the mechanics being able to properly see what they are going; when one cannot do so, the work inevitably suffers in one way or another.

The most obvious signs of inadequate maintenance in wartime, and for some time afterwards, was the large number of engines which used to run around with heavy clanking of their moving parts. The concerted knocking in some British locomotives had to be heard to be believed; those of the LNER were the worst, although other companies could produce some shocking specimens. It seemed that just about everything knocked that could possibly knock — even the enginemen's teeth chattered on quite a few of the clatterbox 'Sandringham' 4-6-0s. The 'Gresley knock' in the 3-cylinder conjugated valve-gear, which was a pleasant jingle when the gear was freshly overhauled, became a $5\frac{1}{2}$-beat syncopated battering when excessive wear developed. The rate of mechanical failure and lost time, due to a wide variety of causes, was a circumstance that would have given rise to grave concern in any administration.

Steam locomotives, however, had a strong, rugged virtue not shared by any other form of traction. They could keep on working under the most fearsome conditions of prolonged neglect, disrepair, or even partial breakdown — long after a diesel in comparable circumstances would have come to a sickening stop with a big-end poking out through the side of its crank-case. The ability of the iron horses to continue slogging away in such a dire state could at times provoke almost a feeling of admiration as for some hero who triumphs against the most daunting odds.

The multifarious unfortunate or risky consequences of failure to maintain steam locomotives properly have been the subject of many a racy story, and one could easily fill a chapter with such anecdotes. There were no end of examples during World War 2, when many of the maintenance staff had been called away to the Forces. For instance in the summer of 1942 I was once standing near Doncaster Carr shed when a 'K3' 2-6-0 (a 'Jazzer') approached, struggling with a mixed-freight train on the Up Goods Line. At every revolution of the coupled wheels there was a cloud of steam enveloping the left-hand cylinder. Going close to it as it passed, I saw that of the studs which should have been securing the cylinder cover steam-tight, only the top five were unbroken. The cover was simply acting as a flap, letting out the live steam at every backward stroke of the piston. And still that engine was soldiering on!

Clearly no maintenance man would knowingly let a locomotive work in the condition described, but through lack of labour and materials many ran about in a state which would not have been tolerated in 1939. There was, so to speak, a marked tendency to trade on the good nature of the beasts.

Some parts of steam locomotives, such as the interiors of steam valves, ejectors and injectors, had to be kept spotless during repairs and assembly, although they usually collected scale and other foreign matter during service. But most of the rest of a steam locomotive would function with amounts of grit and dirt which would be unthinkable in diesel or electrical mechanisms.

Besides their tolerance of much sheer neglect, many parts of a steam engine would stand for an incredible amount of ham-fisted repair work. Although it was far from proper practice, it was by no means unknown for a nut in an awkward position to be *tightened up* by using a hammer and chisel! Also, open-jawed spanners in bad condition were frequently used for removing nuts; in order to apply extra pressure, a piece of steel tubing was commonly fitted over the spanner to obtain additional leverage. If such a tube were not lying handy, or if a fitter were working in an awkward position, he would not hesitate to hammer the spanner.

The motive power depots came out of the war having done a great job under the most arduous circumstances, but the effort had also taken a tremendous toll of them. Many people had become so accustomed to the bad conditions prevailing during wartime that much complacency had developed, and this persisted in several areas well into the 1950s. Many depots were unable to restore prewar standards of cleaning, making life disagreeable for the mechanical staff. However, many achieved an order of maintenance near to 1939 levels; this was true of most express passenger sheds — especially where enlightened local management combined with a favourable staff situation to retain a fair degree of pride in the work. The mechanical condition of locomotives depended heavily on the quality of management, as well as on the calibre of the rank-and-file — either or both of which left much to be desired at too many depots. Unfortunately a shed whose standard of repair was less than satisfactory could have adverse effects over a considerable area, wherever its engines worked.

On many of the locomotives allocated to some freight depots it did not need an engineer to diagnose that something was seriously wrong with axleboxes or rods, or both. Even my wife, standing at a station on one occasion in 1952 remarked 'Surely you would not let one of your engines go around like that!', as some bone-shaker of a 'J39' 0-6-0 went clonking by. I assured her that it was not one of 'mine', but remarked that it was all too easy to let these things get out of hand, with the result that the bad condition of such machines became so familiar as to be scarcely even noticed.

Locomotives were sent from depots to main works ('shopping') for a variety of reasons. Usually an engine had reached its scheduled mileage, but there were many causes for calling an engine in before that was achieved. These included broken parts, such as cylinder blocks, which could only be repaired in the Works, heavy collision damage, and boiler repairs which were beyond the capacity of running sheds.

An occasional task of the repair staff was to prepare engines for storage, or to make them fit for traffic after they were taken out of store. Locomotives which were stored could always be recognised by a piece of tarpaulin tied around the chimney, or a piece of wood or steel plate fixed across the top of it. This precaution was intended to keep rain out of the smokebox, and thus to avoid water going down the blast pipe, which it would have accumulated in the valve chests and cylinders — so rusting the valves and pistons. Bright steel parts were smeared with tallow or grease.

According to the Factories Acts the walls of workshop premises had to be kept whitewashed, but even when this was done, in most sheds they were no longer white after a few months. The workshops were the only part of a locomotive shed covered by the Acts, and they were not visited as often as they should have been — probably because many of them were in out-of-the-way locations. Also the operations going on there were not production processes. In 1955 a long-experienced Inspector visited the depot at Neasden (north-west London) while I was in charge there. At first sight of the workshop he burst out: 'These conditions are Dickensian'. As a result of his report whitewashing and some minor improvements were carried out. It was as well that that depot was closed under dieselisation in 1966, but it was no worse than the average for the country as a whole.

If a serious accident occurs, it is obligatory to call in the Factory Inspector. Being keenly aware of safety requirements, I formed the habit of doing my own factory inspection ,and encouraged all the staff to be safety conscious. It paid dividends to the extent that during seven years of shed-mastering there was never a serious accident to workshop staff under my control.

Apart from general stores (considered later) steam depots had to stock a wide range of items, ranging from expensive articles such as mechanical lubricators and injectors to humble plugs, nuts and split pins — stocked by the dozen, or the gross, or the pound in a galaxy of sizes. Some new items, though expensive, were issued on the simple signature of a chargeman. Whether cost control would have saved more than it would have cost to run may be debatable, but so far as I know it did not even come up for consideration. As against this there was usually unfavourable reaction to any request for new depot equipment such as vices. The most common observation was 'What will it save?' How on earth can you show a saving in replacing a battered, ancient, home-made fitter's cupboard by a new one?

The allocation of engines at many depots comprised quite a miscellaneous collection, and there was even a greater variety of locomotives of other depots which worked in. This necessitated hundreds of items being held in the stores, and more tools being kept than would otherwise have been needed. It was not practicable for every depot to stock spare parts for the many classes concerned.

One of the principal virtues of building the standard range of British Railways locomotives was that at last we were getting spare parts which were common throughout the country, which was more than could be said for the subsequently constructed diesel locomotives. This reduced the overall quantities of stock which had to be maintained.

On many railways nearly every class of boiler had its own types of fire-bar, often of two or three types in one grate — not forgetting drop-sections or rocker-grates. These, togehter with brake-blocks of various sizes, were often kept in the open; being of cast iron, they were not attractive items and it did not matter if they went rusty.

Brick arches, too, varied from class to class and generally necessitated two or more types of brick for each arch.

Locomotives were often out of traffic 'awaiting material', the easiest action in such cases being to send off the defective item to the main works designated to supply spare parts, and simply to wait for a replacement to arrive — especially if the 'crippled' engine was a 'foreigner'. This usually took a week or longer, and a quicker way to release such an engine was to contact a neighbouring depot having similar engines allocated. The likeliest source was usually the stopped engine's home depot, which could send the spare item on the footplate of the next locomotive working in, and so avoid waiting for the (weekly) stores van.

One way of obtaining a spare part was to remove a serviceable, identical item for another 'stopped' engine. This practice — universally known as 'cannibalisation' — was often frowned on by Higher Authority. There were good reasons for forbidding this procedure, because double work was incurred in taking down and in replacing the parts concerned, and because it involved disturbing fittings which were best left alone. However, when two engines were stopped, and there seemed to be no hope of getting the items needed within reasonable time, then any mechanical foreman worth his salt would cannibalise one to release the other. In the dying days of steam traction, when main works were being turned over to the maintenance of diesel locomotives, it became exasperatingly difficult to obtain spares, and therefore each depot had largely to fend for itself. All sorts of unofficial caches were mades, so that items not being used over a long period would not be called in to central stores, and therefore lost to the depots concerned. Under these circumstances cannibalisation became rife.

There were even many depots where engines were withdrawn from service, but could not be sent to the scrap-yard because they had been 'robbed' of essential items, such as axlebox springs.

There then arose the incredible situation that new springs had to be ordered so as to enable the locomotives concerned to be towed away for breaking up.

I had much experience of cannibalisation during World War 2 with the Royal Electrical & Mechanical Engineers, where there was a sound dictum: 'No workshop can provide a better service than its supply of materials'. From that experience I also learned the value of keeping maximum and minimum levels of each item, and the necessity of ordering replacements in good time according to anticipated delivery periods.

Besides spare parts, tools and portable equipment for the workshop had to be stored and occasionally renewed.

I trust that the foregoing remarks have sufficiently illustrated how steam locomotives could keep going in deplorable states of lack of maintenance, and how the repair staff — notwithstanding primitive, rundown facilities in many depots — generally managed to do a creditable job. But how much more satisfactory it would have been if reasonable (even humane) working conditions had been provided at all sheds, and if the details of steam engines had been so designed, or redesigned, so as to get rid of sources of so many annoying defects.

9

Design and Maintenance

For many years leading up to the Grouping of 1923 the main works of some of the companies had been inadequate to their growing work-load, and so the larger running sheds had often done jobs which ought to have been carried out in the Works. Thus until the construction of the Crimpsall Shops at Doncaster in 1900-01 Peterborough (New England), Kings Cross and Ardsley (near Leeds) had even done minor rebuilding. In Great Central days Mexborough frequently changed boilers due to lack of capacity at Gorton, especially during World War 1.

Many of the larger Midland sheds had 'outstation' shops, at which 'intermediate' repairs were carried out, these being done at about half the mileage between Works overhauls. In his book *A Breath of Steam* W. G. F. Thorley describes how this system operated at Wellingborough, and how — through lack of financial control — it was very uneconomic.

At the Grouping in 1923 the LMS, the LNER and the Southern had each inherited a very heterogeneous collection of locomotives, many of which were obsolescent. Some were so unreliable and heavy on repairs as to impede seriously any attempts at planned maintenance. Whatever the quality of the individual classes there was an excessive variety of types for the same kind of work, and many sheds had quite unnecessarily mixed allocations, as may be inferred from Richard Hardy's account of Stratford in his book *Steam in the Blood.*

The allocation of engines to various depots was a source of endless interest to many thousands of individuals and societies — especially as many large sheds had three or four classes, each capable of doing a given duty. Their varied origins necessitated the holding of different spare parts; whenever a fresh class was introduced to particular work there were likely to be difficulties in driving and in maintenance until the staff became used to them. There was often long-lasting prejudice against unfamiliar types.

Each of the pre-grouping companies attempted some standardisation within its own stocks of locomotives, carriages and wagons, but the various companies had no interchangeability of parts, except for that which was essential to the through running of vehicles in exchange traffic. In the sense of retarding standardisation, steam locomotives were too long-lived, and the main works as well as the depots paid a dear price for such diversity.

Much headway was made between the two world wars in reducing the proliferation of types, but difficulties due to diversification persisted until the latter years of steam traction.

In *Steam was my Calling* I wrote about awkward and expensive design details on locomotives. Clearly those responsible for design cared little for the tribulations which they inflicted on drivers, erectors and repair staff, and even for maintenance costs so long as the engines could somehow be made to haul their trains on time without excessive consumption of coal. The railways suffered from this malady particularly because of British locomotive engineers' traditional insistence that neatness should take precedence over almost all other factors.

Several drawing offices used to specify countersunk bolts to provide a flush outer appearance, so avoiding bolt-heads being visible. It was no concern of their's how fitters had to chop nuts off bolts in most awkward and dirty locations simply because one could not secure a hold on the bolt head.

Locomotive design was a prestige function, and each succeeding Chief Mechanical Engineer (or equivalent title) — except on the Great Western — seemed to regard it as an essential part of his position to introduce a new range of designs, often designating them 'standard'. So long as he demonstrated an acceptable management ability, no one on the Board of Directors had sufficient understanding of technical matters to challenge this often unjustified process. Locomotive engineers were not all theoretically qualified in the complexities of design, and even if their chief draughtsmen had a good technical education, it was the locomotive engineer's personal whim which predominated.

Even so prestigious and theoretically capable a designer as Gresley seems to have been deaf and blind for most of the time concerning the needs of running sheds, notwithstanding that those of the Great Northern were his direct responsibility between 1912 and 1923. From early in 1923 the depots of the LNER were administered by a Locomotive Running Superintendent for each area.

Nevertheless, as Chief Mechanical Engineer of that railway he was a man of enormous influence. The explanation seems to lie in his lack of motive power training, which was limited to a few months in a supernumary position at Blackpool shed shortly after he had completed his pupilage at Crewe. From that time until 1912 (ie until he was aged 35) his experience was exclusively in carriage and wagon matters. He would not drive a locomotive, even when invited to do so.

A number of features of his designs betrayed a woeful ignorance of realities in running sheds. The great majority of his 3-cylinder engines had the conjugated valve gear in front of the cylinders, whereas it was a matter of common observation that when a locomotive was being disposed a quantity of fine smokebox char fell on the footplating in front of the smokebox door. On the engines mentioned some of it used to trickle through the chinks around the hinged plates which were provided for access to the valve gear levers, and so formed a grinding paste with the lubricating grease. I frequently saw char piled high on the levers, and even noted cases where one could poke a pencil between a lever-pin and its bush. It was no wonder at all that the middle valve on these engines often lost nearly all its motion at the lower speeds. Whatever Gresley's qualities in other ways, he was oblivious of what was happening over the ashpits.

In 1927 the LMS introduced a system of detailed repair costing in its running sheds — lucidly described by W. G. F. Thorley in his book *A Breath of Steam*. In this respect that railway was ahead of the others, which even by Nationalisation never seem to have understood the difference between accountancy (on which they were very keen) and costing. If the latter had been properly applied and controlled at Board level, then — for example — the Civil Engineers would not have been allowed to dissipate millions of pounds on like-for-like renewals of semi-redundant assets (eg excessively complicated track-work), and on the Southern Bulleid would certainly not have been permitted to get away with constructing all those exhorbitant Pacifics.

At Exmouth Junction in 1956-57 I had 37 of these Southern 4-6-2s to maintain, and at nearly every valve and piston examination we were renewing the drive chains in their weird valve gear. These were costing over £200 per set — which was almost a sixth of my salary as Assistant District Locomotive Superintendent-cum-Shed Master. These engines worked numerous trains which were equivalent to others being hauled on the other regions by 4-4-0s or 2-6-0s. It is no exaggeration to suggest that the 'Britannia' Pacifics need never have been built if a corresponding number of 'West Country' and 'Battle of Britain' Pacifics had been transferred from the Southern Region in exchange for smaller engines from other parts of the country. But in spite of the outstanding performance of these Pacifics, the other Regions showed no willingness to take them with their outlandish valve-gear, welded fireboxes and gargantuan consumption of coal and lubricating oil.

If the Authorities at Liverpool Street or Waterloo were seriously concerned with maintenance costs, the echoes of it at depot-level were limited to general exhortations to economise. After all, how can you expect a depot manager to manage efficiently if he has no detailed analysis of large sectors of his costs? Certainly nobody ever asked me at any locomotive shed 'how much is it costing to run this depot?'. Any shed master of an average-sized depot would have had difficulty in answering such a question to the nearest £1,000 a week.

In the depots of my acquaintance there was fairly close accounting, but no budgeting — perhaps because depot costs were largely determined by the locomotive work required by the operating people. Costing and budgeting must have an arbitrary element, but however rough the assumptions, a crude attempt at costing is better than none at all. It does at least impose a certain discipline to seek out the factors which run away with the 'lolly', and to some extent focuses ideas as to possible reductions of their magnitude. On the Eastern and Southern Regions there seemed to have been no widespread effort to compare the maintenance costs of one class of locomotives against others doing similar work. Gresley's 'B17' class 3-cylinder 4-6-0s would have shown up pretty badly in comparison with almost any 2-cylinder 4-6-0 of comparable power.

A common task for the fitters in a running shed was to attend to glands leaking steam along piston rods and valve spindles. These, by their very nature, were often difficult to keep steam-tight. Yet it was necessary to keep these leaks to an absolutely minimal amount if a locomotive were to do its work properly, and if the footplatemen were to see clearly the track ahead and the signals. When a piston rod or valve spindle became scored, it was no longer possible to ensure complete steam-tightness without dismantling, turning and burnishing — a job which could not be done very satisfactorily with the machines available at the majority of locomotive depots. A certain amount of leakage from glands had to be tolerated — though not without bitter complaint from drivers during frosty weather.

While glands with split cast-iron rings had been fitted to later engines on most railways, their access was deplorable on most locomotives with inside valve gear. In some cases the parts concerned were in total, or near-total darkness. When Bulleid designed his contentious Pacifics he certainly did not do so with sufficient consideration for the unfortunate fitters who would have to work inside that horrible oil-bath. Bad access was often a major cause of the indifferent state of repair of many of the glands concerned, and of numerous other details.

Up to World War 1 it was common for drivers to repack their own valve-spindle glands every few days with soft packing, and to screw it up whenever it started to leak. They often went on duty before their booked time in order to do this work, which on inside cylinder engines had to be done in the dangerously confined spaces above the slide bars. From the time when cast iron cylinder packings were introduced, the maintenance of packings became a duty of running fitters, although many of the older engines were to continue in service for over 30 years longer with soft packing (usually of asbestos rope).

I had some months of experience of glands of that type on the obsolete Ivatt Class D3 4-4-0s working from Boston shed when I was the mechanical foreman there in 1947-48. One could well sympathise with a fitter, who having made a good, steam-tight job of repacking such a gland found it blowing again as bad as ever only three days later, while the drivers reported time and again on frosty days that they 'could not see signals for steam'. The fact that such unsatisfactory design features persisted in service for over 50 years was proof enough that Chief Mechanical Engineers and many of their senior staff were badly out of touch with what was happening in the sheds — or even worse, didn't care.

Designers who arranged two, or even three sets of valve gear between the frame plates of a locomotive in addition to one or two inside connecting rods should have been condemned to dismantle and re-erect them in bad running shed pits until they altered their ideas. Not only did erectors in the works and fitters in the sheds suffer physically from the efforts which had to be exerted with these and other heavy parts in confined spaces, but the time taken to carry out work on these items always exceeded that which would have been needed for the same tasks on equivalent components located outside the frames (as was fortunately recognised by most latter day designers). The preparation, examination and many repairs to engines fitted with inside valve gear could only be done by setting them over a pit.

The maintenance of engines having inside cylinders and motion was doubly costly in the extra time which they had to spend out of action for repairs — sometimes amounting to a whole day in the course of a valve and piston examination. Swindon were perpetuating the avoidable monstrosity of inside valve gears in 1951 — three years after Nationalisation, in spite of the fact that Stanier (an ex-Swindon man) had been building for the LMS thousands of locomotives derived from Great Western designs, but with *outside* valve gears since 1933.

In view of the stripping down and re-erection needed to re-metal over-heated axleboxes, these were some of the most costly defects on a steam locomotive. With proper design they should seldom have occurred. Bad design was not as often blamed as it should have been; after all bearings which let in grit or water were simply not suited to the environment in which locomotives had to work, be washed out and cleaned.

The bearing surface of many axleboxes was not adequate for their load and speed conditions. This was demonstrated when the prestigious 'King' class were rostered to the sharply timed 'Bristolian' under insistence from the Regional Headquarters. In spite of Swindon accuracy in machining and in lining up the horn-blocks, these engines ran hot coupled axleboxes on this duty with disturbing frequency. When Old Oak Common had almost all their 'Kings' stopped for very expensive lifting, 'Castle' class 4-6-0s were put on this working — with appreciably less tractive effort, but with proportionately greater bearing surface — the trouble immediately disappeared.

Likewise the LMS Class 4F 0-6-0s and the Fowler-designed Class 7F 0-8-0s ('Austin Seven's) gave repeated trouble with hot axleboxes since their design was derived from those of Midland 0-6-0s of considerably smaller power. Furthermore the '4F's were commonly pressed into service to work excursion trains which covered fairly long distances nonstop at sustained speeds. Lots of costly, laborious work under a sheer legs was the frequent result, when the staff concerned would have been better employed on keeping examinations up-to- date.

Lubricating oil being an expensive commodity, much work was done on oil-trials, adjusting trimmings, lubricator settings, etc (especially on the LNER), but whatever the multifarious causes of over-heating, nothing like enough research was done on the design and lubrication of so important a component as axleboxes.

Awkwardly placed footplate controls were far too numerous to mention in a single book. Quite a variety of unofficial contraptions were concocted in some sheds to make engines more suitable for their work. These ranged from bits of wire to more sophisticated items of local manufacture. (See W. G. F. Thorley's account of his invention of a supplementary regulator handle on Midland 'Jinty' 0-6-0Ts working at Wellinborough, pages 53 - 54 of his book : *A Breath of Steam* Ian Allan, 1975.)

The designers of the BR Standard steam locomotives went to a very commendable amount of trouble to make the cab layouts convenient to the engine crews, and undoubtedly succeeded in these endeavours, but — alas — in several instances at the expense of the maintenance staff, who had to live with the impaired accessibility which resulted. A case in point was the pipe-joints, etc located inside the pedestal which carried the reversing screw and other fittings. In small items as well as large, locomotive design was a sacred cow; Chief Mechanical Engineers and their design staffs regarded even the most minor of unauthorised alterations as a serious infringement of imperial privilege. But sometimes a depot, or even district management became so frustrated by official obtuseness towards getting necssary modifications adopted that they resorted to quite systematic alterations. (On some railways it is still a long, painful process to have a modification agreed on a diesel locomotive, notwithstanding the efforts of service-experience committees.)

Among the forbidden minor 'adaptations' which I made at various depots, one example must suffice. The 10 Class B1 4-6-0s and the 30-odd Class L1 2-6-4 suburban tanks on my allocation at Neasden in 1954-55 had, like others of their types, a notorious tendency to develop heavy knocking. Even the 'L1s', with their 5ft 2in coupled wheels used to run at speeds around the 70mph mark every day in the course of clocking up the highly respectable mileage of over 7,000 miles per month. Much of the knocking was due to excessive wear in the coupling rod bushes, and one could often hear it a mile away.

These bushes were designed with felt lubricating pads across their full width at the top and bottom. However, after a few thousand miles of running the felt had worn so that the gap cut for the bottom one broke the oil film, and acted as a scraper. The bushes were so badly worn that they were renewed at the 10-12,000 miles exam; so in the interests of reducing future wear, for the sake of oil economy, and as a quicker and cheaper method of machining these bushes, I instructed my turner simply to omit cutting out the bottom pad-way in each bush. There then remained about 330° of uninterrupted oil-surface, and the bushes ran the next 20,000-odd miles without futher attention.

Fortunately this 'crime' remained undetected by the time I left Neasden at the end of 1955.

One of the most annoying causes of hot axleboxes was sand getting into the bearing. On the Thompson Class A2 Pacifics there was a lip around the sand-box filler hole, so formed that if any sand were spilled outside this lip it trickled down on to the coupled axlebox situated below. An official request from New England (Peterborough) District Motive Power Superintendent for a plate to be fitted so as to deflect away any spilled sand was brusquely declined. Indeed a riposte from the Chief Mechanical Engineer's office added that sand should not be spilled in this manner, and that any spillage should be swept away!

Apparently any excuse would do to justify inaction. If the author of such a remark had ever stood near the top of a 7ft ladder, trying to fill a sand-box from a bucket in a strong wind, he would have known that fine, dry sand will blow about anyway. So New England regularly fitted their Thompson Pacifics with the necessary plates of their own manufacture, and thus saved themselves the trouble (and the railway the high cost) of lifting express engines to re-metal heated axleboxes. But they had to be sure to retrieve the plates before any of these locomotives went into the Works.

Such was the extent of taboo fittings installed on certain classes of engines at some depots that it took a day's work to strip off all the illegal contraptions before a locomotive was sent to the Works. And on its return it needed another day to 'modify' it again into serviceable, if unauthorised, order before putting it back into traffic.

Where neither official requests nor unofficial management action sufficed to get necessary improvements made the practical necessities of making engines haul trains to time sometimes led the more resourceful characters to resort to clandestine adaptations. The commonest of these were 'Jimmies', or 'razors' — a device usually concocted with the connivance of the depot blacksmith, or of the repair shop of a neighbouring establishment in exchange for allotment produce or other barter.

These consisted of a narrow bar, arranged to fit across the top of the blast pipe, so as to split the exhaust steam and increase the draught on the fire. It had to incorporate some method of clamping, to ensure that it would remain in position notwithstanding the heavy vibration added to the rapid pulsations of the blast. Yet at the same time it had to be easily removable, so that its owner could retrieve it at the end of each turn of duty with a particular engine.

Quite some ingenuity was needed to contrive such an article, especially if it were required for use on blast pipes of various shapes.

Many of these gadgets were remarkably effective; but while they often counteracted badly designed draughting arrangements there was a constant danger that their use would conceal bad maintenance, such as a smokebox drawing air. Boilersmiths would lodge strong complaints with the management if they came across a 'Jimmy', since they contended that the sharper draught produced by it caused the fire to be hotter, and thus provoked deterioration of the stay-heads and plates in the fire area (meaning the area above the grate where the fire was in contact with the plates).

If one found a 'Jimmy' in an engine of a type which was normally free steaming, this was often a warning sign that it had some defect which should be corrected, or that the driver or fireman were insufficiently skilled in handling that type of locomotive. Difficulties of unfamiliarity occurred, for instance, when wide-firebox engines were rostered to men accustomed to narrow firegrates. There was no provision for footplatemen to be trained on any particular class of locomotive, as is the case with a diesel. It was not supposed to matter if they relieved another crew on an Austerity, or even an American engine for the first time, be it in the dark or any other unfavourable circumstance — they were just expected to know, as if by instinct, plus a couple of sentences exchanged with the previous crew, all that was needed to work a train to time with their strange steed.

In the present age, when so many mechanisms work by push-buttons or switches, and depend on circuit-breakers or fuses, a feature of steam locomotives, probably not appreciated by many, was that until 1940 the vast majority of them in Great Britain were entirely innocent of any electrical circuit. Nearly all Great Western engines and those on the Tilbury line had an automatic warning system, but electric lighting with steam-driven turbines was not generally fitted in this country until World War 2.

The execution of many booked repairs could be reasonably deferred to a later occasion, when an engine was due for scheduled maintenance or washing-out. Otherwise the engine might have to be stopped for attention by the daytime staff. Supervisors had to watch that 'running men' did not cause loss of availability by stopping locomotives in this way when they could have completed the necessary work during their own shift.

It was most desirable for the daily examination to be carried out as soon as possible after the arrival of an engine in the shed yard, since this gave the running foreman or mechanical supervisor the maximum time to arrange for carrying out repairs booked by drivers and/or the examiner (and there nearly always were some such items). Consequently a conscientious examining fitter might be seen tapping around a locomotive while it was still on the ashpit, or undergoing or awaiting any one of the servicing functions. Examination out of doors by day ensured that the parts being inspected could be seen by daylight. At night, however, it was almost always done by the flickering light of a smoky, paraffin-flare lamp.

It was the LMS which introduced — in 1934 — a most detailed system of scheduled maintenance, and which refined this so that the basic mechanical examination coincided with boiler-washing under the title of 'X' Day Exams. That system was extended under Nationalisation to cover all the steam locomotives of British Railways. About half the work involved in the periodical examinations concerned items which were inspected at intervals of 3-5 weeks, 7-9 weeks, 3 or 6 months, or a year, depending on experience acquired with the various types of equipment (injectors, boiler mountings, etc).

It would be excessively lengthy to summarise here all the time-based and mileage examinations, especially as there were exceptions for various classes and for non-standard fittings, besides variations which were introduced to take account of local circumstances, such as particularly bad feed-water. It must therefore suffice here to note that a 'No 1' examination was a visual inspection carried out at 5-6,000 miles; other mileage-based examinations were carried out at multiples of these figures. Connecting rods and coupling rods were scheduled to be taken down at the No 4 Exam (20-24,000 miles), at which they were in most cases re-bushed.

The most extensive examination was the 'No 6' — commonly referred to as the valve and piston exam — which in practice became due on most engines at about half the mileage between main works overhauls. However, many Pacifics received two of these examinations within that period and some of the LNER Peppercorn Pacifics even achieved three 'No 6 exams'. At these the valves and pistons were withdrawn and cleaned of carbon. The steam ports were cleaned, and new rings fitted to valves and pistons. Many slide-valve engines were still running about (mainly ancient shunting tanks) until the last decade of steam traction); these had their valve faces re-machined if necessary at the 'No 6' exam, and the mating faces in the cylinder block also scraped or machined.

Getting rid of the carbon formed by decomposition of the lubricating oil in high working temperatures was important because it tended to prevent valve and piston rings from expanding circumferentially to give steam-tightness. The carbon also added to the weight of reciprocating parts, and reduced the cross-section of steam passages.

Usually material had to be obtained from the Works for the renewal of several parts at these examinations, especially as the depots could not stock all the various sizes of rings required for different classes of locomotives, whose valve liner and cylinder bores wore within quite a wide range of dimensions. The time taken to receive the material often determined the duration (generally 6-10 working days) of the examination. Advantage was taken of the immobilisation of engines at any of the periodical examinations to carry out any boiler examinations or deferred repairs, plus any time-based examinations which were almost due. The whole operation amounted to a minor overhaul, and when it was done in a thorough-going fashion, with axlebox wedges re-adjusted (where fitted) the engine would perform like a new one.

Not content with its sophisticated and highly successful system of preventive maintenance, the LMS combined this with its Repair Concentration Scheme — also described at length by Thorley. By this scheme maintenance was planned on a District basis. All repairs and examinations on engines which were mobile, and which would need more than 24 hours for their completion were concentrated on one (sometimes two) of the largest depots in each district, so that advantage could be taken there of the specialisation of workshop crafts. These sheds also had their range and quality of machine tools brought up to a good standard, at the same time as other modernisation works were carried out (eg provision of mechanical ash-handling).

The concentration depots also held the district reserve of locomotives. Other depots, carrying out generally those repairs which could be completed within 24 hours, were reduced to the status of garage sheds. Responsibility for the condition of engines was strongly localised, whether under the Repair Concentration Scheme or otherwise, each Locomotive Shed Master being answerable to a District Officer. The Concentration Scheme involved more light running than the arrangement whereby each shed carried out all its own maintenance, but this was minimised by the very efficient LMS control system.

Conscientiously applied preventive maintenance could almost eliminate failures, and could reduce lost time due to boiler and mechanical causes very substantially, but could not obviate them entirely. For this reason, all but the smallest depots retained one or more 'running fitters' on each shift, while the largest sheds had a 'running boilersmith' also.

There were many aspects of steam locomotion in which one could take a keen interest. While always happy to ride on the footplate — in spite of the probability of getting face, hair, neck and clothing dirty with smoke and fine coal dust, I found maintenance work to be the most absorbing. No doubt it was partly because of having served my apprenticeship at Doncaster — one of the world's finest locomotive works. Also my army training and duties, which were mainly concerned with maintaining vehicles, had much to do with that inclination. During my early motive power training I had also come to the conclusion that it was possible to make the most effective contribution to the working of a depot by concentrating on keeping its engines in first-class condition. This not only kept failures down to a minimum, but helped materially to ensure a high level of morale — both factors of the highest importance to a good standard of performance.

From several points of view it was as well that steam locomotives were superseded when they were, for numerous depots just could not obtain the skilled men needed to maintain them properly. Also, with progressively rising wages, labour-intensive steam traction was becoming more and more uneconomic. This was particularly evident in shunting, which was being progressively dieselised, even before the modernisation programme was instituted. It was even clearer with stopping passenger services, where diesel multiple-unit sets replaced steam trains at much less than half their running and maintenance costs.

For the maintenance staff, the transition was from having to work under some of the roughest conditions in which men were called upon to repair machinery, to surroundings which will compare favourably with most modern factories. No doubt many of those who had to maintain steam locomotives find the work on diesels less interesting, but I doubt whether any would willingly go back to the conditions which prevailed in most steam depots.

10
Depot Layouts

There was great variety in the means of entry to running sheds, some of which were almost inaccessible to road vehicles. The pedestrian entrance was often by a gate in a fence or wall or through a gap where the gate used to be!

The layout of locomotive depots depended principally on the shape and size of the site selected. Once this was determined, it was then most influenced by the type of shed building chosen — whether of the 'round-house' variety, or a 'straight' shed having parallel tracks.

Many depots were congested for reasons connected with a long, chequered history, while others suffered from a lack of proper planning in the first place. Most often the sites had been adequate for the original quantity of engines, dating in some cases back to the 1840s. Increases in the number of locomotives allocated to a depot generally over-loaded its facilities to an intolerable extent before extension was authorised by a board of directors always grudging to spend capital. In many instances the depot had to be moved to another site.

An example of this was at Doncaster, where by the early 1870s the original shed — lying between the present station and the locomotive works — was badly congested. The only way to provide extra tracks for the station and to relieve the hard-pressed 'Loco' was to remove the running shed to a new site about $1\frac{1}{4}$ miles to the south-east. The station was rebuilt in 1876, incorporating the site of the former shed, thus providing the present No 8 platform, plus tracks and sidings west of it.

A locomotive shed yard was often alive with interesting activities. At any sizeable depot, besides the functions already mentioned, there were arrivals and departures to be seen during most of the day and much of the night. Moreover one was frequently aware of the surroundings — especially the running or shunting of trains on nearby lines. A depot was characterised not only by the types of locomotive allocated there, but also by their hours of coming and going; For instance, some sheds served a high proportion of industrial traffic — such as steelworks. Others provided engines principally for suburban, or other local traffic, but at most places the trains were distributed roughly round-the-clock, and for the most part 6-7 days a week. In effect, running sheds — apart from the smallest ones — never closed.

At many depots some of the points — notably the yard inlet and outlet, and points leading to and from ashpits and turntables — were used over 100 times a day. The permanent way gang therefore had only very limited periods when they could have possession of portions of the track. The ground surface between the tracks was made up of old ballast and compacted ashes; moreover only second-hand rails were used for most of the lines in locomotive depots. The ballast was nearly always fouled with coal-dust, ash, oil and grease; for this and other reasons the drainage was often bad. So areas adjacent to water-columns tended to be water-logged.

Although the movements were always at low speed, they were of the heaviest vehicles, with high unsprung weight. The track maintenance men were therefore understandably not keen to work among moving engines any more than they could help. So it was perhaps inevitable that derailments in depots were often due to track being in inferior condition. There was no signalling within depot limits, so if a derailment or a collision occurred at a strategic pair of points, there would be chaos until the tracks were cleared.

Shed shunting was a regular feature of the working of every running shed, and shed shunters needed to have an intelligent approach to their job, so as not to create difficulties for the running foreman by marshalling engines in the wrong order. At Mexborough there was the Garratt to be shunted at its weekly washout. This had become thoroughly unpopular because of the heavy firing required every time it pushed a train up the 3-mile incline at Worsborough — where it was doing the work of two engine crews. Shortly before that duty ceased, with the electrification of the line in 1951, a shed shunter — unable to move the brute with his shed-shunting engine — hooked more and more locomotives on to the drawbar in order to pull it out of the shed. Suddenly there was a loud bang, and the whole group lunged forward. A cylinder of the Garratt had accumulated a lot of water in it, and a cylinder cock was either closed or blocked. Extra tractive effort had been applied until the hydraulic pressure created could no longer be contained, and a large chunk burst out of the cylinder block. The engine was immobilised in Doncaster Works for several weeks until a new Class 02 cylinder block could be fitted.

Whatever disciplinary action the unfortunate shed shunter may have suffered, it was more than compensated by the popularity he gained among his fellow footplatemen for having put 'Big Bertha' out of action.

While the shed shunters at any depot were pushing and pulling engines about with the shed 'mike', to and from the boilerwashing tracks, the repair shop, the sheer legs, etc other engines in steam were making their way about their own diverse pursuits. At the larger depots, having a mixture of different types of passenger and freight work, there was thus a daily cavalcade of iron horses of all sizes and descriptions. Many depots had a considerable assortment of locomotive classes on their own allocation, and while the personnel of the shed was well acquainted with them all, there was always an element of the unexpected in what might turn up from a 'foreign' depot, especially at a shed occupying a focal position such as Oxford, where engines of all four main line companies were to be seen, or one handling a lot of excursion traffic — such as Blackpool.

The most important feature in planning a locomotive depot was to have a free 'flow' of engines through the various operations, plus a facility for bypassing any of them. When I was in charge of the Eastern Region Shed Analysis Committee (p92 of *Steam was my Calling*) we recorded the time during which locomotives were kept waiting for various purposes, as well as that occupied with the functions themselves. These were plotted on a time-base chart, waiting time being shown as a red bar preceding a bar of another colour for the function concerned. Time and again we observed that the red bar was longer than that representing the time to do the work. This indicated a loss of availability, and often less time in which workshop staff and others had in which to carry out their duties on these engines. Sometimes a delay was incurred from one day to the next before a locomtoive could return to revenue-earning service.

A depot handling an allocation of about 100 engines was probably the largest which could be managed efficiently. Where substantially more than this number of locomotives was needed at one place it was desirable to have two separate sheds — one for passenger and one for freight engines — as at Crewe North and South respectively. Stratford shed would have worked much better if a separate depot had been provided at Temple Mills for freight and shunting locomotives. There probably never was an ideal steam locomotive depot layout, but Carnforth — north of Lancaster — was very good.

Both dead-end and double-ended sheds were wasteful of land in the track-work which fanned out from a single track by a succession of points to form several parallel tracks in the shed building. At many depots this 'fan' covered ground longer than the shed building itself. Restriction of the width of land available might cause a shed to have a limited number of long tracks. Where land was cheap — as it often was in the early days of railways — sheds commonly had a larger number of short tracks. Shed yards tended to be long and sprawly, so that it really required a bicycle to get around some of them.

Numerous depots were unbelievably antiquated in facilities both for men and locomotives. Many were badly planned within the space available, like the old shed at Ipswich or were horribly cramped like Camden (London). Others, such as Kings Cross Top Shed, had notoriously awkward yard layouts — mainly for reasons of piecemeal historical development. (See *Steam was my Calling*, page 95 concerning a very significant track improvement which ought to have been carried out decades earlier at the inlet of the shed yard.)

Many depots were of good proportions, being constructed to generous dimensions, either as replacements for earlier sheds on different sites, or in connection with the opening of new lines. Colwick, Nottingham, was an example of this, being a 'dead end' shed built in 1881, when the Great Northern was empire-building westward with a sprawl of lines which extended to such improbably far-afield places as Burton-on-Trent and Stafford. It had strong similarities to the 'through' shed, built at Doncaster six years earlier.

On page 74 of his book *Locomotive Adventure* H. Holcroft writes of producing drawings at Swindon about 1912 for new GWR running sheds: 'The details of style and construction were standardised, so that sheds could be composed of standard parts: engine pits, coal stages, water tanks, repair shops, etc were all of a pattern. It was largely a case of adapting the shed and its sidings to the land available as a site'. Other railways similarly had standard features, particularly in round-houses, but from the Grouping in 1923 there was very little standardisation in depots until Stanier went from Swindon to take over as Chief Mechanical Engineer of the LMS in 1932.

Holcroft wrote concerning several depots on the Southern Railway in 1934: 'There was no money for improving and modernising locomotive depots, many of which were inadequate for the number of locomotives allocated to them: plant and equipment was obsolete, and repair work had to be done in dismal surroundings and under depressing and uncomfortable conditions. That the locomotive stock was kept in such good order was a tribute to the maintenance men'. These remarks would have been equally appropriate to numerous depots on the LMS and the LNER.

Considerable capital cost was incurred in providing pits between the rails of most indoor tracks and quite a length of outdoor tracks in motive power depots. It was necessary to go beneath locomotives for examination, disposal, repairs, cleaning preparation and washout. It was usual for pits to be provided along the full length of the tracks in straight sheds and in all stalls in round-houses. An engine-length of each track outside each dead-end shed and outside one or both ends of a 'through' shed was almost invariably equipped with a pit, since by daylight it was much easier for drivers, examining fitters, and cleaners to see what they were doing in these outdoor pits.

Sometimes ashpits were awkwardly placed alongside a coaling plant, so that reversal was necessary between one facility and the other. This disposition was almost always due to an ashpit having been originally alongside an elevated coaling stage, so that the two operations could proceed simultaneously, whereas this was not possible with a mechanical coaling plant.

Contrary to general practice the ashpit should have been so located as to allow disposal to be the last function to be carried out before berthing, since an engine needed to be able to move itself about a depot in its own steam. It was certainly better for a locomotive *not* to be pulling cold air through a bare firegrate, and so provoking unequal expansion at the tube ends. Also vacuum-operated turntables required a degree of vacuum which could only be assured if there was about 50lb/sq in to work the ejector. Moreover if an engine were to be blown back to a hot water wash-out plant, then the more residual pressure available in the boiler the better. If it were simply to be stabled awaiting the next duty, it was better to keep the boiler as hot as possible, and so only to throw out the fire at the last practicable moment.

The various activities were accompanied by a great diversity of noises from a succession of whistles to the thunderous rumbling as a coaling plant was being filled, or as engines took coal there. The sounds were further increased during fog or falling snow when detonators and shouts were added to the usual repertoire. As required by operating rules any movement had to be preceded by a whistle blast to alert anyone close-by. With any steam locomotive which has been standing more than a few moments in cold weather it may be necessary to open the cylinder cocks so as to blow condensate water out of the cylinders, and thus avoid their being damaged by hydraulic pressure.

Most other operating noises were also regularly heard in a depot, including the working of injectors (forcing water into a boiler), creating vacuum for the brake (exhaust sound from the ejector steam jet), the 'pish-tish' of a Westinghouse pump, and steam blowing out of the chimney from a smokebox blower-ring. With this latter hangs a true tale pertaining to Camden depot, which supplied engines for Euston. That shed was located in a thickly built-up area, and like others similarly sited it was from time to time subject to residents' complaints about smoke. On one memorable occasion this was raised as a question in the House of Commons. A small group of Members of Parliament were therefore delegated to make immediate enquiries, and at very short notice they called at the shed. All concerned were warned not to put fresh coal on any fire during the half hour which remained before the party arrived. And lo, when they made their inspection there was no smoke to be seen.

They were just departing to report these findings at Westminster when someone discovered that a 'Black 5', due 'off shed' in about a quarter of an hour was low in steam. The natural reaction was to turn on 'the blower' to brighten up the fire, which did not create smoke since the fire was well burned through. But it did send up a shower of sooty water, which by sheer malchance sprayed the visitors from head to foot. Camden was not guilty of smoke on that occasion, but it was nevertheless condemned with some strong, unparliamentary language.

Turntables were of two main kinds, the more common having the girders below the rails — necessitating a fairly deep pit — and those whose track passed between the girders, as favoured at many locations on the Great Western. The latter enabled the circular rails of the table to be laid only a few inches below the running rail, so that virtually no pit was necessary. The latter was of quite old design, and as wider engines came to be constructed in later years, the space between the locomotive and the girders became dangerously restricted. A ladder was therefore sometimes mounted on the outside of the girders, so that men could climb between the cab and the ground without risk of being crushed if the engine should move.

The pit of a turntable constituted a serious hazard to the unwary — especially in the dark. Out of doors it was seldom protected, except that the pit edging was sometimes whitewashed to draw attention to the danger. This was often the situation inside roundhouses, but there in many cases the wooden deck of the table was extended to cover the whole circular area of the pit. This enabled staff to take short cuts across it, instead of having to walk round the edge of the pit. They could thus also keep clear of the front end of locomotives which might move without warning, or shoot out sprays of scalding water from their cylinder cocks.

A less frequent form of protection, offering neither of these advantages, was a tubular fence which revolved with the table. Both this and the revolving stage referred to above required a framework built out from the turntable girders and supported on wheels.

Most turntables required engines to be carefully balanced on them if they were to be turned with a reasonable amount of effort. Unfortunately for many years locomotives were built on most railways close to the limit of the wheel-base length that the tables would take, and this constituted a serious limitation on locomotive design. This was particularly true on the Great Eastern, a circumstance from which the LNER suffered throughout its operations in East Anglia.

With the longest engines on many routes there was no room to obtain balance on the tables: indeed on some tables the rails had been extended by about a foot at each end so that locomotives could be turned whose wheel-base exceeded the original table length. All that the unfortunate crews could do was to fill the tender tanks to the most appropriate level before turning the engines concerned.

There was even a case related to me by the Mechanical Foreman at Peterborough Spital in 1952, concerning the LNWR shed which used to stand alongside the River Nene, about 200yd west of the East Coast main line. In his earlier days at that shed 4-4-0s which were too long for the turntable at Peterborough East were often worked from Rugby. The hapless shed staff had to part the engine from its tender, turn each separately, and then couple them together again — what a way to run a railway!

There were stories galore of tables not turning freely — sometimes causing injury to men who over-strained themselves. Few turntables were ever fitted with roller bearings on the centres — which would have cured most of the trouble — but there were some non-balancing tables which had roller-bearing race-wheels. The circular track of a turntable needed to be dead-level. If it did not have a good foundation, or was not adequately maintained, there could be short lengths of slight gradient, so that whatever weight rested on the pair of wheels at one end of a table had, in effect, to be pushed uphill. Whatever the cause of a table being hard to move, the staff who turned engines on it often acquired a pinch-bar, intended to pinch wagons along a track. While the driver pushed on a turntable handle, the fireman used to prise between the circular track and a race-wheel.

Many turntables were so constructed that the lever which operated the catches also served as the bar used for hand-pushing the table.

The turning of some tables was facilitated by hand-cranks, which by means of a chain drive rotated one of the race wheels; a mechanical advantage was obtained by installing sprockets of a suitable ratio.

The LNER, the LMS and some other railways fitted many of their larger turntables with vacuum motors patented by Cowans, Sheldon, the crane-makers of Carlisle. These took power direct from a flexible brake hose on the locomotive, and this sufficed to turn the engine appreciably faster than could be done by hand. At many LNER depots, in addition to vacuum-fitted engines, there were quite a number which had only steam brakes or Westinghouse brakes. At several such depots the vacuum-motored turntable was equipped with large vacuum cylinders, mounted alongside the main girders. Once these were charged by a vacuum-fitted engine they sufficed for turning one of the others, and also gave a quick start as soon as the motor was coupled up.

At shed such as Mexborough, where the preponderance of locomotives allocated to or coming into the depot were fitted only with a steam brake, the turntable was equipped with an electric motor.

Powered turntables saved engine crews much risk of strain and had the great merit of making it easy to stop the table at the proper moment. Regrettably there was repeated trouble at many places due to enginemen attempting to stop a moving table by throwing in a locking catch. Since the revolving mass of locomotive plus table could be up to 190 tons, the momentum — even at less than walking pace — was enough to break anything if one tried to stop the movement instantaneously. Many men seemed to be incapable of grasping this piece of elementary mechanics. Unfortunately militaristic-minded managers thought that giving an order to stop a table before engaging the catches was all that was needed to ensure its being done. It would probably have been more economical to mount the catches on hydraulically cushioned brackets rather than to incur the repeated expense of replacing smashed catches, but such ideas of economy rarely prevailed on a railway.

Two much more serious, but fortunately very rare troubles occurred with turntables. One was failure to engage the catches properly before an engine ran on to the table. There was then a considerable risk that the rails on the table would not be quite in line with the rails of the approach track, so that one or more pairs of wheels became derailed on the table decking. This happened with a Leicester Pacific at Marylebone, when as the Locomotive Shed Master at Neasden I had to take charge of its re-railment. Fortunately the weight of the wheels was taken directly by the table girders, so that the re-railing could be done with no particular trouble.

The other grave danger was that an engine might be set in motion towards the table when this was not set for the track on which the engine was moving. One or more pairs of wheels would then fall into the pit. Besides the table being immobilised, any locomotives then in the stalls (the tracks radiating off the table) would also be trapped in. If the pit were a deep one, there would almost certainly be damage to the brake gear, coupling rods, sand-gear, etc and the re-railing job could be very difficult. Any men on the footplate would be liable to injury. In the case of a turntable of the type on which engines ran between the girders, the locomotive was likely to sustain only minimal damage by running into the shallow pit, but the race-rail of the table could be badly bent.

Newton Abbot diesel depot has a traverser because it was formerly a repair factory for steam locomotives. Sheffield Grimesthorpe and Old Oak Common also had a traverser; at the latter depot this was used for setting engines in the repair shop in a restricted site.

In order to avoid turning on a turntable, or as a substitute means of turning, advantage was often taken of a 'triangular' track layout where two lines joined so as to form a triple junction close to a depot — as at Mexborough. Some stations without depots, such as Skegness, even had a triangle laid in exclusively for turning locomotives. These, however, required a large amount of land, and it was virtually impracticable to make any adequate use of the land inside the triangle. As notable exceptions to this general observation, New England shed at Peterborough was built within a triangle installed for locomotive turning only, while Farnley Junction depot, Leeds was built in the fork of a traffic junction. A single track forming the third side of a triangle was provided exclusively for turning engines.

Triangles have the great advantage that a succession of several locomotives of any permitted length and weight can use them simultaneously. No effort is required other than the power of the engines themselves.

O. S. Nock has written concerning the modernisation of steam depots, 'instead of spending the vast capital which was laid out on dieselisation and electrification, much could have been done to mechanise some of the shed processes, or to facilitate the manual jobs — particularly fire-lighting. However, this would have left a lot of costly functions, such as boiler-washing and repairs, tube-sweeping and cleaning, in which the labour element would still have been very high. Re-building most of the steam depots to modern standards would itself have involved prohibitive capital costs, and the retention of much valuable land'.

Note: A description of various types of turntable, including systems of power drive is given by H. C. Webster in *Locomotive Running Shed Practice*, pages 192-9, Oxford University Press, 1947.

11

Shed Buildings

Steam locomotive depots were provided with one or more 'round-house' buildings, or one or more sheds having parallel tracks. The latter — which were much the more common in Great Britain — were 'dead-end' or 'through' sheds. Some depots had a combination of these types of building, dating from different periods, or originating with different constituent companies.

Dead-end sheds suffered from the serious drawback that shunting a locomotive to or from any position in the shed, (or on one of the tracks leading to the shed) necessitated withdrawing all the other engines between that position and the points which served that track. Many such depots had space within the building for four or five tender engines on each track, and some of these tracks also had standage for several more outside. Thus to shunt out an engine at the dead-end might involve first having to move up to nine others.

A 'through' shed was open at both ends, with the tracks connected to the yard layout. Certain tracks were reserved for washing out, and others for repairs, but the general method of working was to push locomotives in from one end, and to take them out under their own steam from the other end. This necessitated one or more doors at either end of the shed being open at any time; after World War 2 it was common not to replace doors which became broken. Moreover there were large vents in the roof along each track for the escape of smoke and steam. When there was a wind blowing — unless its direction was roughly square to the tracks — the shed building acted like a wind tunnel. In winter some of those winds must have been howling non-stop from Siberia. A vast amount of heat was given off by engines standing in steam in the shed, but even this enormous source did not suffice to keep the place warm when a freezing wind was blowing, except alongside each locomotive. In cold weather the staff would sometimes rig up rough tarpaulin screens to mitigate the chill blast, but these had to be kept well clear of engines moving on adjacent tracks, and were seldom very effective.

It was usual in straight sheds to have smoke chutes running the full length of each track, so that wherever an engine might be set there was always an escape for smoke directly above each chimney. Some of the older sheds had a number of chutes placed at intervals. Such an arrangement was cheaper to construct, and produced much better natural lighting; it also afforded better access to the top of a locomotive for cleaning or repairs. However, in the latter years of steam traction shed shunters could hardly be relied upon in a large shed for such niceties as setting an engine with its chimney under a smoke chute.

During World War 2 and its aftermath, shortages of labour and materials caused smoke chutes and troughs to fall into disrepair, so that unsafe sections were often taken down, and not replaced. On one occasion in 1949 I was standing in Lincoln shed alongside a 'Springbok' 4-6-0 when it started to move. The rails being greasy, its wheels slipped violently, giving a sharp blast from the chimney. Unfortunately at that point the smoke-chutes were not intact, and the blast fetched down a shower of roof glass, which fell around my head. This let in more light; since the glass was thoroughly grimy, it also let in the rain. Nobody thought much of it, and it is doubtful if the smoke-chute or roof-glass was repaired before the District Engineer's staff came around to do routine periodical repairs — which may well have been over a year later.

The end of a 'dead-end' shed opposite to its dead-end was known as the 'shed front'; this term included also the preparation pits in that vicinity, and was applied equally to that end of a 'through' shed from which most, if not all of the engines departed. In most depots the shed master's office was part of the main building, and was commonly located so as to command a view of the shed front and that part of the shed yard which lay beyond it. There was no 'shed front' at a round-house — locomotives being prepared in the stalls.

'Round-houses' are sheds whose tracks for berthing locomotives — whether for examination, repairs, boilerwashing, etc preparation, or just awaiting the next train working — consist of short lengths radiating from a turntable. Most such sheds had a full circle of tracks, known as 'stalls'. In England the Great Western, the Midland and the North Eastern used this arrangement for their larger depots. At

Guildford, Inverness and many places overseas a round-house was used which had less than a full circle of tracks — often because the site was restricted.

The round-house for stabling engines was one of the earliest types of railway installation. Since such sheds incorporated a turntable, locomotives were turned out for their workings facing in the direction required. The shell of a similar building survives near Chalk Farm Underground station in London, opposite the site of Camden locomotive depot. During most of its service it was a goods shed, but still proclaims its original function in its name 'The Roundhouse Theatre'.

The main advantage of a round-house was that any engine could be placed in it, or withdrawn, without disturbing any other; but there was the drawback that only one engine could be dealt with at a time, and this usually took a minimum of two minutes.

Most depots using roundhouses had two or more tables. Hull Dairycoates had no less than six of them (five in line), plus two straight sheds. Adjacent round-houses had a connecting track, so that in the event of an outlet becoming blocked, access could still be maintained via the other table.

What were called round-houses in Great Britain were in fact almost all square or rectangular so far as the building was concerned. Consequently it was usual to place long tender engines, or two tank engines on the stalls which extended into the corners of the shed. At the turntable end locomotives were often dangerously close to one another; this was a hazard which everyone working in a round-house needed to become aware of in his first few hours of duty there. Visitors and trespassers had to be watched to see that they did not get trapped by moving engines. This danger had become acute in that many round-houses had been constructed for an allocation of inside cylinder engines, whereas (on the North Eastern particularly, and later on the LMS) there was increasing use of locomotives which were much wider on account of their having outside cylinders.

At the opposite end of each stall were conversely a wide open space due to the diverging tracks, and this was nearly always simply waste floor-room. Some advantage was taken of it when engines needed work done on their 'front-ends'; they were then usually set with their tenders (or bunkers) toward the table, and so there was ample room in which to work around the 'front end'.

When engines were not in steam there was a problem of setting them in, or of moving them out of the stalls of round-houses. The simplest way, when the table was appreciably longer than the locomotive to be moved, was to tow it on to the table with a very short 0-4-0T (a Class Y7 in the North Eastern Area), and then to turn the two together. Otherwise an engine had to be placed in the stall opposite to the one in question to push or pull the dead locomotive on to or off the table.

When the necessity of using longer engines obliged a reluctant management to install longer turntables in some of the round-houses, extensive alterations became necessary to the shed buildings. Examples of this, including Gateshead, are to be found in K. Hoole's *North Eastern Locomotive Sheds* (David & Charles, 1972).

Unfortunately not one of the dozens of round-houses which existed in Great Britain has been preserved intact, but the round-house shed at York has been adapted for displaying locomotives as part of the National Railway Museum. A similar arrangement has been adopted by the SNCF, whose museum at Mulhouse is accommodated in the former locomotive depot.

Kings Cross also had the only round-house on the Great Northern, built by that company for rental to the Midland when their trains started running into Kings Cross (via Hitchin) some 11 years before St Pancras was constructed. It survived until 1931, being used in its later life for accommodating tank engines, due to the short length of its turntable.

From 1861 Kings Cross depot had a traverser which must have been unique, since it ran on a curved track. As explained by P. N. Townend in his book *Top Shed* (Ian Allan, 1975) this traverser was installed for moving engines to and from repair bays. It is significant that a steam-driven traverser had been placed eight years earlier in the centre bay of what was then the erecting shop of Doncaster Works (D5 Bay in the LNER area) — Archibald Sturrock being the Locomotive Engineer responsible for both establishments. The original building, occupying part of the site where the electrification depot and the Freightliner depot now stand, had 28 individual 'stalls' for stabling locomotives side-by-side on a graceful curved frontage. Each had its own pair of doors, the adjacent tracks diverging slightly from one another. The shed therefore looked like a terrace of boxes for the iron horses to reside in — inspired no doubt by grandiose stables on a country estate.

This building dated from 1850 when the Great Northern started its operations from London, before the present terminus was constructed. If one takes into account the fact that the terminus itself was modelled on the Tsar of Russia's Riding School, then equestrian thinking in the architecture of the original Kings Cross shed would appear to have been entirely natural. And after all, the vast bulk of the country's transport was at that time still horse-drawn.

The last round-house to be constructed in Great Britain was at Leicester Midland, the stalls being of equal length, and the building a 32-sided polygon. While most round-houses in the United Kingdom were enclosed, this shed was open in the centre, with only the stalls covered. The arrangement had the advantage that it let smoke out and daylight in, besides which the building was less expensive to construct and maintain. Other examples of this were to be found at Stoke and at many places abroad. When the roofs of old round-houses became uneconomic to repair after 1945, it was common to remove the portion over the table, and later simply to strip the roof off altogether.

Pre-cast concrete elements were extensively used in constructing the shed at Leicester — this being a recent development for such structures. The roof was partly glazed, and there were large windows placed high in the perimeter walls, giving good natural lighting. The space below these windows was filled in with brickwork. The turntable was a 70-footer, able to revolve a BR Class 9F 2-10-0, or a Pacific. Part of this shed was enclosed for steam engines under repair, sliding doors being provided across the openings. There was also a 3-track repair shop, containing a drop-pit.

While shed interiors were often gloomy, and not at all favourable to photography, they frequently presented material of intrinsic interest to the connoisseur. Where part of the roof was missing — as was all too often the case after World War 2 — sunlight streaming into the hive of industry beneath sometimes created contrasts of light and shade which were quite artistic. Repairs on stopped engines were usually done in an area apart from locomotives in steam, except at small depots and medium-sized round-house sheds. In shops reserved for repairs there were no smoke chutes to block out the daylight, and doors were provided to keep out the wind. Where a drop-pit was installed this was most often in the repair shop, or occasionally — as at Lincoln (which had no repair shop) — in a separate building.

In all sheds — and particularly in the repair shops — there were heavy wooden benches installed for fitters and other staff. Below these, or suspended from them, was usually an untidy assortment or steel of wooden boxes, made to accommodate a great variety of personal possessions, tools and equipment. Engines needing repairs or examinations were when possible shunted to the ends of tracks near to the benches.

For hanging clothing many sheds had until the latter years of steam nothing more sophisticated than a miscellany of hooks and nails at odd heights on dusty walls. At some depots a cupboard contained a stock of cigarettes, sweets, etc, with which some enterprising character carried an illicit trading to augment his low wages.

Many shed buildings in Great Britain which survived until the latter days of steam locomotion were very old, having been constructed in the great age of railway expansion between 1850-80, when almost all the locomotives in this country were of inside cylinder design — and thus considerably narrower than most of those built in the present century. Consequently many locomotive entrances to shed buildings, turntables having their girders on each side of the decking, coal-stages where the tracks were kept close to the building, etc had restricted clearances. Generally this meant any building or fixed installation which penetrated within the Civil Engineer's structure gauge.

The worst examples I ever encountered were at the Southern Region depot at Yeovil Town, where at footplate-level an average cat could only have squeezed between a locomotive and the wall at the entrance to the shed building if he had been a lean and hungry specimen. Such conditions were dangerous to the point of being death-traps; it said much for the vigilance of supervisors and supervised that in 14 years of motive power work I never came across a case of anyone being crushed at such a location — although there had been such fatalities elsewhere. The danger was, of course, well known to all concerned, but it was not confined to the proximity of old structures. For instance, the platforms provided at coaling plants were necessarily as close to the locomotives as were most station platforms.

Under British Railways administration all such danger points were marked with standard red-and-white, enamelled chequer-boards.

Besides the visual impressions in a depot there were many nasal ones, although these could be detected close to locomotives, they were often most noticeable in the sheds, where several of them were gathered together and liable to be still for hours on end — sometimes in confined spaces. Several of these odours were due to warm oil, usually from oil-boxes or oil-pipes close to the smokebox, boiler, or ashpan. Oil was often thrown by crossheads, etc on to cylinders or other hot parts, and during preparation or cleaning, oil or paraffin was liable to be dropped on to steam pipes. Smell was usually the first indication of a bearing in trouble, although a hot-axlebox could often be detected by blue smoke drifting from it.

The casual visitor (with his ideas probably orientated toward locomotives) would scarely notice the stores, but it was a vital feature of any running shed. At medium-sized and larger depots this establishment was presided over by a store-keeper or stores clerk. There were one or more stores issuers on each shift, plus one or more labourers (later 'shedmen' on British Railways) working daytime hours. Many of these positions were reserved as light-duty posts for men who had sustained injuries, or were partially handicapped after illness, or who had failed eyesight examinations, etc.

There was a great variety of items to be stocked, particularly lubricating oil. This had to be supplied in several grades; axlebox oil, cylinder oil for superheated steam, ditto for saturated steam, and occasional special oils required for some particular purpose. In cold weather cylinder oil became very viscous, and so it was then necessary to heat it in order that it would flow readily. For this reason, at many of the larger depots the oil store was separated from the general store.

Paraffin was stored in appreciable quantities — often in a special lamp-room — being used for the lamps carried on locomotives, and for cleaning. Many depots also stocked various greases, including the special type needed for grease-nipple lubrication. This was supplied to a surprising number of parts on many Gresley engines, for instance on the 2-to-1 conjugated valve motion. Each depot had also to stock paints of the various colours used on its locomotives.

Many items arrived by the wagon-load; these included chemicals and bales of wood-wool for water softening plants, anti-foaming briquettes, oil in drums, iron castings, and sand. The last-mentioned commodity might involve a wagon being used as a sand-store, in which capacity it could be immobilised for weeks at some of the smaller depots.

On many railways nearly every class of boiler had its own particular fire-bars, often comprising two or three types in one grate — not forgetting drop-sections or rocker grates. These, together with brake-blocks of various sizes were often kept in the open; such cast-iron items were not attractive, and it did not matter if they rusted. Brick arches too varied from class to class, and generally needed two or more types for each arch.

Another requirement in considerable quantity was a range of fire-irons. Each engine needed a firing shovel and a coal hammer — although with much of the small stuff which was loaded on to tenders, a fireman could consider himself lucky if there was anything big enough to crack! But occasionally a very large, hard lump would become blocked in the gate leading to the coal space. In the 7 May 1971 issue of *Model Engineer*, Don Young described how an engine crew and himself had to attack such an obstacle when there was no coal hammer on board. It was not an exercise that any fireman would willingly repeat.

Hand-cloths (like domestic dish cloths, but officially known as 'sponge cloths') were stocked by the gross, and occasional shortages of them led to much complaint. They were issued on a daily basis to enginemen, who often received new ones. When washed they were also supplied to other staff, especially for cleaning. (How many thousands of these cloths found their way to non-railway uses was nobody's business.) Whenever they were in short supply from 1940 onwards it was common to issue cotton waste, which could cause trouble in vacuum brakes.

Each depot which had a stores had to distribute uniform clothing for footplatemen, and protective clothing for certain of the shed grades. The measurements of each man were recorded — and altered if a man's dimensions changed. It was akin to a quartermaster kitting out troops in an army unit. The whole management of the stores in a motive power depot was akin to running a wholesale store and a retail shop combined. Maintaining stocks of all these items was a troublesome part of the Storekeeper's duties; it was also a source of worry to the Locomotive Shed Master — a coal-fired locomotive cannot be driven far without a firing shovel!

In the early years of railways artificial lighting was largely by oil-lamps, but as gas supplies became economically available, gas lighting was installed. In many places the railways set up their own gas works and supplied not only their own premises, but often quite a lot of local private property as well. Running sheds were gas-lit if they happened to be conveniently near to a gas supply. Oil-gas factories were also constructed by several railway companies; at Doncaster this was close to the locomotive shed yard, but was mainly used for supplying gas for lighting carriage stock.

Electric lighting began to appear in railway workshops from about 1890, but it is not likely that it was installed in any running shed much before the turn of the century. However, a photograph taken at Woodford when that shed was opened in 1899 shows an electric lamp. Other sheds already fitted with gas lighting no doubt had to wait for many years for such modern illumination. The earliest electrical fittings were not designed to stand up to the smoky, corrosive atmosphere of locomotive depots, and the number of lighting points was not at all generous. Reflector shades and lamps became grimy unless they were frequently cleaned, and except in offices, workshop areas, stores, etc the standard of lighting provided was not greatly better than that which had been afforded by gas.

At the beginning of World War 2 many depots still had gas lighting, and in some odd corners I even saw 'bat's wing' flares in use as late as 1947. Few depots with electric light were illuminated to adequate standards, and indeed only the LMS — judging by those depots which it had modernised — appreciated the importance of this facility.

In Great Britain there was always some form of yard lighting near the preparation pits, but never any in the pits themselves. In the latter years of steam locomotion there was generally a possibility of trailing an electric inspection lamp on a flexible cable to an indoor pit (including preparation in a roundhouse). However, over outdoor pits any work needing to be done in the hours of darkness had to be carried out by the light of a small, flickering flare-lamp — or by candle-light!

In wartime, besides the other hardships to be endured, there was the nightly handicap of the 'black-out', with the occasional shout of an air-raid warden or fire-watcher: 'Put out that light'.

At the beginning of World War 2 it was realised that adequate light for examination could not be provided outside shed buildings during the black-out, and so at the larger depots a 'light-tunnel' was constructed. This was a lightly built shed of semi-elliptical cross-section, equipped with a pit, and long enough to hold the longest tender engine. These tunnels were provided with floodlighting by tubular lamps, and so paradoxically afforded much better lighting than had been seen for such work in any shed before the war. They proved to be most useful installations during the rest of the life of the depots concerned.

Outside the 'tunnels' at these sheds, and at other depots which had no such equipment, it called for much patience and ingenuity to examine or repair a locomotive in the shed yard with all yard lighting extinguished, and without showing any light visible from above.

Other depots (notably on the LMS and LNER) were equipped with lighting trolleys, these being in effect distribution boxes on wheels, by which several wander-lead lamps could be arranged around a locomotive. The idea was good, but there was repeated trouble with the cables being severed due to carelessness, and so some of the trolleys were abandoned along with other junk in deserted air-raid shelters or other out-of-the-way places.

During both world wars the roof-glass of running sheds, in common with that of workshops, stations, etc, was painted over as an air-raid precaution, and at most of them — the staff having accustomed themselves to working in the 'black-out' — it took some years before the paint was removed, or the glass renewed.

Lack of natural light was not only an inconvenience to those who had to work in running sheds, it also cost the railways substantial amounts in extra gas or electricity used, as well as creating less safe working conditions. In later years, as gas lighting was replaced at various sheds by electricity, improvements were made in the type of fitting installed, and more ample illumination was provided by increasing the quantity of lamps and their power.

Trafford Park, Manchester, depot was gas-lit under the Cheshire Lines Committee, being converted to electric lighting after the London Midland Region took it over. The work was only just completed when along came a representative from the Gas Board, armed with an old contract, obliging the railway to take gas for some tens of years. Following these representations, the new fittings had to be stripped out and replaced by new gas mains and equipment.

After Nationalisation, really good enclosed electric lighting fittings were provided in motive power depots, and this at last gave adequate standards of illumination. At the same time power points were installed at numerous locations, so that portable electric lamps and small power tools could be used.

It was incredible, but true, that even when such modern lighting was available, hand lamps other than plug-in types were age-old, paraffin lamps of the crudest variety. These were like an oil-can, with a plug of wick stuck in a fat spout, and a spluttering naked flame burning from it. Using one of these in a strong wind was an absurd handicap in examining or repairing steam locomotives.

At those depots which were fortunate enough to have a blacksmith, a coppersmith, a joiner and/or a painter, these craftsmen each had their own small shop with the characteristic odours of their respective trades. In the case of coppersmithing it was either oil or paint being burned off pipes of other non-ferrous parts under repair, or the pungent fumes which were released when white-metal was being renewed in bearings. The machine shop-cum-fitting shop usually had a warm smell of coolant oil, penetrating oil or paraffin, while the oil store presented a similar mixture of oily odours. Mess-rooms and offices were more likely to reek of tobacco, according to the habits of their occupants.

But the all-pervading smell in most parts of a locomotive depot was that produced by smoke, and as the grades of coal varied, so did the smell. This was never as disagreeable as the exhaust fumes of a diesel motor, yet could not be called pleasant in the sense that smoke from a wood-fire may be. Burning briquettes (particularly in France) gave off a smell quite unlike that from mined coal. The smell from oil-fired locomotives is also unpleasant, being the same as that which comes from the boilers of an oil-fired steamship. At its worst, coal smoke comes in a dense, brown cloud, billowing out of the chimney and the fire-hole of a freshly lit locomotive which has not raised enough steam to operate the blower jet. Where this occurred in a dead-end shed from which the fumes did not escape quickly, a most objectionable kind of fumigation was produced, which could be tasted in the throat like smoke from a brick-kiln; in such an atmosphere it was virtually impossible to work.

The circumstances of traffic working are beyond the scope of this book, but they were often of vital interest to those in the depots who were responsible for maintenance. In particular the noises produced by locomotives could be very significant. Once when I was sitting in my office at Peterborough Spital shed, there was a phone call with a distinct tone of urgency from John Blundell, the keen-as-mustard District Motive Power Superintendent. He had just heard some rattlebox of a Gresley 2-8-0 clanking along past New England Yard on a southbound freight, without being able to observe more than the top of it beyond the intervening sidings full of wagons. It was all too evident that it was in a scandalously run-down condition, and he wanted me to get its number as it trundled through the north station.

Many a depot office commanded a good view of a main line, or was close enough to a running line for engines to be seen from the shed yard as they passed by working under load. Hence one could get a good impression of whether a locomotive's valve events were correct, see whether it was being well handled, where steam blows were being produced, and many other useful indications. If an engine in trouble were not 'speaking for itself' by some plainly unusual noise, its driver would often whistle and then give some vivid sign-language gesture as he passed by the depot, and thus the running foreman would have valuable advance warning that something was amiss.

From the early days of World War 2 the maintenance of locomotive running shed buildings was a constant, costly headache, and no one can have been more pleased than the Civil Engineers to see them closed.

Tail-piece

Most depots had one or more resident cats, almost always strays, who had discovered that the weed-covered waste-land around the depot was a good hunting ground for mice and birds. Being attracted by the warmth of the buildings, they were often adopted by the men of the stores, who would encourage them with scraps of food and milk. A good mouser could earn his keep by keeping vermin out of the stores and offices. Occasionally a litter of kittens would be produced, and then a number of motive power men's homes would acquire a railway-born pet.

ENGINE-HOUSE, PADDINGTON.

45
This old print shows the first Great Western shed in London, at Bishops Road, Paddington, which survived until 1853. The round-house is of all-wooden construction; judging by the roof and walls, it was surely octagonal, having seven 'stalls' and one access track — notwithstanding that the floor details suggest that there were only six tracks. The turntable pit is covered by the turntable decking.

The 2-2-2 tank engine is named *Elephant*, while the 4-2-2 engine named *Rover* (more correctly described as a 2-2-2-2) bears a strong similarity to Sturrock's classic No 215 as it was built by Hawthorn's for the Great Northern.

It was at this shed that Sturrock (Locomotive Engineer of the GNR 1850-66) spent his earliest years with the Great Western. *British Rail*

46
Did you ever see a locomotive running shed almost as clean as a museum? Battersea Park depot in London, Brighton & South Coast Railway days, 30 April 1921. The presence of wheel sets indicates that this part of the shed was used for repairs, although there is no 'engine stopped' board or other visible evidence of repairs in progress on 0-6-0s Nos 527 and 542 near the turntable. They may have been in store, but were more likely out of steam, temporarily not required.

The turntable deck extends to the edge of the turntable pit. The building still survives, its roof being visible at parapet-wall level of the tracks coming out of Victoria, at about 200yd on the right after crossing Grosvenor Bridge over the Thames. *H. C. Casserley*

47
St Margaret's, Edinburgh, depot on 20 June 1937. It would appear that already the near-bankrupt LNER was indulging in 'deferred maintenance', at least on the roof of this shed. Here are four Class Y9 0-4-0 shunting engines — with solid wooden buffers! Left to right they are Nos 9042 (with embellishment around smokebox door handle), 9099 with another behind it, and 9010. *H. C. Casserley*

48
One of the four round-houses at Old Oak Common, Paddington, in 1911, showing an assortment of old-timer tank engines as well as a number of more modern tender engines. These include: extreme left 'County' class No 3809; beyond the turntable catch lever, a 'Star' 4-6-0 of the 'King' series; a Dean 4-4-0; '43xx' 2-6-0 No 4311; an '850' class 0-6-0ST; 2-6-0 No 4303; '633' class condensing tanks Nos 643 and 642 (built at Wolverhampton in 1872); 0-6-0ST No 2778 of '2721' class (built 1900, withdrawn 1947); another engine of the same class.

On railways where the number was not painted on the back of the tender or bunker, it was general practice for locomotives in a round-house to be set with their front-ends toward the turntable, since each engine number was carried on the smoke-box door or buffer beam, the numbers of all the engines could thus be seen by anyone standing on the turntable.

Note the lofty roof, with some very high smoke chutes, and a single electric lamp suspended over the middle of the turntable. The decking of the track across the table appears to have been washed — presumably for the sake of the photograph. *BR Central Photographic Unit*

49
Ex-Midland 0-4-4T, No 1378 at Kentish Town on 30 June 1945. World War 2 had ended in Europe during the previous month, and the black-out covering has been removed from the roof and wall windows. Note the ancient suspended gas-lamp. *H. C Casserley*

50
Unusual function for a motive power depot. Class K4 2-6-0 *The Great Marquess*, restored to its LNER livery and number 3442, and a Class N7 0-6-2T stored at Neville Hill shed (Leeds). The latter engine was awaiting restoration in the ownership of Dr R. F. Ewell for preservation on the Stour Valley Railway, near Colchester. The photograph, taken on 10 July 1966 shows one of two adjoining round-houses which survived after two others (formerly part of the same building) were demolished in 1960. *J. S. Hancock*

51
Peppercorn 'A1' Pacific No 60154 *Bon Accord* poses at one of the shed exits at Neville Hall in 1963. Note the oil lamp above one of the electric lamps — serving only as a head-code marker.

The interior of the shed looks remarkably light, the building being modern — probably as restitution of wartime damage and deterioration. *Ian Krause*

52
The only steam engines still in British Rail service are three narrow gauge 2-6-2Ts of the type seen here on 23 July 1934. Unfortunately they are totally untypical of British practice. In this photograph is shown the Vale of Rheidol shed at Aberystwyth, now demolished.

These few engines now have abundant covered accommodation in the nearby former standard-gauge shed, in which narrow gauge tracks (also for carriages and wagons) have been installed. *J. S. Hancock*

53
BR standard Class 3 MT 2-6-0 No 77012 in the shed at York on 17 December 1966. Most 'round-houses' had high, spacious roofs, with very few columns to cause obstruction.

Even quite small steam leaks could produce a considerable visual impression, and indeed engines in steam usually had one or more such leaks. Note that this engine has the characteristic high running board and huge motion-plate of the BR standard series. *J. S. Hancock*

54
An interior view of Doncaster shed in the early 1950s showing 'A1' Pacific No 60533 *Happy Knight* and behind it Class K3 2-6-2 No 61977 — a 'Jazzer' — both newly overhauled. In front of the Pacific is one of the ageing Class J6 GNR 0-6-0s. The roof, rather unusually, had no smoke chutes, being of recent construction, but had ample vents. *T. G. Hepburn*

55
This picture of Reading depot is believed to have been taken about 1910. The vantage point is close to the line to Taunton (via Westbury), and in the background is the main line to Bristol and South Wales. Note the differences of roof construction of the shed building. The cabin at left foreground is entirely of corrugated iron, while that on the right has riveted steel plate walls with a corrugated iron roof.

The engines shown are (left to right): No 3810 *County Wicklow*, No 3407 and No 3387 *Paddington*. *BR Central Photographic Unit*

56

Stanier Class 8F 2-8-0 No 48083 stops at the entrance to Derby round-house on 2 January 1966, in accordance with the instruction which reads: 'Midland Railway. Engines requiring to enter the shed must be brought to a stand at this board. By order.'

Note axlebox spring on ground. *J. S. Hancock*

57

The round-house at Barrow Road (Bristol) — No 82E under Western Region administration in 1960. The building is of typical Midland Railway architecture, with groups of three round-topped windows to each gable-end wall. The engines shown are BR standard Class 9F 2-10-0 no 92135 behind 'Jinty' 0-6-0T No 47552, and 'Crab' 2-6-0 No 42839.

Note the gas lamp, and the high trestle on to which one end of a footboard can be placed for working on high footplating, or on which tubes can be rested when removing them from a boiler, or fitting new ones in position.
J. S. Hancock

58
Exmouth Junction depot (Exeter), as seen on 18 July 1925. The deplorable state of this important shed was typified by the skeletons of the smoke stacks. This almost entirely timber building was replaced by a reinforced concrete one during the following year.

The locomotives seen here include Class H15 4-6-0 No 333, Adams 4-4-0 No 0162, Class 02 0-4-4T No 228 and (nearest camera) Class K10 4-4-0 No 381.
H. C. Casserley

59
Faversham depot on 30 June 1934. Following the depression of the early 1930s enginemen's promotion was seriously retarded on the Southern Railway, which was also extensively electrifying its London suburban routes. There were therefore plenty of cleaners and even 'put back' firemen, and discipline was high. Its locomotives were thus kept beautifully clean. The engines shown, which had numbers on the front buffer beam and on the sides and rear of the tenders are: Class N 2-6-0 No 1874, SER 4-4-0 No 1186, Class 6 0-6-0 No 1242, and Class D1 4-4-0 No 1494.

The last mentioned is apparently having its tender topped up by hand coaling from the wagon alongside. Note the different roof construction of the two bays. *H. C. Casserley*

60
War Department 'Austerity' 2-8-0 No 90225 standing in front of the offices at Doncaster Carr Shed on 13 December 1964. The shed was built in 1875, and in Great Northern and LNER times the District Locomotive Superintendent had his offices on the upper floor. This engine was one of many acquired by the Great Western Railway after World War 2, and fitted with top clack valves and a chute for fire-irons above the footplating. Its headlamps in the 'express passenger position' indicate that it was going to take the breakdown train to a derailment. *J. S. Hancock*

61
Immingham shed (near Grimsby) photographed on 7 May 1961, as rebuilt in the early 1950s. The main building, sheeted in asbestos, has an unusual roof form.

The present diesel locomotive maintenance shop was built close by on part of the former depot site.

Gresley 3-cylinder Class 02 2-8-0 No 63937 is one of the original Great Northern batch retaining the typical cab-shape of those times, but is coupled to an LNER Standard tender.
J. S. Hancock

62
Bathgate depot was situated in the industrial belt of Scotland, at a junction on the ex-North British (mainly freight) line between Edinburgh and Glasgow (via Airdrie). The shed, with its cladding of asbestos sheets is evidently a utility re-build of a former running shed.

The locomotives (left to right) are: BR Class 2 2-6-0 No 78046, an ex-NBR 0-6-0 (LNER Class J36) and BR Class 4 2-6-0 No 76111. *Ian Krause*

63
Watford Junction depot, adjoining the station on the east side of the West Coast main line, photographed on 9 March 1949. The shed has two quite distinct types of architecture. On the right is the low water tank, and immediately right of that an entrance to the underground air-raid shelter — such as were installed at all depots early in World War 2 where there was any likelihood of bombardment.

The engine on the left is Fowler 2-6-4T No 40010; to the right of it is Stanier 2-6-4T No 42568, in front of which can be seen the back of a London & North Western tender. Besides local duties on the main line, the depot served the branch to St Albans. Its site is now a car park for railway passengers. *H. C. Casserley*

64
The stone-built shed at Fraserburgh is in better shape than the station — to judge from the roof of the latter.

Great North of Scotland 4-4-0, BR No 62279 *Glen Grant* stands ready with its snow plough in mid-summer on 10 June 1953. *S. C. Nash*

65
Fort William shed, with the lower slopes of Ben Nevis coming down to the railway, photographed on 4 July 1960. Edward Thompson would have been well pleased to see this scene for this Class K1 Peppercorn 2-6-0 No 62011 was of a type almost identical to Thompson's rebuild of a Class K4 3-cylinder 2-6-0 — the latter design having been specially built by Gresley for the West Highland line. *S. C. Nash*

12

Getting Engines ready for Work

Steam locomotives were tremendous producers of dirt wherever they worked, particularly when passing through tunnels. Soot adhering to tunnel roofs was fetched down by the exhaust from chimneys, dropping on to the top of locomotives and carriages, whence with rain it left unsightly streaks. Grease droppings and oil thrown up by wheels, rods and valve-gear, added their contribution; and in depots there was often fine ash, dust and smoke carried in the air, attaching itself to exposed surfaces.

Up to World War 1, with most locomotives worked by one regular crew, it was common for the driver and fireman to keep 'their' engine spotlessly clean — often with unpainted brass parts and copper pipes highly polished. Paintwork was thinly smeared with tallow, patterns being often created in it by regular rotary movements when wiping it over with hand-cloths. Following the rapid call-up of men of the armed forces from August 1914 the regular manning of engines began to be seriously interrupted, and maintenance suffered. Until 1923 several railway companies were competing for traffic in many parts of the country, with much overlapping and penetration of one another's territory. Locomotives were symbols of prestige, and their appearance was thus commercially important.

During the 1930s, with considerable redundancy among the Southern Railway footplate staff due to the electrification of most of the suburban lines, the locomotives of that railway were kept beautifully clean. In other parts of the country there was much unemployment and wages outside the railway were low, consequently discipline was high, and cleaning presented no great problem, notwithstanding that it needed a lot of labour to keep locomotives looking really presentable. But World War 2 was to produce insuperable staffing difficulties in such non-essential activities.

When there were not enough cleaners, shed labourers were used so far as they could be obtained. During both world wars women were employed at many depots for locomotive cleaning and labouring, as were coloured immigrants in the 1950s.

Cleaners working in gangs were supervised by a chargeman cleaner or shed chargeman at the larger depots, or by a running foreman at other sheds. This was seldom satisfactory since the latter had much more important duties to attend to, while chargemen were appointed by seniority from among the shed staff — which as any manager should know, is just about the worst way of appointing supervisors.

Well-cleaned locomotives were extremely good for the morale of a depot. From time to time, when enough cleaners were available, and there was some special occasion, I would have an engine cleaned and polished as if for a royal train. The effect on cleaners, shed staff and footplate staff would be quite noticeable for a day or two. When one of our 'Merchant Navy' Pacifics at Exmouth Junction was to be photographed for a film sequence, we had it cleaned up to exhibition standard. Although I did not see the film, the engine looked impressive hammering away up the incline out of Exeter Central station.

Persistent shortages of cleaners caused managements to seek aids to cleaning; these included a hot water lance, fed from an adjacent locomotive. A more sophisticated form of this was a trolley equipped with a hot-water injector. A particular type of this equipment was the Weaver paraffin-fired 'Steam Jenny', which could work independently of a hot-water supply, and also comprised a tank for cleaning agent, so that the parts to be cleaned could first be sprayed with the cleaning solution and then hosed off with hot water. It was possible to feed small amounts of oil to the jets, so as to produce a shiny finish, but one could not avoid spraying some of this on to floor and pit surfaces.

It was a glaring omission of running shed equipment that not enough thought had been given to the straight-forward problem of getting the machine into steam in the first place. The essential difficulty was that of 'cooking' a mass of cold coal until it was converted into blazing lumps, giving off enough heat to boil water. In most instances it was necessary to start with a firebox which was itself cold, and in winter often freezing.

Fire-lighting was done by the steam-raiser (or a fireman acting in that capacity) who had to tend the fires of all engines in steam which were not in the charge of a set of footplatemen. Traditionally scrap timber or oily waste was thrown in a pile on the grate. The steam raiser had a shovel with a specially large, deep blade, with which he carried blazing coal from a sand-drying furnace, or from an engine in steam. One would see him walking with it balanced on his shoulder — the live coal being about 2ft behind his head. This he had to push up on the steel plate between engine and tender to which he climbed, and then threw the burning coal into the firebox. This crude method was still in common use in the 1950s.

At many depots 'fire-lighters' were supplied, as widely used for lighting domestic coal-fires, these consisting of small sticks of firewood, enclosing a bundle of naphthaline-soaked shavings.

The Great Western and some foreign railways had a practice of throwing a layer of coal across the grate, this being sprayed with crude oil, which was then ignited. Others used a burning jet — akin to an army flame-thrower. But whatever process was used, there was a serious problem of smoke. Until sufficient pressure of steam was created to turn on the blower-ring, and so produce a draught, thick, brown, pungent smoke came billowing out of the firehole door, as well as out of the chimney. This sooted up the heating surfaces, and everything in the cab. It was very desirable to shunt engines outside, where smoke could be blown away, before lighting them up. However, this was sometimes difficult due to lack of track space, especially when several locomotives had to be lit up at the same time.

I once experienced a shocking instance of this at Peterborough Spital — an ex-Midland double round-house shed. Close to the north of the shed was the ramp of Spital Bridge, and to the west of it was housing, so that the smoke-clearing effects of northerly or westerly winds were much reduced. As at most depots many fires were thrown out after work on Fridays or Saturdays. Locomotive Shed masters were not normally on duty on Sundays, but one Sunday afternoon I decided to take a walk to the depot, and see how things were going.

They were proceeding well — as far as the usual work was concerned, but the whole place was filled with dense, acrid smoke. The morning-shift steam raiser had lit up about 20 fresh fires, so that smoke was drifting from the chimneys and cabs of most of the engines in the shed. The Running Foreman regarded it as an inevitable feature of the Sunday routine, but this was just another of those situations were people accept what is familiar, without querying whether one could avoid obnoxious conditions. It was not in fact necessary for most of the engines to be lit up until hours later, as they were not needed before various hours on the Monday morning — and many of them could have been lit up outside anyway.

From half-a-ton to a ton of coal was burned by each freshly fired locomotive before it went into traffic, the amount depending on the size of the firegrate and how much time elapsed between the engine being lit up and its driver 'ringing out' to the signalman at the shed outlet. One device for accelerating steam-raising and reducing the smoke nuisance was a compressed air connection on the side of the smokebox on certain engines, with a connection to the blower ring, so that a draught could be produced on the fire before the boiler had generated steam.

Pre-steaming (or 'direct' steaming) — ie filling an empty boiler with hot water and steam from a stationary one — was tried in England (see R. H. N. Hardy's *Steam in the Blood*, page 79) and it was regular practice in North America (see also H. C. Webster *Locomotive Running Shed Practice*, page 177).

Soot in the form of fine dust was an all-pervading phenomenon in steam locomotive depots and in their immediate surroundings. It even penetrated into the drawers in offices, and one's clothes needed more frequent washing than in a more civilised environment. Footplate staff and anyone else working in close contact with locomotives found it necessary to wear some form of head-gear, and even so to wash their hair often. While the railways did not do all they might have done in this matter, they did play an active part in smoke abatement generally. In particular, T. H. Turner, Chief Chemist & Metallurgist of the LNER arranged for regular sampling of the atmosphere on the company's premises at numerous locations in industrial areas.

Preparation was generally the last operation in servicing a locomotive in a depot. It was most often carried out by the men who were due to take an engine out of the depot for a day's duty — or for a fresh turn. An hour, or somewhat less, according to the class of locomotive, was allotted for this task, prior to the booked departure time from the shed outlet signal.

Enginemen booked on duty — as now — at all times of the day or night at a depot or a signing-on point, usually at a station or freight yard. At the busier times and at the more important places there was a timekeeper. At less busy times and at smaller places the men reported to a supervisor, or might simply report their arrival by telephone to a Control Office. In any case it was essential for safety and operational reasons that the men read carefully the daily and weekly notices. These informed them of diversions, special permanent-way notices, or emergencies which might affect the working of trains. Failure to note these properly has been the cause, or at least a contributory cause of a number of accidents. The failure of one of my drivers at Neasden to comply with a 'Late Notice' of a speed restriction led to an express passenger train crashing through a crossover at around 55mph, with most of the train badly derailed, one day in August 1955 (see *Steam Was my Calling*, page 136). Since the driver paid the ultimate penalty with his instant death, it was not possible to determine whether he had read the notice, but the evidence available suggested that he had not.

In many steam depots the gloomy interiors of the buildings, and the general lack of space in congested surroundings posed a considerable problem of adequate display of notices. Weekly booklets of operating notices are issued in addition to those posted on notice boards, and these have to be signed for. They include particulars of track relaying, and any alterations to train running which can be programmed in advance.

Bulleid's original Pacifics (and his 'Leader' tank engine) incorporated a bold effort to reduce preparation time by enclosing the valve gear and other parts in an oil bath, topped up periodically by the mechanical staff. But neither this, nor any other time-saving innovation by locomotive designers caused the enginemen's representatives to concede any reduction in the agreed preparation times.

The driver's duties during preparation were mainly concerned with topping up mechanical lubricators and oiling round dozens of lubrication points. The accessibility of many of these was decidedly awkward on numerous types of locomotive, and a long-spouted oil-can was issued for this work. At the beginning of each preparation duty the driver would collect from the stores an issue of cylinder oil and a 'bottle' (made of galvanized tinplate), filled with lubricating oil — usually referred to as 'axlebox oil'. Heavy mineral oil was issued for cylinder lubrication, its grade depending on whether the particular engine was superheated or saturated.

Meanwhile the fireman collected a firing shovel, a coal hammer and a galvanized bucket. One of each of these was kept in the stores for each locomotive in the depot which was not in the charge of a set of enginemen. The bucket contained a set of tools, a hand-brush, a number of common-user spanners, screwdriver, etc for emergency repairs. One or two spare gauge-glasses were usually kept with the tools.

The fireman also took from the stores or lamp-room the headlamps needed for the particular engine-duty, a tail-lamp and a small lamp for illuminating the gauge-glasses. In Great Britain these lamps were generally paraffin-lit until the end of steam traction. At a few large depots paraffin lamps were cleaned and filled, and the wicks trimmed by a lamp-man, but it was much more common for the fireman to perform this task.

From 1941 a few classes of locomotive were fitted with electric lamps — notably by Bulleid on the Southern and Thompson on the LNER. On a few lines white marker discs were used for route indication, but elsewhere paraffin headlamps were used as train classification markers.

A dozen fog detonators (whose age had to be checked periodically against the year stamped on them) were carried in a cylindrical tin — usually along with two red flags — and kept on the engine.

Besides the daily examination of each steam locomotive carried out by an examining fitter, the driver who prepared an engine was expected to look out for any part which might be loose, fractured, badly worn, or needing adjustment. It was often the vigilance of a driver which averted potential disaster.

There was no set division of duties as between driver and fireman during preparation — this being left to the discretion of each individual driver, but naturally the fireman would occupy himself with trimming coal and pulling it forward on the tender; he would usually fetch buckets of dry sand from the sand-drier, and top up the sandboxes with it.

Firing irons were usually kept on each locomotive, but each set of men had to check that they were present and in good order. When a crew, or pair of crews had their own regular engine there was often a comprehensive set of well cared-for tools locked up on the engine. However, on common-user engines the 'tool kit' generally dwindled to a couple of spanners and a screwdriver, all of dubious quality. With these even the handiest of drivers could only tackle a very limited range of first-aid jobs; some of the more conscientious types therefore used to carry with them one or two personal general-purpose tools, such as an adjustable spanner.

From the early years of World War 2 shortages of hand tools and of fire-irons led to recurrent difficulties at many depots. When this happened many enginemen would find hiding places for a personal cache of such items — thus compounding the trouble. Where all the missing items went to was a mystery, for they were of no disposable value, even as scrap. Firing irons sometimes fell off a tender, due to being insecurely laid on coal which was piled up on tenders and not trimmed, with consequent danger to staff on the ground, or to trains on adjacent tracks.

Enginemen had to be warned of the risks of swinging fire-irons outside of the loading gauge. Such momentary contact with an overhead conductor wire could result in electrocution.

In British practice the sand boxes were just above or below footplate level. These the fireman would fill by fetching sand from the drier in a bucket fitted with a spout. It was not uncommon for some of this sand to be spilled, or for powder sand to blow about, especially when it was being poured in a strong wind by a man standing on a ladder. It was not surprising that some of this loose sand should find its way into working parts, and many a case of a heated axlebox was attributed to this cause.

The various railways used different types of sand furnace — usually of their own manufacture. One of them still exists (although no longer used) at the Great Western Society's Didcot depot, which was formerly the GWR running shed. (Diagrams of another furnace used by that railway are also given by H. C. Webster in *Locomotive Running Shed Practice*.) An ingenious type, designed for universal installation, was that manufactured by the Kelbus Co. It had a beehive-shaped, coke-fired central furnace, around which the damp sand was 'jacketed'; additional drying was obtained by pipes carrying hot gases from the fire passing through the sand.

Whatever kind of drying was used, it was essential to have effective screening of the sand because supplies often contained pebbles, which could cause failures by blocking the small orifices in the locomotive equipment. A great improvement on sand for increasing adhesion was blast furnace grit (or 'fines'), but this was only used in later years. It has the great merit of not clogging, even if it becomes wet.

At the locomotive depot close to each main works it was usual to see new locomotives, or freshly overhauled ones. It was the duty of the depot concerned to run them in before returning them to the shed to which they were allocated. This involved putting right any minor defects, referring any major troubles back to the Works. On the other hand they were able to do work of their own depot with engines of other sheds, but without having to maintain them.

One of the greatest contrasts between the working of steam and diesel depots is found in the departure of locomotives. A depot such as Doncaster, which in the 1950s had three running foremen on each shift for the supervision of enginemen and of depot servicing had more departures during the busiest hour than the present diesel depot has in an average day. In the steam era nearly half the work of the depot was geared to the punctuality of these departures, and this activity seemed like a vital throb, which is entirely lacking with diesel or electric traction.

13

Of Management and Men

The management of any lively concern is an almost constant challenge, and there can have been few forms of management making a greater challenge than that of being in charge of a sizeable steam running shed. However, in spite of the 24-hour activity during seven days each week, they were generally very manageable units, although vastly more complicated than people outside of the organisation could understand. Their work was intimately bound up with that of the Operating Department, which was wholly dependent on 'the Loco' for power, and that department was the only one which they served (save for rare lifting jobs for the Civil Engineer).

Life was challenging enough at an orderly depot with regular commitments and a fairly full staff complement. But from 1940 onwards at most of the London depots and at some in the conurbations, struggling from 'hand-to-mouth' for footplatemen, with locomotives often in dubious condition, and with special workings it was backs-to-the-wall nearly all the way. And if a long-suffering Shed Master should sometime imagine that he could briefly relax, that was the likeliest moment for a breakdown call to come in — or for his District Officer to make a surprise visit.

Many District offices were located at the main depot of a district, and there were even cases where the District Motive Power Superintendent had to share an office with the Locomotive Shed Master. This was so at Exmouth Junction up to the early 1950s, where — following the creation of Districts on the Southern Region — the latter functionary also carried the title of Assistant District Motive Power Superintendent.

Supervision of activities within the shed and the shed yard took up most of the time of the Locomotive Shed Master, and nearly all the time of the foremen. Besides this there was a continuous responsibility for engines and enginemen in traffic, the supervision of whom was bound to be a tenuous business. For instance, at any given time Grantham men could be found anywhere between Kings Cross and Newcastle or Leeds. For contacting enginemen in traffic Running Foremen were dependent on maintaining close touch with control or station staff.

Although 'Control' worked to the 'working timetables' for most trains, they often made short-notice alterations which would involve modifications to engines' and men's duties as the day-to-day, or even hour-to-hour situation demanded. This did not apply to the Southern Region, whose 'trains supervision offices' mainly concerned themselves with registering what happened.

In the 1950s promotion for many younger shed masters was fairly rapid, durations of appointment of about two years being common; so the new appointee had to establish his authority quickly and adapt to strange circumstances. In this my army experience stood me in good stead, particularly the training by which officer cadets were told 'You can command obedience, but you must earn respect'. Without a response of respect one could often not get an order carried out under the conditions of labour unrest which was an undercurrent of British Railways in the 1950s. Some of the martinet managers who had ruled by fear before the war would not have lasted a month in charge of a depot after it.

'The new Gaffer' (or 'Guv'nor' in the south) was at a disadvantage in that he was soon known to everyone, but it took time for him to know more than 'key' staff, plus a few persistently awkward characters. At the larger depots it could take weeks to become acquainted with those conscientious types who habitually stayed out of trouble.

For a shed master there was always something new to learn, new faces to meet — and never knowing at the beginning of a day what the rest of the day would bring. He, for his sins, was involved with almost all the troublesome items — especially enquiries into breakdowns, derailments and time lost due to locomotive causes. At Exmouth Junction in 1956-57 I signed a hundred or more 'Please explain' notes to drivers for trains which had lost 2min or more in running; against this I had the satisfaction of noting numerous cases of time recorded as 'regained by loco'.

Occasionally one would have to investigate an accident to an employee, and once I had to interview a driver concerning a suicide who had jumped off a platform in front of his speeding locomotive.

Whatever suicides think when they jump in front of a train, they evidently do not give much thought for the driver, or for the grisly consequences for those who have to dispose of the bloody remains, or for the great inconvenience incurred by many others who have to hold an inquest, a post-mortem and other time-consuming procedures. For an example of such an incident see *Steam was my Calling* (page 139).

Some of my contemporaries used to start their day with a morning gathering, calling the chief clerk, the foreman and chargemen to their office (sometimes irreverently referred to as 'the prayer meeting'). But in my experience it was better to confer with these worthies on their 'home territory'. First I used to ask if there were any urgent administrative matters. Then to the Running Foreman on shift duty to scan through the log-book; this summarised the events of the shifts, and was often the first intimation of an incident which might have considerable consequences. Thus assured that the wheels of organisation were turning normally — or if not, why not — along to the Mechanical Foreman and Chargehand Boilersmith to find out what was being done about stopped engines, and to agree the priorities for the day.

There were countless occasions when by talking to a man on 'his own territory' useful pieces of information were to be gleaned which would never have come to the governor who believed in commanding the show from the comfort of his office chair. The difficulties of organisation and circumstance about which a shed master could do little were legion, but I found that obtaining the confidence of the staff in the manner described often seemed to diminish problems, even when one could not provide a solution.

Getting to know individuals was a great deal of the battle in a locomotive depot. For instance, there were one or two drivers who had a reputation for refusing the engine booked to them. It was, after all, not difficult to find a pretext to fail some of the run-down, old crates running about in the late 1940s. Here it was often a question of temperament, for it seemed to satisfy the ego of one or two self-important types to take awkward actions of this kind, which could put a Running Foreman to no end of trouble. One day I had a particularly difficult, wordy dialogue with one of these characters, telling him that occasionally refusing an engine with a genuine defect could be agreed as justifiable, but that as he had the habit of doing this, he was evidently seeking to get the best engines, and to leave the worse ones to his fellow-drivers.

He went off the shed in high dudgeon, his own conscience telling him that he had been caught 'doing it too brown'. But so as not to let him nurture a grievance about this, I prepared a sequel for him on the next day. I left word for him to come to my office just after he signed on duty, and as soon as he appeared, said 'I've got something special for you'. Then, pointing to an engine on the shed front, newly arrived from the works with gleaming fresh varnish, continued 'There's your engine for today — now find fault with that!' He broke into a broad grin, and conceded 'OK Guv', you win'. So far as I know he never refused an engine after that.

Even such mundane matters as servicing of the staff facilities could not always be left to take care of themselves. If mess-rooms and toilets were not regularly cleaned, the personnel were soon complaining. When the usual performer of these chores failed to turn up for duty it was often difficult to find a replacement. Regular close contact with the men yielded a valuable reward in that many of them had been there since they were boys — or at least since their 20s. They knew local conditions intimately, so that a supervisor with a willingness to listen could benefit handsomely from their long experience.

This sort of contact worked in two ways, for if a man receives a patient hearing, he is much more likely to listen seriously than if he senses that his remarks have simply gone in at one ear and out at the other. Mutual receptivity thus established, it is much easier to say 'Well, you may always have done it here in this fashion, but we used to do it another way at my last shed, and there it went much easier (or quicker, etc)'. So by getting staff to try other ideas, one could introduce methods which were both to the advantage of themselves and the depot.

The office staff could make a great difference to a running shed; in particular a good chief clerk could keep many minor troubles off the boss's desk, so leaving him free to concentrate on more important issues. The staff clerk needed to be a mine of information concerning conditions governed by national and local agreements extending back over 50-odd years. Some clerks would go out into the shed to discuss any unusual circumstance which came under correspondence. Others could scarcely be persuaded to go into the stores, let alone put their heads inside a firebox to see what a damaged brick-arch looked like.

A typical job for the clerks was arranging attendance at medical examinations; it usually fell to the chief clerk to have to tell a man if he had to be taken off his regular duties on medical grounds. I knew a man at Doncaster who had lost his job on the Great Northern; not only had he suffered the agony of a red-hot spark entering his eye while driving an Atlantic, but had received quite inadequate compensation for his resulting incapacity.

The LNER's precarious financial position had led it to pare its clerical staff to excess in some places. Economy teams, universally detested as 'razor gangs', had cut the establishments to the bone, offering no compensating incentive to the remainder. Thus a depot could well be in serious difficulties as soon as one man went sick, or needed a day off duty at short notice. Extra correspondence was caused through letters being delayed, overtime had to be worked, and it was not long before the supposed savings achieved by cutting out a 'marginal' man were dissipated, with the morale of an office depressed into the bargain.

On of the worst difficulties facing railway management under Nationalisation was not having authority commensurate with their responsibilities. A foreman in charge of quite a small depot could engage recruits, but even a shed master with the rank of Assistant District Motive Power Superintendent could not dismiss the most unsatisfactory of new starters. Apart from the necessity of going through the disciplinary procedure (which always involved two levels of management), this procedure could not even be initiated without having to ask the District Office to supply a charge-sheet. This restriction was perhaps imposed to avoid contentious cases at the outset, but an inevitable result was that disciplinary action was often not invoked where it should have been. The consequent frustration soon led to attitudes of 'what's the use?', or 'couldn't care less'.

During the whole of my motive power career I rarely found it necessary to take formal disciplinary action against an erring member of the staff. This was as well, for the disciplinary procedure was legalistic and time-consuming. If, in a bad case the man concerned could not be persuaded to save everybody a lot of bother by resigning, then one would have to go through the whole process. In a labour market where we had many vacancies many men did not give a rap for the disciplinary procedure, but with the older men it was still a useful means of control, and some of them took it very seriously indeed.

Occasionally the complexities of the work and conflicting interests of individuals gave rise to strife between supervisors and men under their charge. In such cases I never let anyone go away evidently feeling sore about being told that he was wrong, if this could possibly be avoided. In the case of a foreman or a clerk, I would say that I regretted having to decide an issue against him, but that such and such were my reasons for doing so. I would often call in a driver or fireman against whom I had given a ruling, so as to give him a similar opportunity of speaking his mind. The fact of a man having been given the possibility of airing his feelings was enough to remove the smart from many a wounded pride, and this practice often helped subsequent relations enormously.

At some depots there were instances of friction between drivers and fitters, but this was rarely so when the running foremen were mechanically trained, as on the Great Northern Section of the Eastern Region. Such foremen could understand the difficulties of the mechanical staff, and could tell them what to do with surer authority than those who had been promoted from drivers (as on the Great Western Railway).

In motive power depots (as elsewhere on the railways) the management did not negotiate directly with the trade unions. Local agreements were made with Men's Representatives who were elected to represent all grades in particular groups, irrespective of which union (or none) the men concerned might belong to. This arrangement had not always worked to everyone's satisfaction — especially as the great majority of footplatemen were members of the Associated Society of Locomotive Engineers & Firemen — but it had proved at least as satisfactory as dealing directly with trade union officials. The elections were carried out with all the formality of local government elections, sealed ballot-boxes being sent to sub-depots so that everyone could record his vote — at whatever time or place he signed on duty.

At all sheds the workshop staff elected a representative who negotiated agreements with the Distirct Motive Power Superintendent and agreed day-to-day matters with the Shed Master.

All who had occasion to go into depot workshops were exposed to the risks which are common in a factory. In the latter years of steam traction the staff were encouraged to wear industrial safety footwear, goggles and other protective gear. Safety is one of the major considerations on any railway, and anyone who worked in a steam running shed had to be aware of the many dangers which lurked there. Not least of these were oily floors, which were often also wet, and whose surfaces were in many places liable to be uneven or broken.

All supervisors and enginemen had to be on the look-out for trespassers, who might expose themselves to moving locomotives, or who through meddlesome ignorance might cause an accident. The more adventurous of teenage spotters could well be capable of starting an engine, and then find themselves unable to stop it. They might also interfere with water-gauge cocks, and leave a drain-cock open, thus risking an unattended boiler being run short of water.

There were in fact remarkably few accidents in motive power depots, and this can only have been due to everyone being aware of the inherent perils, taking the necessary precautions to minimise the dangers for others. Adequate first-aid facilities were provided at all sheds. Ambulance classes, organised under the auspices of the St John's Ambulance Brigade, were well supported by locomotive running sheds. Much of their fine esprit de corps carried over to the other staff.

Most of the staff who worked in the sheds were employed on shifts. Running foremen and their assistants, 'running' repair staff, stores issuers, boilerwashers, coalmen, fire-droppers and shed labourers (later shedmen) who were trained to relieve several of the above grades were also shift workers. A depot such as Doncaster, with a mixed allocation of about 200 locomotives, needed three running foremen on each shift in order to supervise the servicing functions, to ensure the right-time departure of engines, and to maintain close contact with the Operating Department.

A running foreman could go home and forget the depot after eight hours on duty; not so the shed master, whose responsibility extended over 168 hours a week. Thus while under no obligation to do so, I used to make a habit of going into the depot on Sunday mornings, just to see how things were proceeding — even in a purely freight depot like Staveley, where engines were simply got ready for the following day's work. Up to 1952 one of the essential characters at any depot was the 'caller-up' (or 'knocker-up') who had to advise footplatemen of changes of times of duty. He also had to call out members of the breakdown gang who were not on duty when the breakdown train was ordered out. For these functions he had to exercise a particularly intelligent form of initiative, combined with a detailed knowledge of the locality in order to alert the men concerned in the minimum time. Moreover he was the general fetcher and carrier of anything from pay-packets to packets of cigarettes; and as a purveyor of good news or bad he was the bush telegraph personified. The caller-up had, of course, to be one of the most dependable of the men in the depot — a trustworthy who would not stop at a deep snow-drift to get his messages through.

Dut to changes of address or ill-marked residences, these stalwarts sometimes had embarrassing experiences — such as the caller-up at Retford who wondered why he was getting irate responses to his urgent knocking in the middle of the night. It soon transpired that he had awakened a policeman in mistake for a railwayman.

Motive power depot men who were paid weekly wages, but not included in the footplate or workshop staff were called 'conciliation grades', their conditions being governed by agreements stemming from the conciliation boards set up after the railways were obliged by the Government in 1912 to recognise the trade unions. These grades also elected a representative who functioned in a similar way to the workshop representative. Among the national agreements covering both workshop and conciliation staff was the 8-hour working day, which was put into effect from 1 February 1919 following a promise made by the Government during World War 1.

The conditions of service of all these men was simplicity itself compared with the jungle of national and local agreements covering the footplate staff, which will be considered in the next chapter.

14

The Men who drove the Machines

Up to now this book has been concerned with locomotives rather than enginemen. However, it would not be complete without a closer consideration of the footplatemen themselves — a breed so far apart as to have many conditions of service peculiar to their craft. There is in some industries an expression that 'the work breeds the men'. Locomotivemen, by the very nature of their calling, are tremendously individualist, yet are well able to work with others. A driver in charge of a locomotive is without direct supervision while in traffic. He is often responsible for the safety of several hundred passengers and perhaps a million pounds worth of rolling stock and freight.

In the steam train performance articles which were very popular in Great Britain it was seldom noted that the 'speed kings' of the footplate (such as Bill Hoole of Kings Cross) were in their 50s or even 60s when most of their fast running was done. And unlike France and some other countries, where bonuses were paid for time regained, or even for punctual running, in the United Kingdom the drivers' only incentives were pride in their skill, the esteem of their fellow-men and the sheer joy of hard running. The glamour writing in railway magazines sufficed to show what could be done with good locomotives in the best of condition by men who had the will and the understanding to achieve it.

But many times more numerous were the sparkling trips which went unreported. Seldom indeed were the accounts of praiseworthy driving of freight trains. And whoever wrote about any of the innumerable journeys when time lost was recovered by sustained fast running in the hours of darkness?

Less appreciated still was the work in the depots, where a great deal of the activity was carried out by enginemen; much of the administration and supervision was concerned with what they were doing both in the shed premises and in traffic.

The only way that a youngster could start a career as an engineman in Great Britain was to join the service as a cleaner, to clean greasy, grimy locomotives, and occasionally to be allowed some relief from this chore by doing labouring work, or by relieving shedmen. Thence he would proceed to firing duties on uncompetitive seniority. This system had been handed down to us by the dyed-in-the-wool managements of the last century. A more deplorably unskilled entry to a highly skilled trade would have been difficult to devise. That this was only tradition-bound British habit is plain, since in many Continental and other overseas countries drivers were mechanically trained.

From 1940 to the end of steam traction it was only at the end of each school term that many depots could hope to recruit any cleaners — with the prospect of odd firing trips after a few months' service. With the labour situation existing in most industrial areas in the 1950s, most motive power depots were obliged to engage virtually anyone who could pass a simple medical examination, and who was passably literate. As an example of the education of some of these boys, I once asked one them at Staveley 'Where is London?' — to which I got the revealing reply 'I'm not sure, Gaffer, but I think it's in't middle'. Their scholastic attainment was matched by their negative response to discipline.

I used to ameliorate the cleaners' work within practical limits by putting some of them to work with fitters to clean parts which were stripped down and the surrounding parts of locomotives. This helped to make the working conditions more agreeable for the mechanical staff, especially as it relieved the fitter's mate from this menial chore, and left him free to give more direct assistance to the fitter. Furthermore, the cleaners — being under the watchful eye of older men — did a useful amount of work. That was dubious if they were left with a gang of other youths, all disposed to fool around instead of cleaning. This method of working gave cleaners a better sense of purpose, and taught them something about locomotive parts; it also provided scope for observing how the repair staff approached their various tasks. By asking questions they could learn about the functioning of components and how to detect defects.

Staff training is nowadays regarded as being of prime importance, but it was often not so in steam depots. During the first few weeks of a cleaner's service he was given some elementary instruction in how to heave coal into a firebox. In practice this required a skilled knowledge of where and when this should be done, according to the class of locomotive, the type of train, the route over which it was running, the load and the schedule to which it was working. Cleaners were shown how to manipulate various types of injector for filling boilers with water. Occasional instruction was given by an inspector concerning the burning of coal, rules of the depot, plus some knowledge of the Rule Book for the operation of trains. The classroom was sometimes a redundant coach body, which donkey's years earlier had been dumped in some vacant part of the shed yard as 'staff accommodation', where I have even seen turned-over boxes used for seating.

Alas, such training was as inadequate as the conditions were often primitive, so that thousands of firemen and even drivers were lamentably ignorant concerning the combustion of coal — and so wasted large amounts of that costly commodity throughout their careers.

When a cleaner passed the oral examination for firing he was graded 'passed cleaner' — as his first step of promotion — and received a higher rate of pay when he performed a firing turn.

Prior to World War 2 cleaners would have to serve months (or even years) before they were examined for firing, but during that war and afterwards it became common at many sheds for a cleaner to get his first firing trip in less than one month's service. Cleaners tended to be unruly, but fortunately the practicalities of footplate work soon taught them the need of respecting rules and working procedures. A passed cleaner, when not booked for firing, would sign on at an appointed hour, at which he might still be used casually for firing. A cleaner's first firing trip often produced a reaction summed up in the common saying that once a cleaner had been out firing it became more difficult than ever to get him to do any significant amount of cleaning. (It was said with equal force that after his first driving turn many a fireman had no more interest in firing.)

In prewar days cleaners might have to spend some years on cleaning, with increasingly frequent firing trips according to their advancing seniority; many were adults before they became regular firemen. After amassing 313 firing turns (later 180) a passed cleaner was paid as a fireman, but would still be subject to being knocked up at erratic hours to work in place of somebody who had failed to turn up for duty, or whose turn had had to be altered at short notice. Some men served several years before they accumulated the number of turns entitling them to promotion to regular fireman.

While steam locomotives needed cleaning at least once a week, from 1940 onwards all too often they did not get it. After the war finished, the release of men from the Forces was very protracted, and a good range of attractive jobs in various branches of industry was on offer. At most depots cleaners were passed out for firing with a minimum of training, and then were needed almost daily for that duty. Indeed many a lad was appointed as a regular fireman at the age of 16, and one Locomotive Shed Master of my acquaintance had to face a legal charge under the Employment of Women and Young Persons Act because 16-year olds had been used on night firing turns from his depot.

Astounding as it may now seem the training provided for driving was officially no more than one or two trips with a footplate inspector. To the enginemen's great credit — by force of sheer necessity — they themselves made up the deficiency. Training for driving was largely received in their free time, and at their own expense — often on Sunday mornings in the Mutual Improvement Class. Lectures were given by inspectors, railway officials, or invited 'experts', or by their own members who had taken a special interest in some aspect of locomotive working or maintenance.

Not all the meetings were directly instructional; some had a strong social flavour. For instance I once attended an animated 'rules quiz' at Stratford, London, when a team of locomotivemen from Stratford MIC were ranged against a local team from the Operating Department. The large room in which this event was held was filled to overflowing with supporters — most of whom travelled some miles to attend. Almost every sizeable shed in the United Kingdom had a Mutual Improvement Classroom — some of which were very creditably equipped — even if it were only a condemned coach body, shared with the ambulance class.

However, enginemen were in no way obliged to attend these classes; otherwise firemen and passed firemen simply picked up what they could from the drivers with whom they worked. Thus bad habits of driving and of firing were passed along with the good practices from one generation to the next. Most drivers who had senior firemen working with them would explain what a fireman might expect to be asked when he 'went up for driving' — meaning the verbal examination given by a footplate inspector. I once underwent one of these tests so far as knowledge of the rules was concerned, during my training in motive power management, and was impressed by the standard required.

The footplate inspectors had no easy task, and in my experience there were nowhere near enough of them for adequate supervision and examination of the footplatemen under their surveillance.

As with passed cleaners graduating to firemen, the same sort of prolonged casual transition took place before a passed fireman could become a regular driver. However, before a fireman could drive a train without a driver being present he had to pass the test for driving. This required not only a thorough detailed knowledge of extensive rules and complicated regulations, but also demanded the ability to drive various categories of trains over one or more routes which the candidate had to be closely familiar.

The examination might be taken on one or more types of locomotive — not always in the best of condition. Sometimes an unenterprising senior fireman, burdened by an unsympathetic mate, would go for a driving test having seldom handled the controls of an engine. In this case the examining inspector would have to set about giving him tuition in the matter, and if he failed the test it would probably be necessary to put him with a more understanding driver for a few weeks. When a senior fireman failed his driving examination he would have to suffer the indignity of spending a further period on firing, while men junior to him could advance to passed fireman, and so take driving turns.

In Great Britain drivers were not examined on their knowledge of particular classes of steam locomotive. During the two World Wars, enginemen often encountered an entirely strange type for the first time when they relieved another set of men in traffic. It might be, for instance, one of the American 2-8-0 'Liberation' locomotives, different from their British counterparts in nearly every possible way. Their training on this altogether unfamiliar machine would be literally limited to a couple of minutes — often in the dark under the added difficulty of blackout precautions. It would consist of a few brief remarks from the driver being relieved, somewhat as follows: 'This is the regulator, that's the brake — watch it because it's sometimes a bit fierce, those are the injectors — both good 'uns when you get used to them, that's the sanding gear, nothing worth having in the tool box. The coal's a bit rubbishy, but she's not bad at steaming with it. Tubes need booking — one or two of 'em are leaking a bit. Oh, and keep an eye on the left leading axle-box — inclined to run warm if you go fast with her'.

One or two anxious questions from the bewildered crew who had just stepped on board. Answers based on some four hours' acquaintance with such an engine.

Finally a parting shot from the men being relieved: 'Mustn't stay gossiping — Missus'll have the supper ready — besides Jerry might be over with a few bombs to liven things up. So — she's all yours, mind how you go, — and keep smiling!'

The crew who were relieved might well smile, they had finished sweating under black-out sheeting for one night. They could think about going home to their families and to bed, as they vanished into the darkness.

Of course, it was not by any means always as bad as that. Usually, before having to work a particular engine, the men had seen another of the same class, or one having similar controls, in their own depot, or at running sheds into which they worked.

Lucky indeed was the senior fireman whose driver took an active interest in him, and quizzed him day after day on the subject-matter of the driving test. It was interesting to note how some drivers would regularly take a hand with the shovel, both to keep in their hand at firing, and in order to give their mates a break from the hard physical work. Some of these heroes, especially when they had firemen whose seniority put them within a few months of being passed out for driving, would let the fireman do the driving under instruction for an hour or more. All firemen benefited from something of these traditional forms of tuition, but it was essentially a man-to-man affair, for which the driver received no remuneration, and indeed had no official recognition. Once passed out for driving, our fledgling passed fireman would be expected to know — as if by instinct — the idiosyncracies of all types of steam locomotives.

Even when a senior fireman was qualified to drive by having passed the test, he could not take out a locomotive on a particular route until he had 'signed for the road'. This meant certifying on an individual record card that he possessed detailed knowledge of all running tracks in both directions, including level crossings, catch-points, signals, signalboxes, stations, etc. If his duties would require him to work freight trains over the routes concerned, he would also have to be conversant with the goods yards and sidings along the way. Drivers whose duties over certain routes only required them to work passenger trains would sometimes sign for 'running lines only'.

He would need to be aware of the severity of gradients so far as these affected the working of trains, and would also have to make a mental note of landmarks which would enable him to know his whereabouts by night as well as by day, and in bad visibility as much as in clear weather. These landmarks had to include track-side features from which to judge braking distances for stopping from different speeds with trains of various weights. Thus a driver transferred from one depot to another had usually to spend some weeks on 'road-learning' before he could drive a train. Some Districts in later years used films and slides as an aid to learning routes.

Route knowledge had to be re-certified — usually every six months — taking account of track and signalling changes.

Some excellent descriptions of 'road-learning' and its problems, with a good indication of the amount of time which it could occupy is given by P. W. B. Semmens' biography *Bill Hoole — Engineman extraordinary* (Ian Allan) especially in Chapter IV on Kings Cross.

The route knowledge of individual drivers was a constantly changing factor in the complicated puzzle which was the List Clerk's daily chore. Good list clerks knew each man's latest signing without having to consult the route cards. When there was no job for a fireman he was booked on the daily list as 'spare'. Since this and other causes could lead to unremunerative time, most managements conducted a perpetual scrutiny of enginemen's time-sheets. One of the few ways in which a spare driver could be used — other than sitting in the mess-room awaiting orders — was to send him out on a 'refresher' trip over a certain route for the purpose of keeping up-to-date his knowledge of that line.

Some depots had very little special work, while others — such as Mexborough — had a high proportion of it, particularly excursion trains at weekends and specials for race meetings and football matches, which took them to all sorts of unlikely places. Indeed such work was often allotted to certain sheds because the men there had the route knowledge required. From the introduction of 'rest days', with 11 days being worked per fortnight, there were enough relief and special duties for larger depots to have a link composed of such work. This was extended from early 1962 when the five day week was introduced for enginemen.

Whatever the problems affecting enginemen's turns, a principle which was tacitly applied was 'taking the rough with the smooth', and this — while it did not allay all discontents — generally worked remarkably well.

Many depots on the LMS and LNER concerned with freight workings — had a number of 'Control Order Sets'. These men signed on duty at appropriate times, and sat in the mess-room, waiting for Control to give instructions as to what they were to do, or working to the running foreman's directions when Control gave permission for them to be used. Generally they were used to relieve other men in traffic when the irregularities of running trains made it impossible to predict from one day to the next where and when such relief would be required.

Since passed firemen and passed cleaners were required at short notice for driving and firing turns respectively, they were usually booked on duty at intervals 'around the clock'. There were limits to the extent to which a man might be 'moved' from his rostered time, the chief of these being that he must have at least 12 hours rest since booking off his previous duty. 'Passed' men were, of course, exceedingly keen to obtain the qualifying number of turns as soon as possible, and there was therefore immediately an argument (often backed up by one of the men's representatives) with the list clerk if such a man was not given the casual promotion to which he thought he was entitled. Occasionally a man would have to be 'credited' with a turn which he had not worked when the list clerk made one of his rare mistakes. A more complex system of promotion would have been difficult to devise.

At each depot the enginemen (including cleaners) were represented by a local departmental committee, which stemmed from the Railways Amalgamation Act of 1921. The Chairman of its Management Side was the District Motive Power Superintendent, and the Management side Secretary was his Chief Clerk. The man in charge of the depot was a member, whose functions were to make the local agreements work — and to take the brickbats when they didn't. The Men's Side had a Chairman (often the father-figure of local trade union branch), a Secretary and a member.

All the regular duties of drivers and firemen at a depot were included in 'links' (this applies also with diesel and electric traction). A link could be made up of any number of turns, but most consisted of jobs of similar character. An equal balance was maintained as far as practicable between 'am' and 'pm' duties. Regular turns were shown on a 'Weekly List', casual changes being displayed on a 'Daily List'. Maintaining these was the unenviable task of the List Clerk. At small depots these were compiled by a Running Foreman, or even by the Shed Master.

The composition of the links was a matter for local agreement within the framework of national agreements, and from time immemorial such agreements contained many bones of contention. One needed to have the mind of a solicitor to follow the changes and implications of all the agreements which could affect the placing of any given job in a particular link. Some of the more shrewd men's representatives would surely have qualified for the legal profession if they had had the benefit of a university education.

Both drivers and firemen ('second men' on diesel locomotives) progressed through the links by strict seniority, the 'top link' generally having the best quality of work at the depot. This included 'mileage turns' where an attractive bonus was paid for any distance worked above a certain figure (140 miles for most of the steam era).

Details of the trains which a locomotive was booked to work during a 24-hour period, including its departures from and arrivals at motive power depots, were contained in 'diagrams'. Enginemen's diagrams gave their places and times of signing-on and off, where and when they were to be relieved (if applicable) as well as the departure and arrival times of those portions of a train's journey which they were to work. On the Southern Railway (later Region) the term 'duty' was used instead of 'diagram' and duties for engines and men were often combined in the same duty circular. A locomotive and set of men booked to work a certain diagram were said to be 'rostered' to it.

In the suburban links at Neasden in the 1950s all the engines were Class L1 2-6-4Ts — interspersed with LMR 2-6-4Ts as those locomotives became redundant on the London, Tilbury & Southend line when that section was electrified. Two pairs of enginemen each had one engine regularly rostered to them. One set would work it for the morning turn from, say, 5.45am until just after 1.00pm when they would be relieved by men who would work it for the rest of the day. The next week these two sets worked another diagram with the same engine.

Whatever the constitution of a link, all the men in it worked in rotation through all its turns, and so could tell for weeks ahead at what time they would sign on duty, and at roughly what time they could expect to finish. Thus to a large extent the working lists set the pattern of the men's home-life and social activities. A driver and fireman would often stay together for years, so establishing an intimate relationship.

At most steam depots there was an 'old men's link', which was varied to accommodate drivers (and occasionally firemen) who needed light duties on medical or compassionate grounds — such as a man having to nurse a bedridden wife. This link contained shunting turns, local freight trips or branch line workings most of which had long or frequent periods of low activity, and seldom included night duties. A man might be temporarily or permanently transferred to this link after a long illness, or on recommendation of a railway doctor. Many depots had so much shunting work that they had links devoted to this type of work — one being probably nominated as the Old Men's Link.

During World War 1 exchange turns were introduced so as to reduce the necessity for men lodging away from home — notably on the North Eastern Railway. Much interesting information on the working conditions of enginemen in that part of England is given on pages 11-14 of K. Hoole's — *North Eastern Locomotive Depots* (David & Charles). Scattered throughout the rest of that unique book is a wealth of fascinating detail covering the workings of engines and men. These in many ways were typical of practice in the rest of the country — particularly in the industrial areas. Several interesting indications of the social aspects of lodging may be found in *Bill Hoole — Engineman Extraordinary*, already referred to.

At some sheds promotion to the top link was on a voluntary basis, with the option of transfer to the 'old men's link' — mainly for men who with advancing years had lost their nerve for high-speed running. The top link usually included some semi-fast passenger or freight turns, less exacting than the high-speed, long-distance work. This was also arranged not to concentrate an unduly high proportion of the lucrative mileage jobs in one link. These latter included — at many depots, particularly on the LMS — a number of lodging turns. They were highly unpopular with most men, since they often involved sleeping in barrack-like dormitories, called a hostel. Most LMS sheds had such an establishment; I once slept in the one at Kentish Town (London) and for seven weeks was responsible for the one at Peterborough Spital — both of which offered Army-type accommodation.

I was also responsible during 1952-54 for the one at Woodford Halse, which was seldom used for casual lodging, but like the one at Old Oak Common was occupied by a bunch of young firemen working away from home, and having money to burn. Some of the hostels were occasionally used as rest-time facilities by engine crews who booked off duty for a few hours at the outward end of split duties — such as excursion train workings. Each hostel was in charge of a steward, who needed to be a serjeant-major of a disciplinarian, and was responsible for running the outfit — including the troublesome business of catering.

Steam locomotivemen were extraordinarily individual in their characteristics. While a naturally co-operative man would fit in well with mates and supervisors, one with a tendency to be belligerent would find contacts where this might come into play. Sometimes this was best met by a show of strength, or on other occasions by humoring the man concerned. But always there was the need to understand quickly the underlying cause of the trouble of the moment, and just how seriously to take it. Time and again I was struck by the way that an appeal 'to do what was good for the job' induced men at loggerheads to adopt a more compromising attitude. And then, one way or another, some solution was reached — even if it was not with complete satisfaction to either party. Even more quickly effective was the pointing out of some really funny aspect in the middle of a heated argument.

An incident which once occurred at Staveley illustrated something of the relationship which existed between the driver and the fireman of a steam locomotive. Our senior Running Foreman, Frank Hayward, reported to me one day that a certain driver and his mate could not work together, and wished to be separated. If the worst had come to the worst, this might have been arranged by exchanging them with other mates in the same link. But it would have set a most undesirable precedent, and was not a solution to adopt without first getting to the root of this lack of normal relations.

So I summoned the pair of them to my office, and let them have their say. The driver, a conscientious sort of the old prewar, no nonsense variety, alleged that his fireman would not work according to his instructions. The fireman, an intelligent youngster, who evidently liked to think out for himself how best to fire a locomotive, resented what he considered to be unnecessary interference on the part of the driver.

It transpired almost at once that this was a case of neither appreciating sufficiently the other fellow's point of view. So I reminded the fireman that some day he too would become a driver, and would then have full responsibility for carrying out operating rules and other instructions; he would have to ensure the correct time-keeping of trains and would, so to speak, be 'the captain on the ship'. Furthermore it was pointed out that if he were rostered with another driver he would still have to accept the same kind of subordinate position in taking orders on the footplate. To the driver I suggested that the days of rigid discipline had disappeared with the war, and that leadership by reason, example and persuasion could be expected to produce better results than insisting on militaristic obedience. I added that firemen generally worked willingly under the orders of a driver, provided that the senior man showed a fair degree of understanding of his fireman's ideas.

By now it was apparent that what both had been needing was an opportunity to air their grievances in front of a third party without having recourse to an open quarrel. Fundamentally there was no real lack of good-will between them. So I suggested that they let bygones be bygones, try to look at the situation in the light of what was best for the job, and make a fresh attempt to work amicably together. Sensing a positive response from both of them, I invited them to shake hands about it. This they did, and honour being thus satisfied, from then on they worked together as well as any other pair of enginemen.

A closely similar case was referred to me as Acting Shed Master at Peterborough Spital (Midland) depot in 1952, but this time the same tactics did not work. The driver was 'cheesed off' by a succession of undisciplined firemen, and had found a better paid job in the local brickyards, with regular day-time hours. He had made up his mind to resign, and so to give vent to wider discontents. I could only regret that a long-serving driver should thus quit the railway.

The fireman seemed to be altogether more amenable to persuasion, and since he would in any case have to be placed with another mate, I asked him to give some serious thought as to how satisfactory relations on the footplate could be preserved. There seemed to be fair hopes that this request had produced some positive result, since during the rest of my time there his new driver had no cause to complain. It was as well that this young man found himself with a fresh driver, since it would have been most undesirable to apply formal disciplinary procedure as old-time management understood it.

In many cases a 'suspension from duty' would have been followed by the man concerned finding a job elsewhere during the period of his suspension, so that a depot already gravely short-staffed would have become yet one more under strength.

The proportion of footplate staff to other grades varied considerably from one depot to another, but as a general rough ratio it could be said that from 1919 there were around three footplatemen (drivers and firemen) for every man of other grades — including cleaners. During the 1950s the proportion of men working trains to the total number on the books was even less, since for every day that a locomotive was used in traffic at least two hours were spent by a crew in preparing the engine for work, and in disposing of it afterwards. During the day-shift hours of the clerical and workshop staff there were often as many men of various grades paid for being on the premises of any given shed as there were men of that depot engaged on engines in traffic. Furthermore a considerable amount of time was lost in enginemen walking about, especially going to or from a relief point, or waiting for a relief set to arrive, or waiting for a train to turn up on which others were to be relieved.

At March depot there was even a restrictive practice, enshrined in a local branch resolution, which imposed four engines as the limit which one set of men would dispose, coal and put in the shed during an 8-hour shift. This was commonly referred to as the Solid 4. There were many occasions (as I observed in the course of a shed analysis at that depot) when men confronted with a low amount of ash and well burned coal remaining on a fire-grate, especially with a locomotive equipped with a drop-grate section, or even a rocker-grate plus hopper-ashpan, could easily have so dealt with five or even six engines in the course of a shift. However, those who might have been willing to do so did not dare to because of punitive action by activists at the branch. That ASLEF Branch Minute carried more force in March shed than most of the laws of the land. This sort of negative attitude on the part of footplatemen undoubtedly deterred management from fitting a much greater quantity of labour-saving items of equipment to steam locomotives.

66
The oil stores at York depot on 30 May 1947. On the counter, covered with zinc or lead sheet are two battered oil 'bottles', made of tinplate. The stores issuer is reading a chit, authorising the men to draw a certain quantity of specified oils. Behind him is a gas lamp, and vertical glass cylinders for measuring oils of different kinds. The screen screen of timber and expanded metal was of a type quite common for such purposes in running sheds. The men's dress is typical.
BR Eastern Region

67
Southall depot as seen in the late 1950s; it serves today as a maintenance depot for rail-cars, the shed building having retained much the same external appearance. Surprisingly, although there were eight tracks under the roof (which is of postwar construction) there were only six rows of smoke cowls — these being of a type seen at many other Western Region sheds. *British Railways Photographic Section*

68
I have made it a rule not to illustrate sheds after they were closed, having sought to portray them as hives of activity. However, Central depot is full of nostalgia, as it was my first command. It is shown here (as described in *Steam was my Calling* after it was rebuilt in 1951-52) with three short tracks inside the shed and two extending for the original length of the building.

The two round-topped windows were those of the Locomotive Shed Master's office.

Annesley, Woodford and Neasden sheds were all six-track developments of the original Manchester, Sheffield & Lincolnshire shed on this site at Staveley. *J. S. Hancock*

69
This must be about the shortest locomotive shed ever. This building at the Civil Engineer's depot at Redbridge, near Southampton, was constructed in irregular stonework, probably for an 0-4-0T. The roof is relatively modern, the upper portion of the wall at the rear corner having been removed, apparently for repair work.

Locomotive No 233 carries the prefix DS (Departmental Service). It is of a type built in the USA for service in Europe during World War 2. Note the very short wheel-base for negotiating sharp curves. *Ian Krause*

70
Springbok Class B1 4-6-0 No 1016 *Inyala* receiving attention at York on 30 May 1947. The driver is about to top up the oil pot on the crosshead with a 'feeder' oil-can. The fitter (or examiner), with 'sponge' cloth in hand, is pushing sideways on the return rod to ascertain whether there is excess play in the return crank bearing; there should not have been, for these joints were fitted with ball bearings on LNER engines.

The young man on the footplate is filling a mechanical lubricator, a task which a driver would normally delegate to his fireman, but this man is not a fireman, as is evident from his boiler-suit, which was the traditional garb of the mechanical staff. He was almost certainly a management trainee gaining footplate experience. *BR Eastern Region*

71
Clean locomotives were very good for both publicity and morale, and the LNER recognised it to the extent of having a station shunting engine painted in green livery at Liverpool Street, York, Newcastle and Edinburgh. The East Coast regions of British Railways also maintained a shunting engine at these stations in specially clean condition. Here Class N7 0-6-2T No 69614 ('The Pride of Stratford') is seen at Liverpool Street on 13 March 1957.

The Westinghouse brake persisted on these suburban services until the lines were electrified. *British Railways*

72
Ex-South Eastern & Chatham 0-4-4Ts Nos 363 and 355 at Slade Green shed on 24 April 1926, a few days before the General Strike. Many such depots in the London area were closed, or converted to other purposes in the 1920s and 1930s, as the Southern Railway extended its electrified system. It was 'taboo' to drop ashes alongside the preparation pits unless the ashpits were out of action, eg for repairs.

This part of a depot, immediately outside the main shed building was known as 'the shed front'. *H. C. Casserley*

73
On the east side of the line from Baker St to Aylesbury, close to Neasden Power Station, was the Metropolitan Running Shed. This photograph, taken on 11 July 1936, shows Metropolitan tank engines, which had an attractive chocolate-brown livery. Shortly afterwards all Metropolitan steam workings — except ballast trains — were taken over by the LNER, and powered from their Neasden depot. That railway substituted the stronger Class A5 4-6-2Ts on the Rickmansworth-Aylesbury services (electric locomotive hauled from Baker St), plus Class C13 4-4-2Ts, push-and-pull fitted on the Chesham branch.

The Metropolitan locomotives was transferred to Colwick (Nottingham) District, where the last of them — a 4-4-4T — was running until it was scrapped just before Nationalisation. That class, of which No 103 is seen at the left, and No 105 at the rear of this picture, became LNER Class H2, while the 0-6-4Ts — here represented by Met No 97 — were re-classified 'M2'.

The Metropolitan only managed to provide a small, very low coaling stage. The men who originated with that railway maintained a proud sense of allegiance to it which endured for the rest of their service. *H. C. Casserley*

74
Modified 'Merchant Navy' Pacific No 35022 *Holland America Line* on one of the ashpits at Exmouth Junction in the early 1960s. The firemen is apparently placing an oil 'bottle' on the footplating before topping up one of the mechanical lubricators. It was unusual for this work to be done on an ashpit, but a set of men were commonly given the order 'Dispose and prepare engine No . . . '. As there was a fixed time allowance for these duties, the men would often take short cuts to complete them in the minimum time, after which the foreman would most probably let them go home before the end of their normal day — especially if he needed the engine in a hurry. *J. Parsons*

75
Doncaster locomotive running shed, photographed from the 'north end' in 1965 during its conversion to a diesel maintenance depot. The great majority of the workings have already been dieselised. The structure had been shortened in 1956/57 by some 90ft at this end.

The diesel maintenance shop now comprises the 'northern' half of the building on tracks 8, 9, 10 and 12 — No 11 having been removed in that vicinity. *Ian Krause*

76
The new order at Lincoln. The light and airy diesel rail-car depot, built on the site of the former Great Central running shed, which for some years had been carriage sidings. This location is just east of Pelham Street, where the erstwhile Durham Ox crossing was replaced by a bridge in 1958. *British Railways*

77
Here's double trouble — fortunately very rare. When Strawberry Hill (near Kingston-on-Thames) was a steam depot, it had a breakdown crane — evidently a vintage model displaced from a larger shed. On 25 June 1921, when called out to a derailment, it became derailed itself.
H. C. Casserley

78
Large or small every crane depended on its driver, whose skilful manoeuvring was usually taken for granted. This photo taken in 1964 shows Retford's 15ton crane in action. There was a single-cylinder engine at each side of the superstructure. *B. A. Stone*

79
Two 75-ton Cowans Sheldon steam cranes lifting the body of a 2,000hp English Electric diesel after an accident at Preston-le-Skerne, County Durham on 7 May 1965.
Clyde Crane & Booth Ltd — Clarke, Chapman & Co

80
Wellingborough's 75ton Cowans Sheldon steam crane (built about 1960) preparing to lift a heavy concrete section during the rebuilding of Birmingham New St Station. Behind it is a road-chassis crane.
Birmingham Post & Mail via Clarke, Chapman & Co

COWANS SHELDON

81/82
Waskerley depot in the wilds of County Durham was clearly equipped to cope with anything! Its museum-piece breakdown train included a hand-cranked crane, which could probably lift up to 10ton. The guard had a better look-out than in any modern breakdown train. This and the snow ploughs were photographed on 31 May 1935. The latter were converted from ancient brake-vans, which still carried the safety links common in the last century.

The author worked with a 12ton hand-operated crane at Boston as late as 1947, and once lifted one end of a bogie wagon with it. *H. C. Casserley*

83
This photograph shows a snow-plough at Darlington with two 'Austerity' 2-8-0s, coupled tender to tender behind it; there was a similar plough at the other end of the combination. They had been out clearing the Barnard Castle line early in 1963; each plough is believed to have been built on an old tender frame, on which staff accommodation was provided in the body-work. *B. A. Stone*

15

Preserved Motive Power Depots

The functions hitherto described are covered — even if in a makeshift way — at the locomotive sheds operated by various railway societies. Steamtown at Carnforth and the Great Western Society at Didcot have full-scale facilities purchased from British Rail. These are considered in the following pages, after which I refer to a few sheds which were converted to diesel maintenance.

Several months before main line steam traction ceased in this country in August 1968 a group of enthusiasts, including Dr Peter Best of Hest Bank and Joe Greenwood — a retired mechanical engineer — formed a company with the objective of preserving the Lakeside branch from Ulverston. When this proved to be beyond their resources they decided to preserve Carnforth depot intact with the potential of providing a 'home' for privately owned locomotives whose proud possessors would be looking for a repository in which their steeds could be kept. This expectation has been abundantly realised. Thus was created Steamtown — named after a similar establishment at Bellows Falls, Vermont, USA — with the above-named stalwarts as directors.

Not only was a museum, unique in Great Britain, so established, but the depot was restored almost to working order. There is not the frequent coming and going of locomotives, which was the life-blood of any steam shed, nor the quantity of engines in steam visible when it was in full operation. Neither can there be men of many grades working about the place at all hours, nor the interchange of engines of several depots working regularly and irregularly into others. And, of course, there is not the hard running of trains under all conditions of weather — and the consequent difficulties, which were the daily commonplace of steam sheds.

Still, there are many willing volunteers doing a variety of chores, many authorised by British Railways to drive locomotives within the depot limits. Moreover, most of the installations are used from time to time, so that visitors can see occasionally the

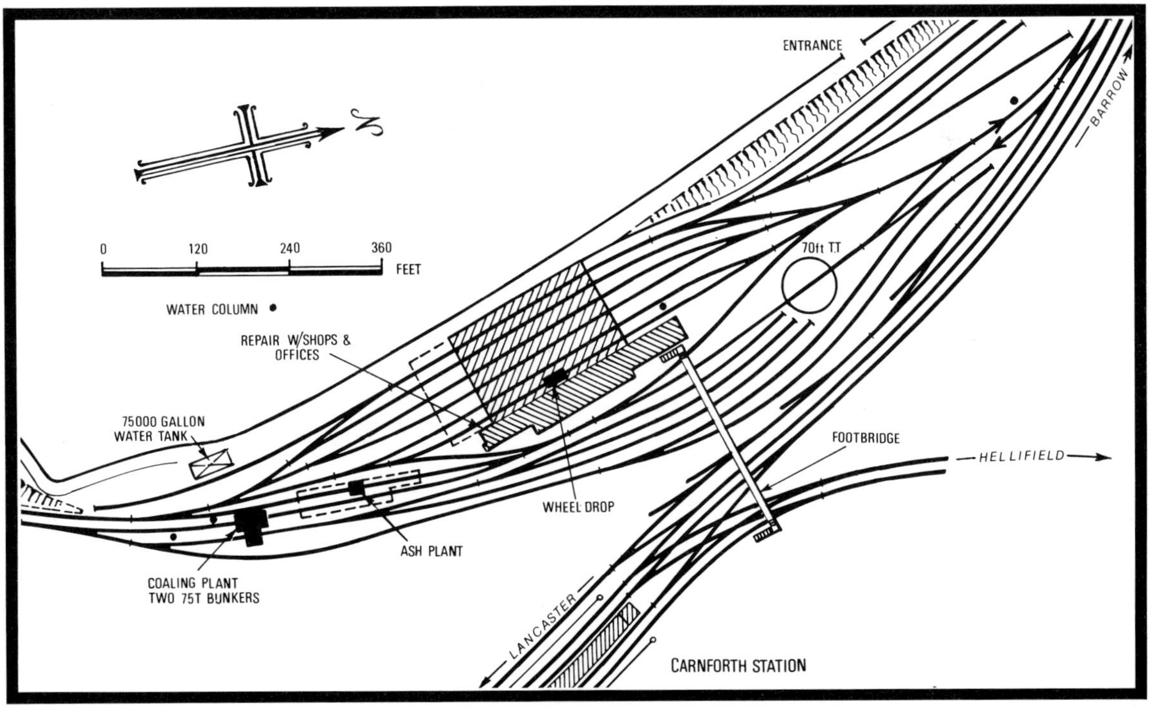

functions described in this book, and savour the characteristic movements, sounds and smells of a running shed.

Furthermore, one can enter the cabs, obtain permission to climb over locomotives, and even examine them from underneath by going into the pits which run the full length of each track inside the shed. This is rarely possible in other establishments, and is vastly better than just looking at exhibits in a museum, polished and cared for, but incongruously placed and pathetically lifeless. Indeed, the public is usually not allowed access to the footplate of engines displayed in museums. One might almost as well examine a stuffed horse as observe a locomotive without fire or steam, and not being able to climb into its cab.

Steamtown lies close to the west of Carnforth station, alongside the line to Barrow-in-Furness, and extends over 37 acres of land (including the site of the demolished LNWR depot) comprising four miles of track. It is equipped with all the usual facilities for servicing steam locomotives.

The mechanical coaling plant contains two 75-ton bunkers, each with jigger-feeds to two tracks, (total capacity about average for the United Kingdom), and is in full working order. Close to this is the concrete ash-elevating tower, identical to many erected for the LMS by Henry Lees & Co, serving one ashpit 162ft long and another 126ft long. The tower, together with the narrow-gauge ash-trolleys alongside the pits. The nearby ashpitmen's cabin now serves as a store for fire-irons and for the boiler wash-out pump.

At the north end of the shed building was the now dismantled sand-dryer. Close to this is the 70ft turntable, equipped with a vacuum tractor. The yard still has five water columns, supplied by the depot's 75,000gal main tank, which was installed during World War 2 by the LMS. Until the end of British Railway's service water was taken from the nearby Lancaster & Kendal canal, and passed through a softening plant.

The shed roof is typical of the best practice, in that for its entire length it is glazed for a width of about 5ft on each side of the continuous smoke chutes.

Visitors to steamtown should look for the engine arrangements board, a huge blackboard, on which locomotive numbers and daily details of the trains which they were to work is mounted on an interior wall. The notice cases are very ordinary-looking ones with wooden frames, but are typical of those which were to be found in almost any steam shed. The former signing-on lobby is now a kitchen-cum-snack bar, while the adjacent room — formerly the clerk's office — is now a dining room. These provide imaginative catering to suit the tastes of a wide variety of visitors. During an exhibition held jointly with British Railways from 11-26 August 1974 there were no fewer than 50,000 of them.

The erstwhile Locomotive Shed Master's office — shared by the District Motive Power Superintendent with his Assistant-cum-Shed-Master when Carnforth was the principal depot of a district — is now the Director's Office. The former stores is now a lively gift-shop, offering a great range of books, souvenirs, etc while the erstwhile fitters' mess-room has been converted to a 'collectors corner', where a considerable assortment of railwayana is sold. The original fitters' lockers are still in use, as a silent testimony to former 'occupants'. What was once the locomotivemen's mess-room now serves very appropriately as a staff-room for the volunteers who keep Steamtown going.

The room once used by guards serves the mundane, but necessary function of a paint store, while the former general and oil stores continue as a store for locomotive spare parts and the usual variety of materials needed for maintaining steam engines. Between two of the tracks in the shed is a typical rack-full of axle-box springs — all very heavy articles (over 40 of them) just as they were abandoned by British Railways, and comprising a remarkable range of LMS and BR Standard types. The erstwhile boiler-house is now a store for heavy tools.

Steamtown makes a business out of restoring other owners' locomotives, as well as maintaining its own extensive collection. It is also empowered to undertake engineering contract work — something no British running shed was ever allowed to do. A typical job was the re-tubing of LNWR 2-4-0 No 790 *Hardwicke* for the National Railway Museum in preparation for the 150th Anniversary Celebrations of the running of the first passenger train, held at Shildon in 1975. All boilers which are repaired receive a hydraulic as well as a steam test.

There is a wheel-drop of pre-1914 origin, capable of lowering wheels up to 7ft diameter. The machine shop remains with its machines, substantially as it was when British Railways left it, and is virtually a museum-piece in its own right. Dr Beet, with a touch of medical humour, has labelled it 'the Surgery'. Besides a 7ft diameter wheel lathe, purchased by the Furness Railway in 1905, there is a range of lathes and a triplex machine of a model supplied to many other LMS depots which were modernised in the late 1930s. This incorporates a centre lathe, a shaper and a drilling machine on a common bed-plate; the great advantage of this arrangement was that a single motor sufficed for all three parts of the machine. Furthermore, while cutting was being done by automatic feed on one part, the turner could be setting up work, or removing it from another. This type of machine was adopted for some sea-going ships. The shaper head of the triple machine had been ingeniously adapted with a large hack-saw, so that the shaper can be used for sawing metal bar, angle-iron etc.

The lifting equipment in the machine shop comprises a $7\frac{1}{2}$-ton electric hoist, which travels on an overhead rail to serve the adjacent drop-pit, and a 1-ton radial jib-crane for lifing axleboxes. There is also an electrically driven heavy-duty grindstone, and the depot is equipped with an air compressor and compressed air mains. The machine shop contains a small forge and a coppersmith's hearth.

Carnforth, like many another town served by more than one railway before 1923, had a running shed provided by each of them, since they would rather face the costs of constructing and operating their own separate installations than have their locomotives and enginemen under the control of a 'foreign' company. The Midland shed lay on the north side of the line from Settle Junction, to the east of the West Coast main line and east of the A6 main road. It consisted of a single round-house; the building still exists, being used by a contractor as a store and a workshop. it is unmistakably identified by its characteristic Midland windows with their 45° panes.

The Furness shed was a 4-track dead-end building demolished by the LMS in 1925, except for the west wall which was also a retaining wall for the public road alongside. That wall still exists to a height of 6ft, being incorporated into the subsequent LMS shed, which ultimately became Steamtown.

The LNWR shed was also a 4-track dead-end structure, some 300-odd yards to the south of the present shed building, its site being incorporated in Steamtown's territory. Although it was a minor one on the West Coast main line, it always had a certain importance due to being at the foot of the succession of three inclines, which culminate at Shap summit. Carnforth itself lies only a few feet above sea-level, the most south-westerly point of the yard of Steamtown being only a quarter of a mile from Morecambe Bay. Under electric traction that formidable climb has lost its terrors (and its banking engines), but with steam power Carnforth used to receive some glamorous casualties. Drivers of northbound trains would seldom pass that depot if they had serious doubts about the mechanical condition or steaming ability of their locomotives, without whistling for an assistant engine or a fresh one.

By the middle of World War 2 the main building of the LNWR depot had deteriorated very badly, its pits being frequently part-filled with water. A new shed was therefore constructed in 1943-4 on the site of the former Furness Railway shed, to a length of 200ft and width of 120ft, following a standard pattern developed under the Stanier régime. The new building (as at present existing) was of reinforced concrete and brickwork, which were the usual materials for such a structure at that time. Skilled labour being in very short supply due to wartime conditions, Italian prisoners-of-war from the Milnthorpe Camp were employed to construct new pits and to build the foundations of the walls. 322 men were transferred to the new depot.

The new building had doors at each end, of a type which folded in three panels per door. One set of this kind still exists, but the remainder were missing when the present owners took over the premises. Replacement doors had to be installed due to the necessity of keeping out trespassers with dubious intentions. These doors were brought from sheds at Bolton and Hellifield, but had to be widened to fit the door-gaps at Carnforth.

There are preparation pits in each shed track at the south end, and formerly also at the north end. The latter were filled in by Steamtown as they represented a hazard to members of the public.

In LMS and British Railways times the normal sequence of operations was for locomotives to arrive 'from traffic' at the south end of the shed yard, or from the Furness direction, take water, then coal at the mechanical coaling plant, followed by ash disposal at the mechanised ash-plant, turn (if required), and lastly stabling in the shed if repairs or boilerwashing were needed. If an engine were not required for the time being, it would be stabled, whereas if it were wanted for a fresh duty, it would be set on a pit for preparation.

The wheel drop was installed in No 1 track, which together with No 2 was equipped with pit lights, a lighting trolley being also provided. Those tracks were reserved for Nos 2, 4 and 6 examinations (see Chapter 9), and for heavy running shed repairs. Tracks Nos 3 and 4 were used for boiler washing (the supply being boosted to 60lb/sq in) and boiler repairs. Tracks Nos 5 and 6 were locally known as 'going-off' roads, being principally used by engines raising steam or needing running repairs. Carnforth, in common with other LMS depots had cold-water washing out, with a controlled system of blowing-down before wash-out.

The pits outside the shed building at each end were used for preparation, while the first space inside the building at either end would be used for examination, preparation or running repairs so long as it were not required for engines undergoing other operations.

Almost all the Furness Railway engines had been broken up by World War 2, but in its hey-day from the mid-1930s to the early 1960s Carnforth had a varied allocation of LNWR, Midland, LMS and later British Railways types, totalling about 50. At week-ends its ample shed yard was often crowded with locomotives from other depots, as well as Carnforth engines, so that the variety was even greater, and the total sometimes in the 80s.

Many sheds suffered once or more from the alteration of district territories. In the latter days of the LMS and until 1951 Carnforth was depot No 11A, with the District Motive Power Superintendent, also controlling some five other depots. From 1950 the LM Region of British Railways down-graded it to depot No 24L in Accrington district. However, since it was equipped for heavy running shed repairs, it retained its function as a concentration depot — a fact which makes its subsequent preservation all the more interesting. The term ' concentration' is explained in Chapter 9. (In 1962 Carnforth District was reconstituted, with Carnforth shed as No 10A — this time turning the tables on Accrington, which was relegated to depot 10E.)

Carnforth was one of the last three British Rail standard gauge depots to remain in service, and on 11 August 1968 — a week after the last day of regular steam traction — 'Britannia' Pacific No 70013 *Oliver Cromwell* and 'Black Fives' Nos 44781 and 44871 were turned out to work the 'Farewell to Steam' Special which was run from Liverpool to Carlisle via Ais Gill. On the following day the last-named was steamed for a BBC TV feature film. The depot was then used to store locomotives awaiting scrapping, and for stabling diesels. It was closed on 4 April 1969, when it was handed over — in sadly run-down condition — to the company which acquired it, as described above. Since then the drains have been cleared, the buildings renovated and the yard made presentable.

Steamtown is open all the year round (except Christmas), and welcomes many thousands of appreciative visitors every year. Almost every weekend and on many weekdays they can see one or more engines in steam, and sometimes see various servicing or repair operations being carried out. Occasionally one of the larger locomotives can be seen departing or arriving before or after a foray to Ravenglass (Cumbria), York, or some other enthusiast-commissioned destination.

At the 150th Anniversary Celebrations of the Stockton & Darlington Railway, held at Shildon in August 1975, Steamtown turned out the largest contingent, comprising: L&NW 2-4-0 No 790 *Hardwicke*, which established records during the London-Aberdeen 'Races' of 1895; GWR 'Modified Hall' No 6960 *Raveningham Hall*; LNER Class B1 4-6-0 No 1306, carrying name-plates *Mayflower*; LNER Class V2 2-6-2 No 4771 *Green Arrow* and the most famous iron horse of them all — LNER Class A3 Pacific No 4472 *Flying Scotsman.* (Because of its universal popular appeal, this engine more than any other spends quite a lot of its time away from Carnforth.)

The remainder of Steamtown's locomotive stock includes: GWR 56xx 0-6-2T No 5643 (built 1926); rebuilt Southern Region 'Merchant Navy' No 35005 *Canadian Pacific*, this engine was received in an advanced state of dereliction, having been abandoned in Woodham's scrap-yard at Barry from 1965; LMS 'Black Five' 4-6-0s No 44871, built at Crewe 1945; No 44932, built at Horwich 1945; No 45407, built by Armstrong Whitworth 1937 and LMS Class 2MT 2-6-0 No 6441 built at Crewe 1950.

Three locomotives have been brought over from the Continent and restored to excellent external condition. These are: Valentine 4-cylinder Pacific No 231K22, rebuilt by Chapelon, DB oil-fired Pacific No 012.104.6 (built in Berlin 1940) and DR 0-6-0 tank No 80014 (built at Magdeburg 1927), though the latter has since been transferred to the Nene Valley Railway, Peterborough.

There are also several industrial locomotives, comprising 0-6-0 and 0-4-0 shunting tanks, one of which is a fireless locomotive owned by Steamtown. The depot handbook gives further details of the engines, carriages and wagons on display. (The admixture of industrial engines and Continental locomotives has made the place less like a running shed. The latter will never go out on BR lines because they are foul of the largest British loading gauge.)

Steamtown uses the ex-Furness Railway carriage shop at the south end of the yard for restoring carriages.

The former sidings of the Furness and the LNWR have been lifted to provide a huge car park with a capacity for about 1,000 cars.

Material for the above notes has been kindly supplied by the gentlemen mentioned above and by retired driver John Easter Roberts, formerly Chairman of Carnforth Urban District Council. He was also for several years Chairman of the men's side of the Local Departmental Committee, the representative body for footplatemen at the depot.

In contrast to Steamtown, the depot at Didcot has been preserved not to house a general railway collection, but to display locomotives, rolling stock and equipment of the Great Western Railway. Up to the early 1930s it had been a smaller-than-average depot, whose facilities were rendered inadequate by increased traffic in the 1920s. A grant was obtained under the Loans & Guarantees Act of 1929 (an Act designed to combat unemployment) for the construction of the present shed, which was opened in 1932.

The depot remained in British Railways ownership until 1972, being used in its later years for storing locomotives. It was therefore not derelict when taken over by its present proprietors — the Great Western Society. The main building, 200ft long by 80ft wide, is a 4-track 'through' shed, although the shed tracks — which can each accommodate three tender engines under cover — terminate at buffer stops three engine-lengths further on. The shed therefore had to be operated as a dead-end shed which was a bad feature.

No 1 track in the shed extends into a spacious lifting-cum-machine shop, equipped with a 50-ton electric crane. For a preservation society this is much more useful than a drop-pit, since it enables the heaviest locomotive to be lifted at one end, and boilers to be lifted out of the engine frames.

There are two ashpit tracks ('fire-dropping roads'), one of which is still equipped with a pit. During World War 2 these were roofed over so as to prevent the glare from red-hot coals being seen by enemy bombers. From the latter track engines could pass directly to the coaling stage. This is an 'elevated' stage on to which the wagons were propelled up a steep incline to a level of about 14ft above the track on which engines stand for coaling. A covered water-tank of 74,250gal capacity forms the roof of the structure — the whole installation being very typical of GWR practice.

The stationary boiler is still in position alongside the shed, but is no longer steamworthy. It was used to supply steam for space heating and water for washing out.

At Nationalisation Didcot had an allocation of 49 engines, representing nine classes. There are now 18 former GWR locomotives preserved there, together with a selection of carriages and wagons; details of all these are given in the Society's brochure.

The Dinting Railway Centre at Glossop, some 12 miles east of Manchester consists of the former British Railways motive power depot, with its single-track 'double-ended' shed plus a sizeable exhibition hall which has been constructed in the ample yard. Some track alterations have been made to adapt the site to its present function as a museum and educational centre.

The original running shed is believed to have been constructed late in the last century by the Manchester, Sheffield & Lincolnshire Railway, which metamorphosed itself in 1899 into the Great Central. The shed served the Glossop and Waterside branches, and provided banking engines for the gradient of 1 in 100/117, up which a succession of heavy freight trains toiled their laborious way alongside the Longdondale reservoirs before entering the notorious Woodhead Tunnel en route for the West Riding. The depot was closed in 1964, after which the premises were abandoned, and were ransacked by vandals.

Its restoration by the Bahamas Locomotive Society from the summer of 1969 was the usual story of a thorough-going renovation of derelict facilities by keen amateurs having very limited resources. The original brickwork shed, which can accommodate two tank engines, now has doors on each end, and retains its inspection pit. It is of no special significance as a building, except that it is typical of hundreds of such sheds which were scattered throughout the country. They were out-stations or sub-depots of larger sheds, Dinting being a sub-depot of Gorton.

The 'parachute' (or overhead cistern) water column, and the coal stage — for direct shovelling into tenders — and the adjacent ashpit are preserved virtually as they were in British Railways service.

The Centre is open every day except Christmas. On display are — inter alia — rebuilt LMS 'Royal Scot' 4-6-0 No 6115 *Scots Guardsman*; 5XP 'Jubilee' 4-6-0s No 5596 *Bahamas*; LNER 'A4' class No 60019 *Bittern*, and 'A2' No 532 *Blue Peter*; LNWR 'Coal Tank' No 1054, and a small quantity of industrial locomotives.

Tyseley, which houses the Birmingham Railway Museum's exhibits, is not a running shed, but is rather a Works, with an Atcost-type building specially constructed for restoring locomotives and rolling stock. It does, however, occupy most of the former Great Western motive power depot site: — the elevated coaling stage remains intact, and the GWR water tank remains in modified form.

British Railways' only remaining steam shed — at Aberystwyth — is used now only to house three narrow-gauge 2-6-2T engines and some narrow-gauge rolling stock, which work summertime passenger traffic on the Vale of Rheidol line up to Devil's Bridge. Moreover the locomotives, with their deep outside frames, long side-tanks, extending forward to the buffer beam, and with centre couplers are completely untypical of British practice.

The shed building is the former straight 'double-ended' shed, remaining as it was constructed in brickwork by the Great Western before World War 1. The standard-gauge tracks have been removed, and the pits filled in; in their place a few narrow-gauge tracks have been installed in the building. However, it requires little imagination to envisage it in its original form with a variety of GWR 4-6-0s, 2-6-0s, 2-6-2Ts and 0-6-0Ts standing about gently simmering.

The earthworks and the structure of the coal-stage were left intact, since this supports the water tank which is still in use. The engines are coaled at ground level by hand direct from wagons. The shed has only the most rudimentary facilities, but these are at least better than those of the original Vale of Rheidol depot, which a former Divisional Superintendent responsible for that line aptly described as a cowshed.

The workshop, stores and staff amenities remain substantially as they were when the shed was providing locomotives for standard gauge services, but there are, of course, no longer the administrative, workshop, or shed staff of those times.

It will no doubt seem strange that I should include Thornaby-on-Tees, Doncaster and Chester among preserved sheds, whereas no one made any special effort to keep their buildings in the form which they had as steam depots. Indeed the installations and equipment relative to steam traction were removed after dieselisation, but the main shed buildings remain intact substantially as they were in the early 1960s. They were among very few in Great Britain which were considered suitable for conversion, since their location, access and layout were all convenient, and the space which they occupied was not required for any other purpose. The offices, mess-rooms, stores, etc were adapted to suit the new needs.

During the steam era Doncaster was one of the most important locomotive depots in the country. The depot was laid out on flat land, having a capacity for around 100 engines. It would have been possible to put all of them under the vast shed roof. The workshops included separate shops for minor trades. There were huge wooden doors at the ends of the main shed until after World War 2. Occasionally one or other of these would be smashed, with a noisy splitting of timber, when from time to time there was careless shunting of a line of engines. It was sometimes due to a door not being properly fastened in the open position, and then a gust of wind blowing it foul of moving engines. Such doors were a confounded nuisance at depots such as this, where locomotives were being propelled through the shed at all hours of the day and night.

Alongside No 12 track, and integral with the main building is a two-track dead-end shop (tracks Nos 14 and 15) constructed with pits for repairing steam locomotives. On No 15 track is a hydraulic wheel-drop, for which power was originally supplied by a steam-driven pump. When the depot was dieselised in 1966 the two stationary locomotive boilers, the hot-water wash-out plant, and the steam-hydraulic pump were removed and an electrically driven hydraulic pump was installed. Space heating and hot water were from that time supplied by oil-fired boilers.

The continued existence of the repair shop in its original form owes much to the fact that No 14 track was leased by Mr Alan Pegler for housing Pacific No 4472 *Flying Scotsman*, when it was in his possession from 1963 until it went on its ill-fated tour of North America in 1969. A spare boiler and a large quantity of other spare parts were kept there. The building was renovated (principally re-roofing) at a cost of some £60,000 largely for this 'garage' function. The original, slow, hand-operated gantry crane was retained. During my time at Doncaster shed in 1942 on one occasion when the drop-pit was otherwise occupied I saw a gang of brawny muscle-men climb up on to the decking of that crane, and sweat away at the hand-cranks until they had raised the front end of a Pacific!

This workshop crane was de-rated a few years ago to lift only 7½tons — being now over 100 years old. It is, however, occasionally used, since the shop is frequently occupied with the repair and maintenance of a variety of mobile equipment for the Civil Engineer.

When the depot was dieselised in 1966 a wall was constructed along the line of No 7 track for about a third of the length of the shortened building at its north-west end, and the space between this and the offices, etc was enclosed and converted to the present four-track diesel locomotive maintenance shop. No 12 track was retained for the whole length of the shed as a repair track, since it contains the 'Atlas' ground wheel lathe — ie a machine on which the tyres of locomotives and rolling stock can be turned without the wheels having to be removed.

The whole roof over tracks 1-12 being relatively new, was retained when the depot was converted. Tracks 7-11 are used at the south-east end of the shed for vehicles awaiting tyre-turning or other repair, these tracks being truncated by the wall of the maintenance shop. Tracks 1-6 are used for stabling diesel locomotives, the breakdown train, snow-ploughs and other service vehicles. The breakdown crane (now a 75-tonner) is thus kept under cover —

which was seldom the case at a running shed during the time of steam traction.

There used to be pits along the full length of all the tracks in the shed, and for an engine length outside it at the London end, but these have all been filled in — except where required for diesel maintenance.

The extensive open yard space remains mainly as it was, save that the track-work was reduced when the coaling plant, the old coal-stage and the turntable, etc were removed and the ashpits filled in. In the 1940s and 1950s there was a turning triangle on the open land at the north-east side of the shed, near to the erstwhile LNWR depot which survived as a wagon repair shop, then as a scrap depot, and for years was derelict until it was demolished about 1973. Around 1960 the Civil Engineer was needing land for a permanent way depot, and so a 70ft turntable which was redundant at Southend Victoria was installed at the north-east end of Doncaster depot and the triangle removed.

Chester running shed was most unusual in having two 3-track 'double ended' sheds within 100yd of one another, but separated by running tracks (now rail-car washing sidings). Both buildings have been converted for the maintenance of diesel rail-cars, the pits being deepened, faced with concrete, and provided with built-in electric lights. The most easterly shed survives from the original Great Western depot being about 200ft long, and has round-topped windows, distinguished by numerous small panes. It had a hand-cranked sheer legs for lifting locomotives until the end of steam traction.

The other shed building is believed to have been constructed by the Chester & Bangor Railway and to have been taken over by the GWR from the LMS about 1934; it was re-roofed for steam traction in 1957. It is about 130ft long, and it too has round-topped main windows, but of a different style of architecture from the other shed. Railcars began to replace steam services at Chester from about 1960, and were maintained at the ex-Cheshire Lines depot at Northgate until the above-described sheds were converted to their present purpose.

The magazine *The Locomotive* published in its issue of July 1958 an illustrated description of Thornaby depot, which had been opened in the previous month to replace out-moded sheds at Middlesbrough and Newport. The new main buildings consisted of a straight 'garage' shed for washing out, 'running' repairs, etc and a straight repair shed under the same roof alongside it. The latter was equipped with two Cowans Sheldon wheel-drops and other machinery. This shed was also constructed with facilities for maintaining diesel shunters. There was also a 'round-house', which was in fact octagonal, built around a 70ft diameter electrically driven turntable. This had 22 'stalls' plus two inlet/outlet tracks, and was called the 'bull-ring'.

Pits were installed in the tracks in all the abovementioned buildings. Outside the main buildings were four covered inspection pits and four covered preparation pits. All the engine pits were fitted with fluorescent lighting built into the walls of the pits.

In the yard was also a separately accessible 70ft turntable.

Ash disposal was done on a large wet ashpit, and the mechanical coaling plant — of 350 tons capacity was provided with three outlets.

Across the whole east end of the depot was a gantry supporting water and sand - filling pipes.

For boiler-washing a high-pressure hot-water system was installed.

The depot was laid out to handle up to 220 locomotives. These were a variety of freight and mixed traffic tender types, passenger tank engines and shunting engines.

To sum up, anyone who saw Doncaster, Thornaby, Aberystwyth or Chester sheds during the steam era would find there a great deal which has changed little.

All depends on what the enthusiast or casual visitor wishes to see, but for anyone seriously interested in a locomotive running shed, visits to Steamtown at Carnforth and/or Didcot should be considered indispensable.

16

Breakdowns and Snow Clearance

Each depot having repair staff had a breakdown train, or at least tool vans equipped for re-railing locomotives and rolling stock. In almost all cases the train was stabled in the shed yard, without cover. Wherever there was a steam crane it was kept in steam, with a very low fire — except when its boiler needed wash-out, inspection or repairs. Such cranes as are still in service are a last vestige of steam traction; on British Railways a programme of conversion of the larger ones to diesel power is now in hand.

Originally 'packing and dragging' was the most common method of re-railing. Ramps (eg Kelbus) are a sophistication of this process, whereby a steel surface is provided at the optimum angles to lead the flange of a derailed wheel up to the desired height on the correct side of the rail. Such ramps have been in use in marshalling yards for decades, but heavier ones are provided for breakdown trains. These are in sets, comprising a right-hand pair, a left-hand pair, and a pair of point ramps, for use according to which side of the rail the wheel is on, or is derailed at points. (Webster gives details of these on pages 18 and 19 of his book *Locomotive Running Shed Practice,* Oxford University Press.)

Until the 1950s heavy, water-filled jacks of various capacities were in use with all breakdown trains, but from that time these were gradually replaced by oil-filled ones with aluminium alloy bodies which were much lighter. For use with both ramps and jacks a plentiful selection of hardwood blocks and wedges were provided — indeed the term 'packing vans' derives from this material being the principal means of re-railing from the earliest days of railways.

Blocks and tackle (eg Kelbus hauling gear) can be used to obtain increased pull by mechanical advantage, but with a degree of risk to the anchor points (usually trackwork). Some special equipment is almost indispensable in tunnels or under bridges where it is impossible to use a crane, and is particularly handy in hauling a vehicle back to the track after it has fallen down a bank, or in parting wreckage which has become impacted together.

The hand tools required in a breakdown train are more or less the same as those needed in a maintenance depot, although the increased use of sheet steel in rolling stock has made it useful to carry a long-handled tool with a claw-shaped cutting head — for use as a giant's 'can opener'.

A range of chains, steel-wire ropes and hemp ropes is also needed, accompanied by links, shackles, hooks and slings. With diesel and electric traction virtually every different class of locomotive or multiple-unit stock necessitates that different types of lifting brackets should be carried in the tool van of each breakdown train covering the areas in which they work. For all the smaller items of equipment 'shadow boards' are much to be recommended. Among the heavy items to be found among the equipment of every breakdown train are steel plates of various sizes and a few lengths of steel rail. These should be underslung, where possible from one of the vehicles, so as to ensure ease of access.

A most useful fitting on each side of the tool van is a radial jib, able to swing inside and outside the van. It may also be advantageous to have an overhead rail with a pulley block running along part of the length of the inside of the van.

'Walkie-talkie' sets may also be used between the man in charge of the breakdown train and the crane driver, or between him and an official of another department, assisting at the scene of an accident.

Whatever apparatus is carried, large or small, it is essential that it be restored to first-class condition after each occasion of use, also that it be carried in the most convenient position possible, so that it can be produced with the minimum of delay whenever required.

During the time of steam traction, and in areas of intense freight activity — particularly in colliery districts and where there was a multiplicity of ill-maintained private sidings — derailments were quite frequent. It was by no means uncommon for breakdown cranes in busy areas to be called out six or seven times a week.

I obtained my first impressions of breakdown work on the LNER with a Doncaster gang in 1942, who had about as wide a variety of this kind of duty as one could wish. Being in training there for three months in 1942, I was on call day and night, and so went out on average about four times a week. We always took the crane, for information concerning the extent of an incident was very often inadequate. What was described as a simple derailment might well be complicated by a damaged structure in unsafe condition, or track distorted in such a way that much more than ramps and packing were needed to deal with the situation.

The gang had to go out in all states of the weather — often under conditions which many men from the Works would hardly have tolerated. The train contained a 45-ton steam crane, whose operations were generally supervised by Mechanical Foreman Charlie Walker, who had the unenviable task of keeping Doncaster engines fit for traffic under the arduous circumstances of war.

From 1939 to 1945 breakdown work at night-time was made much worse by the black-out, in which all lights had to be shielded, and hand-signal lamps could only be used with the most careful precautions. In many parts of Great Britain, besides direct bomb damage there were derailments caused by signalling having been put out of action, or trains running on to track which had been destroyed by bombing. Frequently rescue gangs continued working while there were 'yellow' warnings (danger of bombardment) in operation. Such emergency duties were often carried out after a full day's work in the shed, or after very little sleep.

Breakdown work is complicated wherever there are conductor rails or overhead contact wires. I had experience of this as Locomotive Shed Master at Neasden during 1954-55. Early in my time there I went over to the Metropolitan shed to discuss with the London Transport shed master common problems relating to breakdowns, so that we should be better prepared to work together. In fact Metropolitan and Bakerloo tracks still run alongside the ex-Great Central tracks between Finchley Road and Harrow-on-the-Hill, beyond which British Railways stock runs over Metropolitan tracks beyond Rickmansworth (at that time the limit of electrification).

Neasden 'Met' shed had its own breakdown facilities including a crane of no special merit. But their permanently manned rescue lorries, equipped for getting aid to a train in trouble in one of the tunnel sections were a model of ingenuity. (One of these is described with illustrations in a most informative paper presented by K. R. M. Cameron to the Institution of Mechanical Engineers in 1970.)

Any incident outside the shed necessitating a turn-out of the breakdown train was also likely to produce a reaction in inconveniences. For the running foreman it involved providing a suitable locomotive at no notice at all. Nearly all sheds had a reserve of engines to cover such a demand without difficulty, but it was not always so. Most depots had a set of men available at nearly all times to cover absenteeism, or out-of-course working, but when a depot was already on the point of cancellilng a train because of a shortage of firemen (as happened all too often in London and some industrial areas in the 1950s), then finding a set of enginemen for the breakdown train — plus probably a relief set about eight hours later — could become a matter of conferring with Control as to which train was to be cancelled in order to release a fireman and/or driver.

To the Locomotive Shed Master and/or the Mechanical Foreman a breakdown call meant a sudden switch of current activity, and involvement at very short notice with other departments. They were often much concerned about the prolongation of repairs which would result from workshop staff being away from the depot for hours. To those members of the breakdown gang already on duty it was usually regarded as a welcome change from their normal tasks in the shed, unless the weather happened to be particularly bad, but even then the payment of the breakdown bonus, plus the possibility of overtime at enhanced rates was enough to make the turn-out welcome.

For those of the gang who were off duty, being 'on call' imposed the continual obligation to leave a message with the running foreman's office as to their whereabouts at all times.

When a breakdown call is received (now as during steam traction) the questions on everybody's minds are: 'Just where is it? What train or trains and vehicles are involved? How bad is the accident?' and 'what are the circumstances?' Then, of course there is speculation as to how long it will take for the breakdown train to turn out, what time will be needed for it to reach the scene of the incident, and how long it will take to recover derailed vehicles and to clear the site. If lines are blocked, the operating staff are anxious to know how long it will be before reduced traffic can pass, and what further delay will ensue before normal working can be resumed. The locomotive depot personnel — usually cinderellas of the railway — are for a brief spell in the limelight.

One of the earliest references to breakdown trains was contained in a letter of 1851 from A. Sturrock, Locomotive Engineer, seeking permission from the Board of the Great Northern Railway to convert certain ballast wagons into 'tool trucks' for transporting screw jacks, crow-bars and other breakdown equipment for use at derailments.

Little is known of railway breakdown equipment during the last century, but breakdown cranes did not keep pace with locomotive developments. Many hand-cranked cranes were in use for the purpose, a number of which survived until after Nationalisation. Considering that there were over a million small four-wheeled wagons running about on the lines of British Railways at that time, it was not quite so antediluvian as it now sounds. Many steam cranes at that time were of quite old construction and had a lifting capacity of only 15ton.

During the first 60 years of this century there were over 330 locomotive running sheds in Great Britain. Breakdown trains in this country ranged from elementary rescue apparatus with three or four men to use it, to a train with a 50ton steam crane. The latter had a bogie riding van, fully equipped for a squad of a dozen men to spend up to 60 hours on a collision job, and a couple of vans with all manner of re-railing tackle. The whole train was rated for running at speeds up to 60mph. In emergency, under favourable conditions, even this speed was sometimes exceeded.

Each depot had its clearly defined breakdown area, the breakdown crew being composed of men who lived near the shed and agreed to be 'on call'. Those depots not equipped with a crane called on the neighbouring depot which did have one whenever a de-railment could not be cleared in a reasonably short time by the traditional methods of packing and dragging.

(*Note*: A number of the subsequent remarks in this chapter are couched in the present tense, where the observations are equally applicable to breakdown work under diesel or electric traction.)

According to the size of the depot staff and the extent of any particular breakdown job to be tackled, the train goes out with one or more fitters and their regular mates. One fitter is nominated as the breakdown fitter, part of his duties being to ensure that jacks, chains, wire ropes, ramps, lamps and other equipment are in good condition, and properly stowed in the vans.

Some specialisation in any emergency gang is desirable, so that — for instance — lamps can be prepared and distributed during the journey to the scene of a de-railment. It is also most useful for each duty to be covered by a reserve man, so that in the absence of the regular nominee of any task the reserve man can be called on to take the duty right away. This is also necessary, particularly in the case of the crane driver, for relief after long hours at work.

A de-railment or collision may result not only in parts being jammed together, but they may also be entangled with rails, point-rodding, signal wires or lineside equipment. Before the introduction of oxy-acetylene cutting apparatus in general railway use, separating such interlocked parts was a matter of forcing wreckage apart — by means of locomotive, crane or jacks, or — where this was impracticable — laborious, time-consuming muscle-work with hand tools. A depot which was fortunate enough to have a blacksmith would usually include this worthy with his striker in the gang, especially as in latter years they were seldom fully occupied in the shed Gas-cutting has been commonplace since World War 2, and it is most desirable to have at least two men in the squad who possess that skill.

An essential member of the gang is the mess-van attendant; it is he who has to have tea and food ready whenever the circumstances of a breakdown job allow time for the men to have a pause. He will also do the 'housekeeping' in the mess van. It is useful if he is something of a humorist, for when the gang goes back to the van tired and dripping wet after a long, heavy spell of work in bad weather, they need something more than tea and biscuits to revive their spirits.

For non-urgent calls, such as run-of-the-mill siding derailments, not causing any serious blockage, one could usually take up to an hour before leaving the shed. But for urgent jobs I have sometimes taken a tool van at express speed, with a scratch crew of whoever happened to be around the depot, leaving the rest of the regular gang to follow up with the remainder of the train as soon as the squad was complete.

In order to give the reader an inside view of a breakdown gang in action in the steam era I offer the following recollections of work which resulted from the de-railment on Sunday 7 August 1955 of the 10.35am Manchester-Marylebone express south of Rugby. (That line was closed in 1966, and the tracks removed from Calvert Jct to beyond Leicester.)

The train had backed over to the Down track at Rugby, over which it was to travel in the facing direction, single line working being in operation there because of track repairs on the Up line. Under these conditions the train should have been driven at 'Caution'. The cross-over at Barby Sidings was set to return the train to the Up track, and the movement through it should have been at not more than 10mph. The Ministry of Transport Inspecting Officer recorded that the train had been travelling at about 55mph when it hit the cross-over. Neasden Driver Charlie Simpson was killed in the ensuing crash, but his fireman, Nethercott was able to give evidence seven weeks later.

All the circumstances pointed to the conclusion that Simpson had not expected to cross over to the Up line until Braunstone & Willoughby, two miles further on — had been notified in the original printed circular. A subsequent cyclostyled circular, shortening the length of single-line working to Barby Sidings was posted on the 'late notice' boards at the signing-on points, but he had evidently not seen, or had forgotten it.

Notwithstanding the altogether excessive speed of the train, a green flag was held steady at Barby because the rule-book prescribed such a hand-signal as indicating the track set for the train to take the cross-over. I never understood that provision, when such a movement at caution would appear to have necessitated a yellow one. Furthermore, the rule book then in use (but now superseded) gave — according to different circumstances — 13 different meanings for the use of a green flag.

The locomotive involved was No 60820, a Class V2 2-6-2, quite recently overhauled, and on loan from Kings Cross to Neasden while one or our Pacifics was in Doncaster 'Plant' Works. It took the left-hand curve, but could not, of course, negotiate the reverse right-hand bend of the 'S' at that speed; it mounted the rails, plunged down a 15ft high embankment, and slithered to a shuddering stop on its side in a pasture about 120ft beyond the point of derailment.

The coupling between the tender and the first coach was wrenched apart, and the first coach — also on its side — overshot the locomotive, but was further away from the track. Two 'Buck-eye' couplers separated vertically in the final hideous moments. The rest of the couplings, most of which were 'Buck-eyes, held fast. Most of the bogies were shorn off the first five coaches, and were jumbled together like a child's toys. These coaches finished up in an erratic reverse Z-formation, their ends being heavily impacted or otherwise damaged. The following two coaches also left the track, but the remaining three were still on the rails. The up track was destroyed for a length of about 200ft, and the down track damaged over a similar distance. The left-hand side of the leading carriage was crushed and some coach-ends were stoved in, but no telescoping occurred and the bodies were otherwise intact — a remarkable testimony to the soundness of their construction. It was undoubtedly this which prevented serious injury to the passengers, who had a miraculously lucky escape; 19 of them were taken to hospital, but only one was detained.

When the engine pitched into the ground Fireman Nethercott was partly buried under coal; he could not see his driver, who was completely covered by it. A steam pipe in the cab had been broken in the crash, so that steam and boiling water were scalding him from the waist downward. With an excruciating effort he managed to extricate himself, and was seen running — minus a shoe — to fetch help for his mate. In contrast to this presence of mind and devotion to duty by a badly injured man, the restaurant car crew — whose coach was tilted over — locked up their pantry, and abandoned a train-load of injured or badly shaken passengers, and made their way to the nearest main road in order to hitch-hike home. Other railway staff, searching the wreckage, had to break open the pantry in order to give sustenance to those most in need.

Several soldiers in Barby Army Camp, some short distance to the north, hearing and seeing the crash rushed over and gave valuable help. Afterwards they were put on a disciplinary charge (known in military slang as a 'fizzer') for breaking out of camp!

Thousands of accounts of de-railments have been written, and in Great Britain there is a Ministry of Transport enquiry into every major accident and every one involving loss of life. However, I have not seen a description of the problems facing a breakdown gang which has to recover de-railed vehicles, and clear up whatever wreckage may have been produced. The following notes are therefore offered as indicating what took place on the occasion mentioned above.

Colwick (Nottingham), Leicester and Woodford breakdown trains, supervised by their shed masters (Messrs Levick, Micklethwaite and King respectively) were summoned. The work of clearing the last

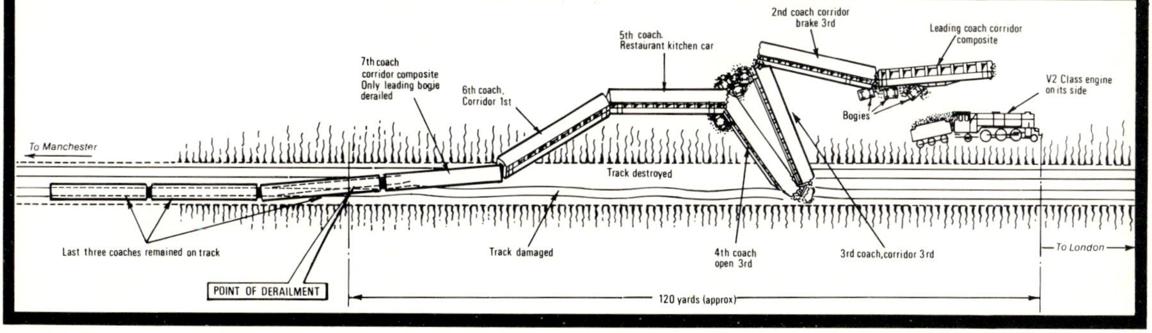

five coaches, and clearing the main line of wreckage, directed by John Blundell, the District Motive Power Superintendent, Colwick continued until four o'clock the following morning. The third and fourth coaches, which had come to rest astride the main line, had to be swung round into the field to be recovered later. By 10 o'clock the following morning, with a new length of track laid in the Up line, and the Down track repaired, traffic was allowed to pass at reduced speed.

The breakdown train from Colwick was ordered out for the next two Sundays in order to take part in retrieving the locomotive and the remaining carriages. Although Woodford's crane was capable of hoisting 35 tons, it did not have sufficient length of jib for the lifts required, and Leicester did not have a crane, so Neasden's breakdown train under my supervision was ordered to participate. We had to travel 76 miles to the site, and I arranged to stop at Woodford in order to pick up a number of their gang as reinforcements. It was good to work with some of my former staff again — even if the occasion had its sombre aspect. Fortunately the two Sundays were fine, and we had firm grass-land to walk about on (a ploughed field can be most tedious under such circumstances, especially if one has to slither about in mud or snow, handling heavy equipment).

The first Sunday was occupied in recovering the engine and tender; the locomotive was lying fairly close to the Up track, but not close enough for our cranes to reach it. Although the larger crane could take lifts up to some 30ft from its pivot (ie at the middle of the track) its maximum lifting capacity was only obtainable at about 12ft radius. Thence it diminished at an increasing rate. So in this case a set of 'Deutschland' re-railing equipment (recently received at Stratford for use under electric traction wires) was brought to the site. This gear consists of long-travel, portable hydraulic jacks, a portable pump to feed the fluid to them at high pressure, steel wire cables and pulley blocks. Three of these jacks were used to roll over the engine to its normal upright stance, and this brought it within the radius of maximum lift of our cranes.

The Civil Engineer's staff had built a stout platform of old sleepers, cut into the side of the embankment, on to which the 'V2' was rolled. When a steam locomotive is thus tipped over it rocks heavily on its springs, and looks alarmingly as though it might go right over to fall on its other flank. But such is the energy-absorbing capacity of its leaf-springs, combined with that of a solidly packed sleeper platform, that it rebounds back to near-upright at the first oscillation. Although this engine had been lying out of steam for over a week, when rolled over it gave a puff from the chimney, as the ashes in the firebox and smokebox were thrown about, giving the illusion that it might still have some fire in it.

At track level the permanent-way men had constructed massive sleeper bases to give support to our crane outriggers. The latter were required not only to take the weight of the locomotive, but also to act as a fulcrum on which the major part of the dead-weight of the two cranes was to counter-balance that of the engine. Neasden crane weighed approximately 60tons. That being used by Colwick was one of the biggest ex-LNER cranes, being on loan from Gorton (Manchester) while their own was under repair. It had a lifting capacity of 45tons, and a dead-weight almost equal to that of the derailed 2-6-2.

The Colwick gang attached their crane-hooks to the dragbox at the rear end, while Neasden's crane was attached to the frame above the buffer beam (at the south end) by pins through the holes provided in the frame-plates. The Colwick crane-driver who was having persistent trouble with his gear-shifts, for a fitter's mate was having to help him with a crow-bar at every change of the gears. The crane had been hurried out from an overhaul without the gears having been run in; to my great relief and that of the Neasden crew our trustworthy old crane behaved impeccably.

Blundell, tall, slim and good-looking in his late 50s, energetic and good-humoured as ever, conspicuous in a white smock, was in charge of the operations; as an ex-Lieutenant-Colonel of the Royal Engineers he was clearly in his element.

The cranes took the initial strain: a moment's pause while he and I satisfied ourselves that all was in order to hoist. We signalled to our respective drivers to give full steam; it was a perfect lift. The load was over 90tons — almost as much as a Pacific — and although Colwick were lifting the heavier (firebox) end, Neasden's crane (rated at 35 tons) had around 42tons on the hook! In a couple of minutes No 60820 was hanging suspended over the field — at about a foot above rail-level. It was then only a matter of the cranes slewing round to lower her on to the track between them. This was done with no further trouble, the wheels being then gauged and found correct in spite of the heavy lateral shocks which they had sustained.

In spite of the engine having lurched through the cross-over at speed, and having ploughed itself to a dramatic, sudden halt on its side, with a 10-coach train acting as a 350ton battering ram behind it, the only serious damage was a fractured cylinder block. We took down the connecting rods, this being all that was needed to make the 2-6-2 ready for towing away to Doncaster Works. Rolling over and re-railing the 51ton tender with two cranes was by contrast a simple matter.

On the following Sunday we retrieved the five coaches, which by then had lain under tarpaulins for a fortnight. The same cranes were used, Colwick having by then sorted out their gear-troubles. Either crane would have had the capacity to lift a carriage by itself, but we decided to use them in 'tandem' on each coach. By that means it was possible to obtain a more easily controlled lift, and to be sure of not causing any more damage. We first tackled the leading coach of the train. After uprighting it and lifting it we had to lower it on to the Up line between the cranes, so as to permit a train to pass on the Down line. Thence it was slewed over to the Down track, and lowered on to temporary bogies, on which it was towed to a nearby siding to be made fit to haul away for repairs.

During both Sundays I was greatly helped by Mechanical Chargeman Norman Claxton from Neasden's sub-depot at Aylesbury, son of a previous foreman fitter at Neasden. He was a huge fellow, 6ft 6in tall, and endowed with a rare combination of muscle and initiative. He had been a Sergeant under Blundell, later became a Warrant Officer, received the MBE for military services, and was twice mentioned in despatches.

We continued with the other coaches, but had much difficulty in detaching the fourth coach from the fifth — with which it had been heavily impacted. There was no foothold on which to stand in order to burn apart some of the interlocked wreckage, because of the smooth, steeply sloping surfaces. So Claxton called to our crane-driver to give him a ride on the crane hook, from which position, with one foot on a carriage roof, he carried out the oxy-acetylene burning.

About mid-day we had to suspend work while the Operating people took possession of the Down track, so as to pass traffic over it in both directions. This was therefore a lunch-break, and one for which more-than-usual preparation had been made. Unlike the vast majority of breakdown jobs, we had had ample warning of this one, and anticipating having about 20 men away from home over 12 hours, I decided that they should be adequately fed. Authority was therefore obtained to purchase special rations, and Claxton brought copious quantities of fresh vegetables from his garden. I think that our mess-van-attendant-cum-cook must have had some home instruction from his wife, for everyone agreed that they had never fed so well on duty. This very noticeably improved morale, and increased the rate of working.

About mid-afternoon, when with more interruptions to allow traffic to pass it looked as if we might have to work until late that evening to get the field cleared of wreckage, Claxton came to me with an unusual proposition. 'If you will arrange to stop at Aylesbury for half-an-hour before closing-time, I'll bargain with the lads that we'll have this job cleared up by 8 o'clock.' To which I replied: 'If the opportunity to drink a few pints will achieve that, then it's a deal'. I sent a message through to Control, saying that we expected to be ready to return to London about 8pm.

The two gangs had worked well on a fine, warm day, and one might have expected their energies to have been flagging, but now fortified by visions of ale in Aylebsury, the Neasden men set to work again with a will. They began to chaff the Colwick men with remarks such as 'Come on there, we don't want to be out all night with this job'. They too had received some hints from Claxton about 'closing time', and it would have been quite in character if Blundell had stood his men a round at some convenient 'stopping point' on the way home.

The other coaches presented a certain amount of difficulty, one of them needing some dragging on its side to get it within reach of my crane. But true to Claxton's word, the last bits of debris were removed just after 8 o'clock and by about 8.15 our guard gave the 'Right-away'. With a clear road, and a bogie crane (she had a sort of 4-6-0 wheel arrangement and ran steady as a rock at 60mph) we had no difficulty in making a stop at Woodford to set down our reinforcements and still reaching Aylesbury by just after 9.20pm.

I had instructed our driver to stop at Aylesbury, where the gang scrambled down on to the track and away to a nearby hostelry where they were soon supping their favourite brew. Meanwhile I went up to the 'bobby', and asked him to put the train in a siding 'so that I could examine the crane'. A few minutes after 10 o'clock the drinkers were back in the mess-van, as per gentlemen's agreement — and so, tired, but somewhat refreshed, back to base.

Snow-clearance has certain features in common with re-railment work, particularly since it involves clearing blocked lines. It too is a motive power function, but instead of sending out the breakdown gang, it is usual to send out the breakdown fitter and his mate, plus a locomotive inspector, relieving them after they have worked about eight hours in the freezing cold.

During winter in cold areas, such as Scotland, the running sheds used to fit small snow ploughs to their main line engines. At these depots, and at most other large ones in areas liable to snowfalls, it was usual also to keep one or two engines in steam fitted with a large snow-plough. Ploughs intended for clearing blocked lines are constructed at least to buffer-beam height, and may be symmetrical or unsymmetrical; the latter are arranged so that on double track they throw the greater part of the snow to the 'cess' side.

Snow ploughs are either attached to the front of a locomotive, or are mounted on a heavy vehicle which is propelled directly by it. With steam engines it was usual to remove the front buffers, and to attach the plough in place of them. However, diesel locomotive cabs are not built to withstand the shock of snow, plus any objects which might be embedded in it, coming up over the plough and striking the front of the cab. Also it is most desirable to protect the bogies from the sudden thrust of impact with a snow drift. Thus it is usual for the plough to be fitted permanently on to a heavy vehicle, which is not required at other times. This is almost always the tender of a steam locomotive, but now, over 14 years after the last steam engine was withdrawn from service, such tenders have become very rare.

At the same time shunting duties have decreased enormously, due to the virtual elimination of shunting passenger stock, and to the very heavy decline in wagon-load traffic (closure of many marshalling yards). Many 350hp diesel shunters have thus been made redundant, although they have served much less than a normal life-time. Doncaster diesel maintenance depot has found a new use for some of these by stripping out all the traction gear and removing the coupling rods, but retaining the brake pipes, cylinders and rigging. A snow plough has then been fitted on one end of each of these vehicles, which is permitted to run at 40mph.

84
Snow in North Devon, January 1963; Class 700 0-6-0 No 30689 had gone out from Exmouth Junction to force a way through snow-drifts, and itself became snowed in near Sourton, on the north side of Dartmoor. This picture shows it having been dug out four days later, being rammed by Class N 2-6-0 No 31846 to break the ice from its mechanical parts, while Fitter Reg Lang of the same depot (with steel bar) and his mate Albert Davey observe intently. After seven hefty collisions, under the supervision of Chief District Motive Power Inspector Sam Smith, it was free to move. *Western Morning News, Plymouth*

17
Finale

The Armistice of World War 2 in Europe was followed by the election of a socialist government in Great Britain which ensured that nationalisation of the railways was only a matter of time; the railway companies therefore had little incentive to make good the backlog of six years of wartime 'deferred' repairs and sheer neglect from which most locomotive depots were suffering.

After the war, with its heavy running down of physical assets, there was an inexorable rise in the costs of maintenance and other motive power functions. 'Outside' industry recovered rapidly in its efforts to make good the unsatisfied demand of the years of hostilities, and there was fierce competition for labour in many areas. With the nationally agreed rates of pay which the railways were able to offer it was increasingly difficult to meet the needs of labour-intensive steam traction. Locomotive depots compared most unfavourably with modern factories, an increasing number of which were offering a 5-day week, without shift duties. Manufacturing industries, whose staff negotiation procedures were often locally based, were much more flexible than the railways, with their cumbersome national negotiating machinery, and in many places they quite blatantly poached many of the best railway staff. Furthermore, thousands of railwaymen (of whom the author was one) were retained in military service for up to two years after the war had ended. It was thus not at all surprising that nearly all running sheds were chronically short of repair staff. Indeed it was rare to find more than one or two apprentices in most steam depots in the 1950s or 1960s. To make matters worse, the desperate shortage of cleaners at many sheds caused a large proportion of engines to be disgracefully dirty.

Improvements were made at numerous sheds during the late 1940s and the 1950s where some rebuilding was done, mainly to make good war damage and severe deterioration which had occurred since 1939. The dieselisation of shunting power proceeded apace from the early 1950s, the shunting engines being maintained in steam loco depots until special facilities were provided. The replacement of steam-hauled passenger trains by diesel railcars, added to the replacement of steam engines for other traffic under the 1955 Modernisation Plan, caused great reductions in the requirements for motive power staff. These effects and electrification led to closures of depots and transfers of personnel on a considerable scale. Problems abounded for the staff offices, but taken overall, the transition was remarkably smooth.

It has been unfortunately belated until now for the history of steam locomotive depots to be recorded in the present amount of detail. However, I trust that I have painted a sufficiently clear picture of the various depots to show that each had very much its own atmosphere and individuality. In a sense any locomotive running shed had something of the character of a village — even if it were located in a town — because virtually everybody knew nearly everyone else.

I was most fortunate to have been in charge of four depots, all of which had adequate, even generous shed buildings, yards and facilities — especially pits of decent depth and condition. Staveley and Exmouth Junction both had very acceptable Shed Master's offices, while Woodford and Neasden both had offices that almost any executive might have been glad to occupy. All had a commanding view of the shed front, and were generally the sort of premises in which a manager could take a considerable degree of pride. I had loyal clerical staffs who, as far as it lay in their capacity, had kept me out of difficulties. The mechanical and boiler repair staff had produced standards of maintenance from fair under most adverse conditions at Neasden, to excellent at the other depots. The failure rates were correspondingly creditable, all this being matched by a fair-to-good response from the ill-paid shed grades at these depots, and a considerably good performance on the part of nearly all the highly individualistic footplate men.

I had not always been able to keep out of trouble — being much to disposed to innovate, and to query established practices for that. But troubles as they arose were generally met on a basis of mutual desire to find solutions acceptable to both management and men, even if this sometimes required extensive arguments, and often compromises which one side or the other might not have been prepared to consider at the outset.

For all this I would not claim any special virtue beyond a measure of luck in my promotions. Most of my contemporaries had it much rougher in many ways — especially in some of the hole-and-corner sheds which abounded on the Southern and some other Regions. Such depots which come to mind were Guildford, built in a cutting adjacent to a tunnel, so that under certain atmospheric conditions it was virtually a smoke-trap; Ispwich, with its hopelessly outgrown facilities so admirably described by Richard Hardy in his book *Steam in the Blood*; Colchester — another depot on the same main line, and impossibly congested. Everything depended in such a depot on the shed shunter never putting a single engine out of place. Then there were Yeovil Town, with its dangerous restrictive clearances, St Margaret's, Edinburgh, producing its smoke, like so many others, in the thick of a built-up area; Neepsend, Sheffield — so bad that even the impecunious LNER had to replace it by a new shed at Darnall — etc, etc.

But all were animated by the iron horses, large and small, with their infinite variety of conditions and characteristics. And all were driven and fired by men who in their own manifold ways were devoted to the objective of keeping the wheels turning. Come hail, rain, fog or snow, the trains must go through, and — so far as it lay within the power of 'the Loco' — on time!

85
The best lifting facilities possessed by any railway preservation society in Great Britain are those of the Great Western Society in its premises at the former GWR running shed at Didcot. Here 4-6-0 No 5900 *Hinderton Hall* is being lifted in order to run out its bogie during restoration work in November 1974.

The motor, flywheel and belt seen behind the legs of the fixed portal crane are part of the mechanism driving the overhead reduction gears. *Great Western Society*

Index